THE
SPECTACULAR
STATE

POLITICS, HISTORY, AND CULTURE

A series from the International Institute at the University of Michigan

Sponsored by the International Institute at the University of Michigan and published by Duke University Press, this series is centered around cultural and historical studies of power, politics, and the state—a field that cuts across the disciplines of history, sociology, anthropology, political science, and cultural studies. The focus on the relationship between state and culture refers both to a methodological approach—the study of politics and the state using culturalist methods—and a substantive one that treats signifying practices as an essential dimension of politics. The dialectic of politics, culture, and history figures prominently in all the books selected for the series.

THE
SPECTACULAR
STATE

*Culture and
National Identity in
Uzbekistan*

Laura L. Adams

Duke University Press   Durham and London   2010

© 2010 Duke University Press

All rights reserved

Printed in the United States of America on acid-free paper ∞

Designed by Heather Hensley

Typeset in FF Scala by Keystone

Library of Congress Cataloging-in-Publication Data appear
on the last printed page of this book.

CONTENTS

ACKNOWLEDGMENTS

My list of intellectual debts begins with one to my parents, Rodge and Ruth Adams, whose love of theater and music has influenced my interests and choices throughout my life. I seem to be the only one in the family without musical talent, but my brothers, David and Brian, and my extended family continually inspire me to pursue the arts through scholarship. In my intellectual biography, several key events, including the USA/USSR hockey match in the 1980 Olympics, the availability of a performing arts high school magnet program in Minneapolis in the 1980s, reading *Anna Karenina* in AP English, and the engaging professors in Macalester's sociology department laid the path to this project. I want to thank my mentors at Macalester College, especially Jim von Geldern, Michal McCall, and Victor Rios, for nurturing the enthusiastic kid who wanted to study places they'd barely heard of and topics that nobody else had written about yet. In graduate school, Ann Swidler gave me valuable feedback and enthusiastic support from the first day to the last, and beyond. I want to thank Neil Fligstein for showing me how to make sociological theory work for me and Yuri Slezkine for pushing me, but not too hard. In addition to gratitude, I want to express my admiration and affection for Michael Burawoy, an exemplary teacher, scholar, and citizen of the world.

In my postdoctoral days, the Georgetown Center for Eurasian, Russian, and East European Studies rescued me from a fourth year of a 3/3 teaching load and gave me the opportunity to refine a lot of the ideas that appear here. The book really took shape during my time at Princeton, where the support and encouragement of

Miguel Centeno made a huge difference in my life. The Princeton Institute for International and Regional Studies, the Comparative Politics Working Group, and the Sociology Department all provided collegial and stimulating environments. It is to Stephen Kotkin, however, that I owe the biggest thank you, because he not only made it possible for me to stay in academia long enough to finish writing, he gave me hope that it was worth doing.

A number of institutions have provided material and intellectual support for this project over the years. The Jacob Javits Foundation funded my early graduate training. The Berkeley Program in Soviet and Post-Soviet Studies administered Foreign Language and Area Studies funds that enabled my advanced Russian language study and supported two research trips to Uzbekistan, and the University of Washington's Near Eastern Languages and Civilizations summer language study funds gave me two years of training in Uzbek. The International Research and Exchanges Board supported my dissertation year in Uzbekistan, as well as a follow-up trip in 2002. The Davis Center for Russian and Eurasian Studies and the Harvard Program on Central Asia and the Caucasus have provided me with a scholarly community and an academic home base for the last twelve years. Finally, the Harvard Writing Program provided funds to support the publishing of this book.

I want to recognize my friends and colleagues in Uzbekistan for all they did to make this book possible. The Tashkent State Institute of Culture, the Ministry of Cultural Affairs of Uzbekistan, and the Tashkent City Department of Culture and their staffs all assisted my work in various ways. The Rakhimberganov and Alimov families provided me with material and emotional support and with very pleasant introductions to everyday life in Tashkent.

Along the way, this book has benefited from the advice and input of numerous additional colleagues, friends, and reviewers. I want to shine the spotlight of gratitude on two people in particular: Michael Kennedy, whose interest in my work and advice about publishing were encouraging and helpful in a very concrete way, and Doug Northrop, who is a generous and conscientious colleague who has held me to his own high standards, much to my benefit. I want to thank many others here because creativity is collaborative and besides, we all like seeing our names in print: Alisher Abidjanov, David Abramson, Sada Aksartova, Gulnora Aminova, Doug Blum, Cassandra Cavanaugh, Kathleen Collins, Alexander Dillon,

Paul DiMaggio, Adrienne Edgar, Hilda Eitzen, Bruce Grant, Fran Hirsch, Jen Hunter, Daniel Goldstein, David Guss, Alisher Ilkhamov, Pauline Jones Luong, Marianne Kamp, Shoshanna Keller, Adeeb Khalid, Umida Khikmatillaeva, Saodat Kholmatova, Charlie Kurzman, Ted Levin, Morgan Liu, Kelly McMann, Nick Megoran, Neema Noori, Usmon Qoraboev, Michael Rouland, Ed Schatz, John Schoeberlein, Said Shermukhammedov, Kelly Smith, Anara Tabyshalieva, Joshua Tucker, Kristina Vestbo, and Russell Zanca have all contributed to this book in ways large and small. Finally, thanks and love to Todd Horowitz, with whom I have shared everything that makes me me.

The introduction to this book was shaped by feedback I got when I presented it at Princeton University. Chapter 1 of this book benefited from comments I received during public presentations of the material at Harvard University, the University of Toronto, and the University of Illinois. Parts of this book have been published previously in a different form. Chapter 2's discussion of the Olympics and cultural form can also be found in "Globalization, Universalism and Cultural Form," *Comparative Studies in Society and History* 50, no. 3 (2008), 614–40. Chapter 4's analysis of the seduction of cultural elites draws on parts of "Cultural Elites in Uzbekistan: Ideology Production and the State," *The Transformation of Central Asia: States and Societies from Soviet Rule to Independence*, ed. Pauline Jones Luong, 93–119 (Ithaca, N.Y.: Cornell University Press, 2003).

THE POLITICS OF
CULTURE IN UZBEKISTAN
1991-2002

It was a blisteringly hot day in Uzbekistan's capital, which is to say, it was a typical August day. I was sitting in a breezy corner of a room that was command central for the spectacular concert that would be held in Tashkent on the eve of the fifth anniversary of Uzbekistan's independence from the Soviet Union.[1] The mood in the company around me ranged from sullen to frenzied as chore-ographers, composers, and directors rushed in and out of the room. A deputy mayor of Tashkent was on the phone, yelling at someone from the Ministry of Culture, accusing them of sabotag-ing the celebration. The staff accountant reported that he had met with someone from the Ministry of Finance, who had delivered the bad news that the Ministry of Transport would not give free bus passes to the hundreds of students who had to attend daily rehears-als for the show. More talk of sabotage, improper priorities, and lack of patriotism ensued. Out on the square, dozens of workers labored under the scorching sun to build a temporary stage that would hold ten thousand spectators and as many performers for the ninety minute, $1.5 million dollar spectacle. Later in the day, I attended one of the first rehearsals for the amateur folk groups from Andijon, Bukhara, and other provinces who were perform-ing in the show a month hence. The directors of the groups had fulfilled their instructions to incorporate patriotic phrases into their songs, such as "O'zbekiston, vatanim manim" (Uzbekistan, my homeland), but they got scolded for not coming up with original choreography, costumes, and theatrical flourishes that clearly reflected the culture, products, and monuments their region was known for.

This mass mobilization of bodies and talent for the goals of nation building was not just a result of the authoritarian techniques of power employed by President Islam Karimov's government, nor of old Soviet habits dying hard, although these were both important factors in Uzbekistan's politics of culture. This politics of culture must also be seen as a way that highly educated professionals, intellectuals, and artists organize their work. While some of Uzbekistan's intelligentsia actively resisted this top-down, ideology-oriented way of producing culture, the vast majority tolerated or even enjoyed such an arrangement because it provided them with opportunities to feel they were influencing the public and the future of the nation. In this book, I examine culture production in general, and in particular the production of spectacular concerts on the two biggest national holidays, the spring equinox holiday Navro'z (the Persian New Year) and the day marking Uzbekistan's independence from the Soviet Union, Mustaqillik Kuni (Independence Day).[2]

Over the course of my research between 1995 and 2002, my goal was to investigate what Mary Kaldor has called "spectacle nationalism."[3] Using ritual and celebration as a lens for analyzing identity and ideology has a long history in the social sciences.[4] More specifically, the literature in sociology on the production of culture emphasizes the importance of analyzing not just the content of public ceremony but also the form and manner of production in order to fully understand the dynamics of agency and resistance.[5] In putting together these performances on national holidays, the organizers were making conscious and concrete statements about how they saw the world. For example, there were real concerns among the producers of the holiday spectacles about what peoples would be represented as "nations" versus "nationalities" (that is, ethnic minorities within Uzbekistan) and how many minutes should be allotted to performers from each of Uzbekistan's regions when whole nations were only getting two to three minutes for the musical number devoted to them. When one of the artists asked, "How can you give a whole nation less time than a single *oblast*? [province]," he was indicating the assumption that the performance should, as much as possible, be a fair representation of the world, a geopolitical and ethnocultural *tableau vivant* of Uzbekistan's worldview. When viewed as both works-in-progress and finished products, these holiday spectacles provide us with considerable insight into the schemas of culture producers and their bosses in the political elite.

Spectacle is an object of study in social science because it has properties that enable elites to close opportunities for input from below, but without making the masses feel left out.[6] As Lisa Wedeen noted in her excellent analysis of the cult of Assad in Syria, political spectacles also "help to foreclose possibilities for political thought and action, making it hard either to imagine or enact a truly democratic politics."[7] Spectacle monopolizes discourse by privileging the definition of truth and reality belonging to the elites and by using technology such as the mass media to create a one-way flow of communication, speech without response, which isn't really communication at all. In silencing response, spectacle turns its participants into spectators. Clear examples from U.S. society are the national conventions of the Republican and Democratic Parties, which are contrived to feel like events where candidates are being chosen and the party platform is being shaped by delegates. In reality, for the last several decades, these things have been decided in advance and the convention is an opportunity to reward and motivate party activists, while getting a very carefully crafted message out to the voting public via the television broadcast. These kinds of spectacles enchant and persuade, and their audiences feel included without feeling responsible for action.

I was interested in studying national holiday spectacles for two additional reasons. First, I thought that it was important to study performance as an expression of national identity since so much of the work on Soviet culture has focused on literature and visual art, often with an emphasis on Russian culture in Moscow and Leningrad.[8] Because they are fixed in time and space, literature and the visual arts have been a readily available source of data for scholars, but focusing on these genres may give a distorted picture of artistic freedom in authoritarian societies. Since they are reproducible and available for mass consumption, such art forms are especially vulnerable to censorship. Performances are more fleeting and are exposed to a much smaller segment of the public, so their producers are more free to express a range of styles and themes.[9] Second, the discourse of cultural preservation is much more intense around song, dance, and costume than around what Michael Billig would call banal nationalism: ways of buying and selling, how people cope with sun and rain, closeness or distance between riders of public transportation.[10] As a novice scholar studying a country about which little had been written, I wanted to start with the most concentrated expression of national identity and work outward from there, from the blatant to the banal. In Uzbekistan, I observed various sites dedicated to national identity performance (national holidays, festivals, contests, theatre and musical performances, and so forth) in order to more quickly distill both the methods and sources of the nation-building project of Uzbekistan. Uzbekistan's holiday spectacles in particular caught the eye of many observers of post-Soviet life in Uzbekistan, both because they were unusual compared to the kinds of celebrations seen in most of the other post-Soviet republics (for example, military parades or more purely folkloric celebrations) and because they were strikingly familiar examples of both totalitarian propaganda and globalized entertainment (for example, Olympics ceremonies).[11]

This striking form of holiday celebration is the apparent preference of one man in particular: Uzbekistan's president, Islam Karimov. From the time it became independent from the Soviet Union in 1991 until the time of this writing in 2008, Uzbekistan has been governed by Karimov, an authoritarian and increasingly repressive leader, and the state-society relationship closely resembles its Soviet predecessor.[12] In many countries, holidays are used as opportunities to propagandize government policy, but in Uzbekistan holidays were often the first time many people heard about government policy, for example, when a presidential decree was published in the newspaper around the time of the holiday. In many countries, policies are framed by the slogans of the administration in power, but in Uzbekistan, policies were crafted to contribute to whatever campaign had been declared that year by the government (2008, for example, was "The Year of Youth"). In many countries cultural events are used for political purposes, but in Uzbekistan nearly every political event was adorned with the trappings of Uzbek national culture. As Andrew March has also argued, Islam Karimov is unique among his peers in his attempts to formulate and transmit an "ideology of national independence" that would legitimate the new regime.[13] In this book, I examine the question of how states like Uzbekistan use ideology for legitimation and use expressive culture as a means of communication and control. Uzbekistan in the 1990s, like contemporary regimes such as Assad's Syria, Hussein's Iraq, and Kim's North Korea, took the political uses of culture to an extreme that made it what I call a *spectacular state*.

A spectacular state is one where, more than in most countries, politics is conducted on a symbolic level, promoting the state's domination over the shared meaning of concepts such as heritage and progress. Typically spectacle is a technique of mobilization, and thus it is used more in totalitarian regimes than in other types of states.[14] However, although Uzbekistan was among the least free states in the world, it was not strongly characterized by the defining institutions of totalitarian, and many authoritarian, regimes: a highly elaborated and constraining ideology, a party-state and its attendant societal organizations, a widespread cult of the leader, and militarization or a reliance on widespread terror (at least until 2005 or so, when the population became increasingly afraid of the state security apparatus).[15] Islam Karimov, unlike his former comrade in Turkmenistan, Saparmurat Niyazov, was cautious about fostering a cult of personality and instead found ways to invest a number of families in the stability of the regime while publicly deflecting adoration to a cult of Amir Timur, which was essentially a cult of personality by proxy.[16] The absence of a full-fledged cult of Karimov make Uzbekistan stand out from its peer spectacular states such as Syria, Iraq, and North Korea, though Uzbekistan's limited cult of the leader was in line with its late Soviet predecessors, both the cult of Gorbachev and the former head of the CPUZ, Sharof Rashidov. In the absence of the mobilizational and repressive characteristics possessed by other authoritarian states, Uzbekistan relied on the techniques of power it inherited from the Soviet system, such as mobilization in mass spectacle, without fully investing in them organizationally or ideologically the way the Communist Party had done.

Unlike many studies of authoritarian states, this book examines the state not as a set of institutions or discourses, but as a collectivity of actors who were in the process of making difficult decisions about the future of their country and their culture. This study of nation building in Central Asia makes a useful contribution to the comparative literature on post-independence states. After the breakup of the USSR, Uzbekistan (and the other states of Central Asia) experienced a transition that was unusual in the history of both postcolonial and postcommunist regimes, in that the transition was never pushed forward by an oppositional or proindependence movement apart from the state. In Uzbekistan, almost as soon as the nationalist intelligentsia began to mobilize, the state adopted their goals and co-opted their rhetoric, creating a continuity in the state's monopoly on ideology between the Soviet and post-Soviet period. The lack of alternative discourses in post-Soviet Uzbekistan has meant that the state had a large degree of control over the shape of culture in the early years of independence. It also created a situation of strong Soviet legacies for the interpretation and production of culture.

This book examines these legacies and the constraints, both institutional and cultural, on nation building in the context of independence. In the language of the sociology of organizations, institutional constraints can be described as sunk costs, internal or external political constraints, legitimacy constraints, and legal or fiscal barriers, all of which make organizational change difficult.[17] More specifically, I examine the nexus of institutional and cultural constraints imposed by cognitive models or schemas, which reproduce institutionalized behavior "because individuals often cannot even conceive of appropriate alternatives (or because they regard as unrealistic the alternatives they can imagine)."[18] Furthermore, along the lines of the "new" institutionalism in sociology, I analyze the way that institutions do more than just constrain options by establishing the criteria by which people discover their preferences and enabling people to make choices that have consequences quite the opposite of those the institution was designed to bring about.[19]

These constraints are especially sharp in societies such as that of Uzbekistan, which lack pluralism due to the weakness of nonstate sectors of society. As argued by Mansoor Moaddel and others, the nature of a society's discursive field is directly related to the content of intellectual production: existing ideas serve as the targets of new discourses, thus shaping their content.[20] Discursive fields are the terrain upon which contests for meaning occur; they set the rules that impose limits on the discursive game but also provide the players with the tools they need to make meaning in the first place.[21] When there is a monolithic ideology that dominates the discursive field, "ideological producers often tend to reproduce in a different form an idea system similar to what they are criticizing," but in a field with multiple targets of discourse, intellectual production is diversified.[22] The research for this book began in 1995, when the task of building a new nation was firmly under the control of the same government officials who had been building communism a few years before. This institutional continuity explains why the campaign for cultural renewal in Uzbekistan continued to reproduce Soviet discourses, practices, and cultural forms. Rather than breaking away from Soviet-style culture, Uzbek cultural "renewal" was dominated by kitschy didacticism, extreme centralization, and the demands of official ideology.

Continuity with the Soviet era was not just preserved in the way culture was produced, it was also apparent in the way that cultural elites understood Uzbek national identity and culture.[23] Cultural renewal in the decade after Uzbekistan's independence was not so much a rejection of Soviet power as it was a reappropriation of Soviet interpretations of Uzbek national culture and identity. Uzbek culture producers simply removed the socialist ideological content of Uzbek identity, leaving the Soviet constructions of place-centered heritage and "universal" human values (such as peace, development, progress, international cooperation), while also elaborating what were commonly understood during the Soviet period as traditional Uzbek values (such as hospitality, respect for elders, large families, and the practices and beliefs of Hanafi Islam).

There were many ways this official national identity was manifested in the public sphere: through the media, in workplaces, in arguments at the bazaar about what was a fair price to charge whom and why. One of the main showcases of national ideology was the massive outdoor concerts the state sponsored on national holidays. A striking feature of this type of consciously produced cultural performance is the medium of a distinctly international cultural form (Olympics-style spectacles, the internationally recognizable genre associated with Olympic opening and closing ceremonies) for all aspects of ideology, whether they refer to national or international values and practices. The producers of Uzbekistan's national holidays used Olympics-style mass spectacle to demonstrate regional folk dances and military bands, traditional classical music and contemporary fashion. The holiday extravaganzas were both a mirror and a medium of the spectacular state. These mass spectacles allowed periodic, limited mobilization of society to take place within an ideological framework that appealed to both nationalists and cosmopolitans. Political elites were happy with how the tightly controlled spectacle form allowed them to shape and monitor the production of meaning and the participation of spectators in these events. Cultural elites like spectacle because it is a form that expresses their national identity through universalistic culture, demonstrating their equivalence with their international peers.

The story this book tells is that, between 1991 and 2002, Uzbekistan's cultural and political elites engaged in a highly directive, largely successful program of nation building through culture.[24] The primary objective of this program was to create an ethnically based national identity (with civic elements)[25] drawn from three main sources: distant historical events that took place in the territory of contemporary Uzbekistan, common stereotypes about Uzbeks and other ethnic groups inhabiting Uzbekistan, and a globalized idea of what it means to be a modern nation-state. Each of these sources was originally heavily dependent on Soviet techniques of knowledge/power (historiography, ethnography, and internationalism),[26] but over the course of the fifteen years following independence, Uzbekistan's culture producers gradually began to use these sources in new ways that were shaped by, or a reaction to, international influences on local politics and society.[27]

National Identity and Postsocialist Culture

In this book I will argue that during the early independence period, culture in Uzbekistan was characterized by national content, modern forms, and Soviet-style production. One contribution my analysis makes to the literature on culture and national identity is this breakdown between the production, form, and content of culture. The literature devoted to colonial and totalitarian culture indicates that struggles over meaning are conducted through culture wars over content, rather than over genres or methods of cultural production. But in this book I pose the question: are cultural forms simply neutral vehicles that can be used to put forth ideas, the space within which ideological battles are fought? Or are forms themselves an essential, if often unconscious, part of cultural domination and transformation? I argue that the Soviet use of modern cultural forms was essential to its success in transforming Uzbek national culture and that these cultural forms continued to have significant effects apart from their content.[28]

Scholars writing about Uzbekistan have failed to present a comprehensive picture of the content of Uzbekistan's national identity, focusing instead on critiquing the distortions produced by tailoring history to ideology.[29] Sometimes in their efforts to demonstrate that Uzbekistan is a "nationalizing state," they ignore the internationalism that is at the heart of much of the rhetoric about national identity, and they fail to recognize aspects of the ideology that strive to conform to global models of nation-hood. While the gross manipulation of history is both distressing and an easy target for mockery, every modern nation claims a foundation myth based on historical events.

The new historiography, however, was only one of three main parts to the government's nation-building activity in the cultural realm. The second was the weakening of identification with the multinational Soviet nation and strengthening of identification with a tradition that was institutionalized during the Soviet period as (ethnic) Uzbek national culture. This project struck directly at the core identity of Uzbekistan's non–Central Asian citizens, many of whom had considered themselves not Russians or Poles, but rather Soviets.[30] The third part of the nation-building project was the identification of Uzbekistan as a normal nation, homologous in form to other nation-states and worthy of the esteem accorded such an entity in the international community.[31] The elite's concern with these issues was reflected in every realm of culture, from the repertoire of the Hamza Uzbek Drama Theater, to the articles in the culture journal *Guliston*, as well as in the content of national holiday spectacles.

Although it may seem ironic that the new national identity was made from old materials that the rhetoric of independence celebrated rejecting, in fact, this continuity in both method and substance was one of the reasons the new national culture was so widely accepted. Rather than casting this kind of hegemony as a form of cultural false consciousness or some sort of postcolonial baggage, I argue that the "modern" idioms used by cultural elites in Uzbekistan point to their desire to communicate in a common language with other cultural elites around the world.[32] The medium of universalistic cultural forms gives cultural elites a common standard by which to judge their culture's modernity, quality, or normality and a common language through which to communicate their ideas internationally. But as Rick Wilk also points out, by naturalizing certain orders, even those that perpetuate local, ethnic, or national heterogeneity, global universalism suppresses other kinds of differences, with different consequences for the global circulation of power.[33]

The focus of my research on national identity is its conscious construction by elites. While intellectuals are key actors in any nation-building project, in socialist and postsocialist states, they play a particularly important role. In any society, Michael Kennedy and Ronald Suny argue, intellectuals do the "imaginative ideological labor that brings together disparate cultural elements, selected historical memories, and interpretations of experiences, all the while silencing the inconvenient, the unheroic, and the anomalous."[34] Katherine Verdery argues that in socialist societies, not only were intellectuals important in the construction of "the nation," but the nation was important in the constitution of intellectuals. Shortage economies of highly centralized socialist states made exclusionary mechanisms such as ethnonational identity a field of contestation between rival groups of intellectuals, each of whom competed for scarce resources in terms of a discourse of what was best for the nation.[35] Valery Tishkov explains that the nationalist intelligentsia continued to hold a place of power in many postsocialist societies because "totalitarian inertia has facilitated the replacement of a tyranny of party programs by a no less rigid tyranny of group thinking and myths. . . . A striking feature of post-Soviet societies is the disproportionately high presence and extremely influential role of intellectual elites in positions previously held by the now demoralized and ousted old guard. A struggle for power by means of knowledge has become a sign of post-Communism."[36]

States are also key actors in the construction of national identity. Nation building through culture is an explicitly political project in which a state attempts to unite its citizens and enhance its legitimacy as the representative of those citizens. Montserrat Guibernau outlines the political dimension of national identity as using one or more main strategies: the construction and dissemination of a certain image of the nation based on a dominant ethnic group; the creation and spread of a set of common symbols and rituals intended to create a sense of community; the advancement of common citizenship rights and duties; the identification of common enemies; and the consolidation of national education and media systems.[37] The interesting thing about examining national identity in Uzbekistan is that most of these processes were already complete during the Soviet era.[38] Because of this, national identity in the case of Uzbekistan must also be seen in terms of the broader phenomena of revolutionary and postcolonial culture. Much of the literature on the political use of holidays and commemorative events has focused on revolutions and other liminal moments in a nation's history when opportunities for making new meanings are there for the taking.[39]

One of the main arguments in this book is that in the years following independence, Soviet models of cultural development provided a template for the cohort of nationalist elites who were charged with projecting an image of Uzbekistan to its citizens and to its peers in the community of nation-states.[40] While the Soviet template was hegemonic, its former content was rejected in favor of what these elites saw as "normal" culture, which contained referents both to the past and to other contemporary nations.[41] The irony of using the conceptual tools of the oppressor to achieve liberation from the oppressor is an element in many studies of colonial and postcolonial nationalism. As Bernard Cohn writes about India, "When Indians, particularly in the first years of their national movement, came to develop a public political idiom of their own, through their own organization, what idiom did they use? I would suggest that in effect they used the same idiom that their British rulers employed."[42] Benedict Anderson argues that the very institutions colonial powers created to control their empires (for example, censuses, maps, schools) had the unintended side effect of creating solidarity among the individuals, especially the elites, within a given territory, leading eventually to anticolonial movements based on ideas of national liberation.[43]

This pattern was no less true in the Soviet Union, whether or not one agrees that it was a colonial empire in which nationality was institutionalized to a degree found in few other states.[44] Though the aims of Soviet nationality policy were to harness nationalist tendencies by co-opting elites and to gradually attenuate the significance of ethnicity by draining national culture of its content, as Rogers Brubaker and others have argued, the unintended consequence of employing nationality as an organizing principle of social life was to strengthen the significance of ethnicity.[45]

In addition to examining the institutions that created a sense of Uzbek national identity during the Soviet period, this book presents an analysis of contemporary national identity along the lines of Eric Hobsbawm's *The Invention of Tradition*. Though used as a discursive strategy to legitimate present practices in terms of their continuity with the past, tradition is always an interpretation of the past in terms of the needs of the present.[46] *Invented tradition* is Hobsbawm's term for "a set of practices, normally governed by overtly or tacitly accepted rules and of a ritual or symbolic nature, which seek to inculcate certain values and norms of behavior by repetition, which automatically implies continuity with the past."[47] Like Hobsbawm and his colleagues, I will examine the link between the creation of new ritual practices and their implied continuity with the past. I will also make use of Benedict Anderson's concept of imagined communities in understanding Uzbekistan's national identity, not only because I agree with Anderson's stress on the importance of subjective perceptions for collective practices, but also because I found the empirical reality I encountered was heavily dependent on cultural elites' imagining of their national and international "others." Unlike Anderson, my analysis does not rest on any assumptions about the role of capitalism in nation building since in the case of Central Asia, capitalism is clearly tangential to the development of national identities.

One of the most prolific authors on national identity, Anthony Smith, critiques the views of Hobsbawm and Anderson as "modernist," preferring to see national identity as a deeply historical phenomenon that can best be understood through "ethnosymbolic" analysis.[48] Although some of Smith's analysis is relevant to this work, I take a modernist approach, not because it provides more insight into the phenomenon of Uzbek national identity than an ethnosymbolist approach, but rather because my research question is framed in modernist terms. The object I am investigating is not Uzbek identity per se, but rather its contemporary reinvention.

Smith also critiques some modernists for taking an excessively instrumentalist approach, where national identity is just something to be crassly manipulated by political and cultural elites for their own ends.[49] I must point out that my modernist approach is adamantly not an instrumentalist one. Rather, building on a Foucauldian approach to power, I see national identity as constitutive of power rather than an instrument of power; national identity constitutes its subjects, both institutions and individuals.[50] In this view, power, in the form of discourses about the nation, works through Uzbekistan's elites, and through all of us, making up part of who we are as social actors. We, Uzbek elites included, perceive ourselves as wielding power by shaping what other people think, or building up the nation by engaging in patriotic activities, but to a large degree, we are ourselves instruments of a more abstract, diffuse power that shapes the choices we make and the actions we take.

In addition to understanding national identity in a broader context of Soviet modernism, we must also understand culture in Uzbekistan in the broader context of socialist and postsocialist culture. However, while the literature on Soviet nationalities policy is fairly well developed and is part of the established canon of nationalism theory, theoretically informed analyses of contemporary Central Asian culture are rare, though this is beginning to change as the first wave of scholars who were allowed relative freedom to do field research in the 1990s are beginning to publish their research.[51] As a result, it is a challenge to study Central Asia both because of the lack of empirical data for comparison (although Soviet sources are available, they are not entirely reliable) and because theory developed in other parts of the world must be adapted to the Central Asian context. Much of the best literature on socialist and postsocialist culture has been written about Eastern Europe, but can Eastern Europe provide any valid basis for comparison with Central Asia? Many authors seem to view cultural differences as an insurmountable barrier to applying postsocialist theory to Central Asia.[52] Such culturalist arguments, however, are too simple. While Eastern Europe and Central Asia have very different political traditions and claim different cultural values, they also share a similar recent history and their trajectories during the late Soviet era were structured by similar institutions.[53]

In fact, the theorizing of Katherine Verdery, Michael Kennedy, Caroline Humphrey, and other social scientists studying Eastern Europe provides valuable frameworks for interpreting socialist culture across what we might initially assume to be impassible geographic and ethnocultural divides. Central Asia shares the following features of postsocialist culture with many other newly independent nations: postcolonial dilemmas that are expressed through public debate about belonging (to Europe, to the East) and the alternatingly respected and resented role of Russian culture; discourses of normalcy that were often framed in national terms; hybridity of Soviet, traditional, and globalized culture in the postsocialist reconstruction of national identity; and the lasting importance of a Soviet habitus in shaping how post-Soviet national cultures were reinvented.[54] These themes, common to postsocialist societies, are part of the core analysis presented in this book.

In *National Ideology under Socialism*, Verdery presents two main devices that help us to theorize about socialist cultures. First, Verdery's analysis of "bureaucratic allocation" as the fundamental engine of socialist societies challenges the assumptions inherent in the work of Pierre Bourdieu and other theorists of cultural politics in market societies.[55] In socialist societies, a social actor is "always trying to get more allocable inputs (e.g., shortage goods) than others at one's level, so one can move up closer to the privileged circle that always gets whatever it asks for. . . . Within this context, social actors at all levels must justify why they, rather than some other actor or unit, should receive allocations."[56] This is important for understanding how resources for cultural production are allocated: unlike Bourdieu's theory of economic and cultural capital, Verdery argues that the field of socialist culture was structured by political status and cultural authority. Cultural authority could be established in much the same way that cultural capital is gained, but in socialist societies, the capital is not exchanged for economic capital, but rather for political status, which in turn allows access to greater resources. Since bureaucrats were in charge of allocating these resources under socialism, bureaucrats became the main patrons of artists and intellectuals, while the public was only of secondary concern, a point that I will return to in later chapters.

Verdery's second main contribution to theorizing socialist societies is her analysis of "symbolic-ideological" strategies of control, which supplement the remunerative and coercive strategies employed in different combinations in different socialist societies. Symbolic-ideological strategies "entail outright exhortations and also attempts to saturate consciousness with certain symbols and ideological premises to which subsequent exhortations may be addressed."[57] This kind of control is different from hegemony (where consent to being ruled is taken for granted, as common sense), as Verdery is careful to argue, because socialist states did not achieve hegemony; their legitimacy was always conferred at least in part through coercion. However, in the Soviet Union more than in Eastern Europe, symbolic-ideological control was largely successful, and Verdery's analysis of this strategy is very useful for understanding the relationship of culture producers to power. While all regimes attempt to "capture" intellectuals and the fruits of their labor, socialist states in particular need intellectuals in order to implement the strategy of symbolic-ideological control as much as they need the security forces to implement the strategy of coercion. Similarly, in post-Soviet Uzbekistan, coercion was not one of the primary instruments of power and, indeed, as my argument about the spectacular state implies, symbolic-ideological control was the main strategy employed by the Karimov regime in the early years of nation building.

Of course, there were some important differences between the experience of the countries of Central Asia and other postsocialist societies. Again, I am not arguing that these differences result from innate cultural or ethnic differences between Central Asians and East Europeans, but that they were a result of the differing paths the regions took immediately after independence. For example, the rise of a nationalist intelligentsia is a feature of socialist societies in the late 1980s, but rather than rising to state power as their peers did in Eastern Europe, the co-optation of Central Asian intellectuals' agenda by the state was made possible by the slower pace of development of the nationalist movements in Central Asia and the continuity in administrations between the Soviet and post-Soviet periods.[58] Once the former Communist Party leaders started promoting the national-ist cause, many Central Asian intellectuals, especially in the more repres-sive states of Tajikistan, Turkmenistan, and Uzbekistan, found themselves paralyzed by the dilemma of having gotten more than what they asked for: their own state.

The Context of the Research

I use the term "cultural elites" to refer to the general category of people I was studying who received higher education in the arts or cultural studies and who were employed professionally in the arts or culture. Though the similar educational and work experiences of these individuals have led them to think in like ways about culture, I do not mean to imply that there was *a* cultural elite who constituted a cohesive social, economic, or political category. I also want to stress that this is a study of culture production, and I devote very little attention to the reception of spectacle nationalism in Uzbekistan.

Who were these culture producers who envisioned international audi-ences for their work and whose creativity operated within a rigid bureau-cratic framework? Over the course of four trips to Uzbekistan (six weeks in 1995, ten months in 1996, and one month each in 1998 and 2002), I conducted in-depth (one- to three-hour) interviews with thirty-two people I characterize as cultural elites, several of whom I interviewed more than once. Seventeen of these elites were involved in the creative aspects of culture production, ten were academics or critics, and five were bureau-crats. Additionally, I conducted about thirty-five shorter interviews with other cultural elites from Tashkent and various regions of Uzbekistan, including Karakalpakistan, Surkhandarya, Samarkand, Andijon, and Jiz-zakh. Nearly all of my interviewees were male, reflecting the gender composition at the level of culture production I was studying, for example, lead choreographers and theater directors. (During the 1990s, apparently there was only one female theater director in Tashkent, a city of 2 million people!) Additionally, I conducted a few in-depth and several shorter interviews about culture and national identity with people who did not fit the definition of cultural elite. In addition to conducting interviews, I did more than two hundred hours of ethnographic observation of culture production. I was present at holiday planning meetings and rehearsals on a nearly daily basis in February–March and July–August 1996, and between 1995 and 2002, I attended more than twenty plays, concerts, and folk festivals.

Since I conducted most of my research in the capital city, what I saw was mostly well-funded cultural production that was closely intertwined with apparatuses of the state. In the provinces, though, I did see the way older cultural forms, ways of celebrating, performing, and so forth, existed as "residual" forms alongside more modern forms.[59] The old forms do not seem to die out, but since they are not useful to the state and to cultural entrepreneurs, they do not play nearly as large a role in public culture in Uzbekistan, and they have also been transformed by the modernization process I analyze. Even the traditional forms of self-entertainment I saw in rural areas took on modern characteristics because they were removed from the traditional place of performance (the courtyard or teahouse), the sexes danced together, and the groups themselves were organized by state culture houses.

The majority of people in positions of creative control in Tashkent, and therefore most of the people I interviewed, were from a cohort that completed higher education in the 1970s. This cohort was trained at the height of the Brezhnev era and came to the apex of their own careers in the eras of perestroika and independence. They were an especially vulnerable generation, fully invested in the old way of doing things, yet at an economically demanding stage of life because of the need to finance their children's educations and weddings. Those who had not abandoned their artistic careers for more lucrative pursuits at home or abroad were forced to work within the existing institutions and power structures if they hoped to secure their future financial and social status. And while some cultural elites had key roles in ideology production at the top levels, others had more peripheral roles and at most were called in to the Presidential Council occasionally to consult on matters of ideology and culture policy.

Because of the observational and interview components of this research, I am able to go beyond analyzing the content and presentation of the arts in Uzbekistan in order to explore where the tensions and debates were among the producers of public culture. For example, a content analysis of the Navro'z holiday concert in 1996 would not be able to reveal the fact that a dance dramatizing Zoroastrian rituals and the symbolic link between Iran and Turon (Turkic Central Asia) had been cut at the last minute by political authorities. A comparison of the 1996 concert with its predecessors would reveal the sudden absence of a performance of the dances of Uzbekistan's various ethnic groups, but it would be a mistake to then conclude that ethnonationalism had suddenly increased. Instead, what happened was that the composer responsible for organizing that performance had gotten quite ill the week before the holiday and hadn't been able to put something together in time.

However, aside from the research I conducted specifically on holiday concerts and theater, much of the other evidence I present in this book was collected in a less systematic way. In other words, I did not seek to sample all newspaper and magazine articles on culture and national identity, though I sought out newspaper accounts of holidays, and I skimmed the major newspapers and magazines from the 1980s until the present that I could find in libraries and for sale in kiosks. Similarly, I happened to run across uncatalogued documents while working in the Ministry of Culture's Department of Public Creativity, and I perused and took notes on everything I found there. I sought out Soviet-era handbooks on mass spectacle production from the public library, but I have no way of knowing for sure that the people working on spectacles today ever read these handbooks. And as is always the case in ethnographic research, often what I report about the daily lives and opinions of people in Uzbekistan relies very much on the coincidence of who my acquaintances were. However, in most cases when I present a claim in this book that is based on this haphazardly collected data (haphazard in the technical sense, in that it was a convenience sample rather than a probability sample), I have attempted to make sure that the claim can be supported by more than one piece of evidence. Thus with these layers of evidence, I hope to provide a rich portrait of Uzbek national identity's public face, the world of its creators, and plausible arguments about the form, content, and organization of public culture in Uzbekistan in the 1990s.

Elsewhere, I have argued that researchers doing ethnographic fieldwork must analyze their knowledge as a product of a relationship between themselves and their informants, and that we must strive to understand the way that we are perceived by our interlocutors in order to correctly evaluate the information being presented to us in those interactions.[60] This approach is part of a feminist methodological tradition that emphasizes that this relationship between the knower and the object of her knowledge is a socially organized practice.[61] The researcher-informant relationship brings into play dynamics of race, gender, class, nation, age, and so forth that give both the researcher and the informant a partial perspective of reality, and the researcher is answerable not for the objectivity of her data but for the situated knowledge she has collaborated with her informants to produce.[62] The concept of situated knowledge implies that the data do not simply exist "out there," being hidden or revealed by informants in response to the researcher's presentation of self, but rather that the data themselves are a product of the relationship between the researcher and her informants. Though the researcher almost always gets the last word as author of the research findings, during the course of fieldwork, power flows between the researcher and her informants, and it is important to recognize informants' agency in the research relationship and how their reactions to us fundamentally affect the knowledge we are able to glean.[63] The responses people gave to my questions about national identity, for example, affected not just how my situated knowledge was produced in collaboration with my informants, but also my understanding in the sense that the informants' reactions to me gave me significant data about how they felt about their culture and what they were making of their national identity.

Because of the conventions of academic writing and the difficulty of claiming an authorial voice when advocating a methodology that produces "situated knowledge," authors rarely analyze the actual knowledge produced in terms of the researcher's uniquely situated experience in the field. Throughout this book, I will try to integrate comments on methodology into the narrative by pointing out places where my role as a researcher and my particular characteristics seemed to be especially important in determining what I was shown or told, or in having some sort of effect on my informants that presented ethical challenges for me as a researcher. I will also attempt to illuminate aspects of my identity, as a scholar and as a person, that will give the reader some insight into how I have shaped the knowledge I have produced. In so doing, I am not intending to be self-indulgent or to set up this book as nothing more than my own perspective, but instead am trying to be as transparent as possible about the partial perspective presented here on the phenomenon of Uzbek national identity.

In chapter 1, I introduce the main issues related to culture and national identity in Uzbekistan, giving the reader a brief history of Uzbekistan and an overview of the ways that the politics of national identity played out during the 1990s. The rest of the book's chapters are organized around a breakdown of culture into form, content, and production. In chapter 2, I discuss general issues related to modernity, globalization, and cultural forms in Uzbekistan, and then focus on the form of the mass spectacle that the government has chosen to represent the culture of Uzbekistan on the main national holidays. The focus of chapter 3 is cultural content, and in this chapter I emphasize the civic and ethnic components of Uzbekistan's national identity as it is expressed through public culture. I examine elite attitudes about the renewal of Uzbek culture and the ways that postcolonial critiques of Russian domination and international discourses of global norms affected the content of national holiday spectacles. Chapter 4 provides an overview of changes in the system of culture production since the Soviet era and takes a closer look at the way that politics influences culture. Specifically, I look at the ways that participation in culture production expresses certain relationships between the state and society. In the conclusion, I discuss changes in Karimov's ideology of national independence since the completion of my fieldwork in 2002 and the implications of these changes for the arguments in the rest of the book.

Chapter One

| | |

MAPPING THE LANDSCAPE OF NATIONAL IDENTITY IN UZBEKISTAN

| | |

Clarice, the glorious city, has a tormented history. . . . Populations and customs have changed several times; the name, the site, and the objects hardest to break remain. Each new Clarice, compact as a living body with its smells and its breath, shows off, like a gem, what remains of the ancient Clarices, fragmentary and dead. . . . A given number of objects is shifted within a given space, at times submerged by a quantity of new objects, at times worn out and not replaced; the rule is to shuffle them each time, then try to assemble them. Perhaps Clarice has always been only a confusion of chipped gimcracks, ill-assorted, obsolete.

| Italo Calvino, *Invisible Cities* |

In January of 1990, as a senior at Macalester College, I did a research project on the urban geography of Russian colonial cities in Central Asia. I was fascinated by the twisty streets of Tashkent and Samarkand's "old cities" that wove around the marketplaces and public squares. Equally striking was the way the nineteenth-century Russian city abruptly confronted the organic tangles of the old city with its radial design, capping the unruly indigenous head with an orderly imperial crown. Further out, in the parts of the city developed during the Soviet era, the linear aesthetic was carried to its logical extreme in the rectangular grid pattern of superblocks subdivided by narrow paths that would barely accommodate a single vehicle. Since this was back in the days of rudimentary word processing, I carefully pasted pictures by hand to the essay's pages: maps of Tashkent and Samarkand, and photocopies of the kinds of buildings to be found in each section of the city: adobe buildings with interior court-yards in the old city, Italianate candy-colored buildings in the Tsarist city center, and monolithic concrete apartment blocks in the contemporary Soviet developments.

Five years later, when I finally arrived for my first visit to Tashkent, my expectations of the city were shaped by these earlier images. I had become infatuated with pictures of the blue-domed buildings and colorful mar-ketplaces of the old city, but I was equally enamored of the stark Soviet aesthetic, exemplified by the apartment buildings and grocery stores I had encountered several years before in Moscow and St. Petersburg. Since declaring independence from the Soviet Union in 1991, Uzbekistan had entered yet another new era, represented to me in my first tour of the city by the construction of a new type of building: the glass skyscraper, future home to banks and hotels. What was it like to live in this place, with its juxtaposition of cultures, histories, and ideologies? What was it like to be so far from Moscow and yet to have shared with Russians (and with Arme-nians and Yakuts, for that matter) a self-concept as Soviet? What was it like to come of age in the stability and security of the Brezhnev era,[1] only to find yourself reaching mid-life in the wild uncertainty of independence and in a period of rapid globalization?

The answers to some of these questions came from my first host in 1995, a woman several years my senior named Saida. Saida opa[2] grew up in a *hovli*, an adobe courtyard-style house, in a village outside the city of Namangan. As a young adult, she lived in Namangan and rose through the ranks of the local Communist Party apparatus. After independence, her facility with English allowed her to find a job in Tashkent, working for a foreign nongovernmental organization (NGO). Saida opa accepted and in-tegrated the various parts of her life, from the obligations she felt toward her elderly parents back home to the demands of being a single profes-sional woman in the city; from her ardent Communist past to her compe-tence at aiding the progress of democracy in the post-Soviet era. She read mystery novels in English in her free time, spoke Russian at work, and communicated with her family in Uzbek. She struggled, of course, with the normal hassles of everyday life in a disintegrating economy and cor-rupt bureaucracy, and she agonized over being single and childless late in

Figure 1. A Brezhnev-era building with a newer façade on its front section. During the 1990s, many older buildings were spruced up with these kinds of contemporary-looking sheaths. PHOTO BY AUTHOR.

her thirties, but her conflicts were far from exotic. Saida opa was by no means a typical Uzbek woman, yet her experiences gave me insight into some of the key issues that other Uzbeks struggle with in crafting a collective identity: mixing traditional lifestyles with Soviet education and ideology, and then retooling to adapt to the realities of a post-Soviet jumble of nationalism, Islam, market socialism, and authoritarianism.

One way this politics of culture is negotiated by the Uzbek government is through the reinterpretation of history, but political and cultural elites working on the official nation-building project are limited by what had been commonly understood as historical facts during the Soviet period, by the national borders established in 1924, and by what "significant others" in the world community will accept, ignore, or reject. The state was also limited by the exigencies of the present, such as the perceived need to create new national heroes, the political requirement that explorations of Soviet atrocities not taint anyone presently in power, and the common sense that Uzbeks and Tajiks were two entirely different ethnic groups rather than a revival of the multiethnic category of Sarts (a name that designated the inhabitants of urban oases) that existed in pre-Soviet times.[3]

The evidence and arguments in the rest of this book deal with the form, content, and organization of holiday concerts in particular, while this chapter focuses more broadly on the complexities of the contemporary politics of culture in Uzbekistan. In order to understand the contemporary situation, this chapter first provides a brief overview of the history of Uzbekistan. However, as a sociologist, I am interested less in history as an attempt to present a narrative that reflects an actual past than in the past as experienced in contemporary social memory. Studies of social memory give us a valuable way to investigate how collective identity is shaped by presentist interpretations of the past.[4] This method recognizes that memory is not something that takes place inside one's head, but rather is a fundamentally discursive act and, as such, requires references to connect to a shared system of ideas.[5] Every statement about personal or societal history must make sense both in terms of what are agreed upon "facts" as well as within the framework of how people make sense of their world.

Just as Saida opa gave me valuable insights into Uzbekistan even though she was not a typical Uzbek woman, my perspective on culture and national identity in Uzbekistan also comes from a particular social location. Although studies of social memory do a brilliant job of deconstructing both history and collective identity, many lack reflexivity on the part of the author about her own role in interpreting the local interpretations of the past. This becomes especially problematic when an outsider is reading a different story in the landscape than would a native.[6] The collective identity that I present in this chapter is inextricable from my own background and interpretation. For example, the fact that I grew up in the 1970s with liberal, egalitarian values that made me question both the cold war anti-Soviet stereotypes and the Soviet stereotypes about "exotic" Uzbekistan. Therefore, my interpretation of Uzbekistan's collective memory needs to be seen as just that: my interpretation, shaped by my own knowledge and perspectives. Unlike those who take a more ethnographic approach to studying social memory, I do not claim that my analysis in this chapter presents the worldview of my informants.[7] The story I tell emerges from a dialogue with people and places in Uzbekistan, but it is still very much my own story, crafted for my audience of Western readers, and not necessarily the one a native would tell.

A Question of Identity

As Italo Calvino demonstrated so poignantly in the epigraph to this chapter, cities tell stories. Social memory, embodied in the ill-assorted artifacts of urban landscapes, museums, and recorded histories, is always a bricolage with more stories to tell than its official interpretation.[8] While history can be recorded and lie undiscovered for centuries, collective memories have to be experienced to exist. Memory can be renewed in many ways: through books, storytelling, recollection, or strolling through a city, but it is always ephemeral, always open to interpretation and vulnerable to distortion.

Questions of social memory are highly charged because although both individual and collective memories are subject to inevitable distortions, we rely on them as if they were objective. Though memories are malleable like clay, we treat them as if they were etched in stone. Memories in the distant past fade: details are lost, new perspective are gained, and old stories are recast into more contemporary forms. Selective remembering and forgetting takes place in a society when present interests determine which events or persons are publicly commemorated and which are collectively ignored. Other cases of remembering and forgetting are shaped, not by conscious manipulation, but by the conventions of memory, the common features of national narratives such as the battle for independence and victories in international sporting events.[9] Triumphs are more often recalled than failures, though a failure of the past may be recast as a triumph of the present. In collective memory, though outright fabrication will fail to convince most people, often the bald-faced truth is also unwelcome, especially when it threatens the very myths that hold a community together.[10] A significant collective memory (such as the Vietnam War, in the case of the United States) can unite a society, but it can also lay out the society's divisions, both past and present, even as other aspects are in the process of being lost from collective memory.[11]

I weave together my exploration of national identity in this section with examples of how social memory is written in the cityscape of Tashkent. Tashkent is a city of more than 2 million, the most populous of the former Soviet Union's Central Asian republics. The features of Tashkent's urban landscape dramatize the city as a point of cultural, temporal, and spatial convergence.[12] During the 1990s, the geographical and symbolic center of

Figure 2. Workers begin construction on Mustaqillik Maydoni in preparation for the Independence Day spectacle. During the concert, hundreds of students will hold up colored cards to form pictures underneath this pedestal where a statue of Vladimir Lenin used to stand. PHOTO BY AUTHOR.

Tashkent's urban landscape was Mustaqillik Maydoni, Independence (formerly Lenin) Plaza, an enormous public space in central Tashkent that used to have a kilometer-long parade alley, designed for the military parades of the Soviet era (and this space will feature prominently in later chapters as it is the location of the Independence Day concert). On the plaza were beautiful fountains, walking paths along the Anhor River, and several important buildings, including the building housing the offices of cabinet ministers. Standing in the middle of the plaza, looking to the east on a very clear day, one could see stunning, snow-capped peaks of the Tien Shan Mountains. Turning toward the west, there was a large, red stone pedestal upon which a statue of Lenin used to stand. After the statue was taken down and unceremoniously dumped in a nearby vacant lot, a (supposedly temporary) monument was put in its place. The monument was a golden globe with a relief outline of Uzbekistan that was so outsized, it took up a good part of the globe's face.

Figure 3. Part of Tashkent's new memorial to the Second World War. The names of soldiers who died are engraved in alphabetical order on metal plates connected by a hinge, like a book. Each viloyat (province) has its own set of plates that visitors can page through.
PHOTO BY AUTHOR.

Looking around the plaza, some of Tashkent's most important land-marks were visible, including the stadium of the Pakhtakor soccer team. To the north was the Turkiston Theater, a performing arts venue designed in the style characteristic of Tashkent buildings of the 1970s and 1980s: blocky but stately, using white stone or concrete, with ornamentation such as blue tile, mosaics, or screen work that evokes Oriental themes. There was also a movie theater on the plaza, with a sign on its roof commemorating the date of Independence: 1 September 1991. On top of the building was one of the first slogans of Islam Karimov, the first and (so far) only president of Uzbekistan, though the part of the sign attributing the quote to Karimov himself was removed between 1995 and 1996. The slogan was *"O'zbekiston Kelajagi Buyuk Davlat"*: in the future, Uzbekistan will be a great state. The plaza also looked to the past in its memorial of the Second World War that was remodeled for the twenty-first century, going from a Soviet-style minimalist design to a more elaborate one that reflected both

Islamic architecture and the contemporary international trend of remembering the dead by name.[13]

Mustaqillik Maydoni was filled with the symbols of modern nationhood. When viewed in the context of the rest of central Tashkent, including the Eski Juva, the old city district, the urban landscape narrated a story of national identity as it was conceived by government officials in the 1990s. While many citizens of Uzbekistan lived their lives in a rural landscape that told a very different story of Uzbek identity, Tashkent's story told of a glorious history and the hope of a glorious, or at least prosperous, future. However, often the government seemed less concerned with the material prosperity of the country than with its international cachet, resulting in a Potemkin-village effect when a visitor passed through a spectacular mosaic archway only to confront litter on a crumbling marble staircase. The government was also interested in the spiritual renewal of the people, but they wanted that renewal to resonate with universal human values and internationally accepted models of secular nationalism. The synthesis of Uzbek and international culture was an elusive answer to the puzzle of identity faced by Uzbeks and other groups experiencing rapid social change: where do we come from and where are we going?

To answer the question "where do we come from?," the government sanctioned the exploration of the history and traditions of the people who had lived in the territory of Uzbekistan (many of whom were not ethnic Uzbeks). To answer the question "where are we going?," the government had to grapple with the role of tradition in the modern world, with its desire to become a "normal" nation, and with the legacies of Soviet institutions. Before I embarked on my field research, I expected cultural and political elites to be preoccupied with a search for authenticity, the elimination of Soviet themes and symbols that didn't "make sense" to Uzbeks, and a recovery of the "true" Uzbek culture that had been repressed or neglected by the Soviet authorities. What I found instead was less a concern for authenticity than an interest in normalcy. In the 1990s, many Uzbeks in Tashkent did not seem to feel strongly that Soviet culture had been difficult to make sense of or had been somehow incompatible with Uzbek culture. They did, however, feel that Uzbek culture was more normal than Soviet culture, that certain Soviet impositions such as Russophilia and the prohibition of private markets were deviant, and that Uzbek culture on its own was much more compatible with global norms than Soviet culture had been. At the same time, they did not hesitate to use dialectical materialist theory to explain why Uzbek culture was "advanced," and they gave credit to the Soviet system for helping Uzbek culture become more normal, through modernization and so on.

As the Karimov regime consolidated its power in 1992, the particular answers to the question "where do we come from?" were narrowed down to a select few and only gradually expanded over the next ten years. What is surprising is the extent to which the historiography of post-Soviet Uzbekistan was firmly rooted in what Olivier Roy calls the "Soviet conceptual matrix," which mapped out the great figures and events of Soviet Uzbekistan's past. The job of the new historiography was simply to reverse the negative evaluations of certain figures deemed by Soviet ideology to be feudal tyrants (such as Amir Timur) or so-called bourgeois nationalists (such as the Jadid writers Cholpon and Fitrat).[14] Contemporary historiography in Uzbekistan shares with its Soviet predecessor the desire "to obliterate the [pre-Soviet] Turkestani identity in favor of an Uzbek ethnic identity, but with the added ingredient of Uzbekistan's desire to pose as a legitimate rallying-point in Central Asia."[15] These official tropes of social memory gave a clear picture of what the government's answers were to the questions of who they were and where they hoped they were going.

Where Do We Come From? Heritage and Social Memory

Walking from Mustaqillik Maydoni to the Jasorat (courage) Monument a kilometer to the north, one travels from the collective memories of 1991 to those of 1966, when the earthquake erased some of the tales that had been etched in its landscape. The monument tells one story, but the ordinary buildings of Tashkent embellish the story and distort what is remembered about "before." Many of Tashkent's older neighborhoods and monuments were destroyed by the earthquake, giving the government a wonderful opportunity to retell the story of Tashkent. The rubble of homes was cleared to make way for cement block apartment buildings. New parks and public spaces were built and dedicated to heroes such as Marx, Lenin, and Yuri Gagarin. Boxy skyscrapers made of glass and blue tile (a secular echo of the former mosques and madrassas) were built in the center of the city, replacing indigenous, colonial, and Stalinist architecture alike. After independence, the government rewrote parts of the story again, replacing the statue of Marx in the city center with one of Amir Timur, renaming many streets, and making over the drab exterior of the Soviet cityscape with shiny glass facades and newly built skyscrapers. The Soviets had given Uzbekistan a useable past, however, so many things stayed the same. The theater named after the fourteenth-century Turkic-language writer Alisher Navoiy retained its Soviet-era name, while Pushkin Street stayed to remind the citizens of Tashkent of their cosmopolitan orientation (see table 1 below).

A Useable Past? The Soviet Era in Uzbekistan

In the 1990s, a quick taxi ride down Sharof Rashidov Avenue (named for the locally well-liked leader of the Uzbek Soviet Socialist Republic (SSR) Communist Party from 1959 to 1983) to O'zbekiston Street took one from the "Courage Memorial Complex" earthquake monument to the "Peoples' Friendship Monument" on Friendship of the Peoples Square (Xalqlar Do'stligi), another of the main public spaces in Tashkent. These two monuments commemorated events of the Soviet era in order to emphasize how misfortune brought out the best in people of different nationalities who worked together to overcome obstacles. Though these monuments, constructed in the Soviet period, stressed the interdependence of the Soviet republics and the great things the Soviet people could do when they cooperated, they remained celebrated parts of the collective memory of independent Uzbekistan. There was much about the Soviet past that Uzbekistan actively remembered in its urban landscape. While political monuments were quick to go after the collapse of the Communist Party, monuments such as these that emphasize humanistic values (friendship and cooperation among people of different nationalities) reminded citizens of the importance of interethnic harmony and spoke to outsiders such as myself of the universal aspects of Uzbek culture.

While the earthquake monument celebrated the way that people from all over the Soviet Union came together to help rebuild Tashkent, the friendship monument celebrated the ways that Uzbekistan aided people from other republics of the Soviet Union during the Second World War. The general principle celebrated was hospitality, one of the particular (as opposed to universal) Uzbek values that was seen as distinguishing Uzbeks from other ethnic groups. Uzbekistan hosted hundreds of thousands of refugees and orphans from the European part of the Soviet Union

Figure 4. Xalqlar Do'stligi Plaza. To the right of the monument to the Shomahmudov family is the Tashkent Circus. PHOTO BY AUTHOR.

during the war, some of whom stayed and made Uzbekistan their home. The friendship monument celebrated a particularly legendary gesture of hospitality made by an "ordinary Uzbek family." The Shomahmudov family took in fourteen children of various nationalities, all of whom were portrayed in the statue on Friendship of the Peoples Square. These monuments and the events they recall were still an active part of Uzbek social memory after independence and demonstrated that despite the dominance of nationalist rhetoric in the public sphere, the integration as part of the "brotherhood of Soviet peoples" was still a meaningful part of Uzbek national identity.

Changes in street names were another indicator of what aspects of the past were retained and which were let go of in the first decade of Uzbekistan's independence. These name changes were part of Uzbekistan's erasure of the Communist elements of its Soviet past, the Russian leaders (but not the Uzbek leaders) and political thinkers, especially. Street renaming in central Tashkent reflected the desire to replace Communist commemoration with national commemoration. Table 1 also shows that some aspects

Table 1. Selected place name changes in Tashkent, as of 2004.

SOVIET ERA NAME	NEW NAME	COMMENT
Engels Street	Amir Timur Street	
Rustaveli Street	Usmon Nosir Street	Shota Rustaveli was a medieval Georgian poet; Nosir was a writer killed during the Stalinist purges.
Lunacharskii Shosse	Buyuk Ipak Yo'li Kuchasi (Great Silk Road Street)	Anatolii Lunacharskii was the Soviet Union's first commissar of education.
Lenin Prospect	Sharof Rashidov Street	Rashidov was the leader of the Uzbek SSR during the Brezhnev era.
50th Anniversary of the Uzbek SSR	Abdulla Qodiriy Street	Qodiriy was an Uzbek writer (1894–1938).
Kuybyshev Street	Yo'ldosh Oxunboboev Street	Kuybyshev was the head of the revolutionary Turkistan Commission; Oxunboboev was the leader of the Uzbek SSR during the Terror.
Karl Marx Street	Hamza Street	Hamza Haqimzoda was an Uzbek writer (1889–1929).
Proletarian Street	Movarounnahr Street	Movarounnahr is an old Arabic name for the land Uzbekistan now occupies.
Revolution Square	Mustaqillik Maydoni (Independence Square)	
Karl Marx Square	Amir Temur Hiyoboni	
Komsomol Park	Alisher Navoiy Milliy Bog'i (National Garden)	Alisher Navoiy was a fourteenth-century poet and is considered the father of literary Uzbek.
Exhibition of the Economic Achievements of the Soviet Union	"Tashkentland" amusement park	The amusement park was built by a Turkish company.
Navoiy Street	Unchanged	See above.
O'zbekiston Street	Unchanged	
Pushkin Street	Unchanged	Alexander Pushkin was a nineteenth-century Russian poet.
Gorkii Street, metro	The street is Academic Habib Abdullaev Prospekti and the metro station is Byuk Ipak Yo'li (Great Silk Road)	Maksim Gorkii was a twentieth-century Russian writer. Abdullaev was a geologist and president of the Uzbek SSR Academy of Sciences.
Friendship of the Peoples Square (and street)	Unchanged	
Muqimi Street, theater	Unchanged	Muqimi was an Uzbek poet (1851–1903).
Hamza Theater	Uzbek National Academic Drama Theater	See above.

of Soviet identity, such as a reverence for Russian (and Uzbek) writers, continued to be meaningful to people in Tashkent.

Some of Uzbekistan's shared memories provided a solid basis for national identity, while others were cast in doubt either because of the suspicion of Soviet repression or because of the uses to which they were being put by the current government. For example, in the early 1990s, the Uzbek language press began to publish articles about writers who had been killed by the Soviet government in the 1920s and 1930s. The authors of these articles had the goal of restoring the public image of authors who had been portrayed during the Soviet era as subversive nationalists. A decade later, the government of Uzbekistan took a stand on the issue, devoting display space in the new Museum of the Victims of Repression to writers such as Fitrat and Cho'lpon and politicians such as Fayzulla Xojaev and Akmal Ikramov, who had perished in Stalin's purges. The museum tells its story carefully, however, commemorating victims without blaming perpetrators. The villains in the story were Russian and Soviet power run amok, and little attention was given to the meaning of the victims' lives other than as martyrs for the nation.[16] In general, post-Soviet history portrayed Uzbeks as "pristine" victims of Russian and Soviet exploitation without exploring the past from a critical perspective.[17]

Uzbek collective memory continued to be affected by other traumas it experienced in the 1920s. These traumas, engineered by the Soviet government, could be seen as both beneficial and detrimental to the post-Soviet reconstruction of national identity. On the one hand, they limited what most people could know about their past, but, on the other hand, they constituted the only frame of reference for Uzbekistan as a nation with its own distinct culture and history.[18] Before the Soviet era, the region that is today Uzbekistan was composed of several kingdoms that were in turn made up of a variety of ethnic configurations. After 1924, when the Soviets drew the present-day borders in Central Asia, the idea of an Uzbek nation began to take shape for the first time in history.[19] However, the emergence of this idea entailed a certain amount of violence done to other ideas about how Central Asian communities might be organized.

One of the first traumas for the Uzbeks was alphabet reform. The Soviets implemented two new alphabets during the early decades of their rule in Uzbekistan: first the Arabic script was changed into a Latin script similar to that in Turkey; then, in order to strengthen the ties between Rus-

Figure 5. The Museum to the Victims of Repression in a Tashkent memorial complex devoted to the "martyrs (*shahidlar*) who have given their lives for the homeland (*vatan*)." PHOTO BY AUTHOR.

sia and Uzbekistan and to erect barriers between Turkey and the Turkic regions of the Soviet Union, another reform changed the alphabet to Cyrillic, the alphabet used by Russia. While these reforms had little effect at the time on the largely illiterate population, in the post-Soviet period an equally small percentage of the population could read the Arabic script (the study of Arabic was considered somewhat suspect), thus limiting their access to documents from their own, pre-Soviet past. Even though the period of secular Muslim reform in the early twentieth century (known as the *Jadid*, or reform, period) was of great interest to people curious about how Uzbekistan would find its own "path to progress," most of these people had to rely on the official academic interpretations of literature from this period, which were tailored to support the particular reforms favored by the government. Adding to these fractures with the past, the Karimov regime implemented a new reform of the alphabet back to Latin script in an attempt to facilitate communication with the West, making Soviet-era literature much less accessible to future generations. This also worked to symbolically exclude Russophones from public life. By 2004, for example, the signs inside the metro stations had all been changed over to Latin letters. One afternoon, a young woman approached me in a subway station and asked in Russian, "Do you know where the museum is?" I looked up at the sign, which clearly said *"muzey"* and pointed to it. "It's that way," I said, bemused.

A second trauma suffered by the collective memory of Uzbekistan and its neighbors was the process of national delimitation, which in 1924 drew the borders that divided the region of Turkistan into separate republics. Prior to this, the territory inside Uzbekistan's current borders was occupied by three feudal city-states (the Emirate of Bukhara, and the Khanates of Khiva and Kokand) and various nomadic tribal configurations. People's local identification corresponded to geography or kinship, rather than ethnic group, while their broader identification was with the Muslim *umma* (broader community) rather than the nation. Porous boundaries that permitted trade, migration, and alliance building were codified by delimitation into actual borders. These boundaries did not simply delimit one territory from another; they served as the foundation for delimiting one ethnic group from another. This had an especially negative impact on the people in places such as Samarkand and Bukhara, where the population borrowed freely from both Persian and Turkic cultures. The drawing of the border between the homeland for the Persian Tajiks and the Turkic Uzbeks began the institutionalization of distinct national identities.[20] However, these distinctions were never fully institutionalized, and an Uzbek-speaking visitor to Samarkand gets asked, "Don't you speak Tajik, too?," as if Uzbek linguistic competence in that part of the country is naturally accompanied by competence in Tajik. Similarly in rural areas around Samarkand, people will avow that there are no real differences between Uzbeks and Tajiks in the region.[21]

The Soviets employed a strategy typical of territorial nationalists in helping the Uzbeks develop a sense of pride and identity by annexing the cultural artifacts of all of the past civilizations that existed in the same territory.[22] By drawing the border in such a way that Samarkand and Bukhara were both included in Uzbekistan, the Soviets gave the Uzbeks the rights, as it were, to a rich and glorious heritage, artificially cutting off the Tajiks from a legacy that was also theirs. Uzbekistan's monopolization of legacies (such as Samarkand's "glorious" Timurid period following the rise of Amir Timur) was contested by Tajik intellectuals, but given Tajikistan's dearth of institutional and material resources to back up their claims, there was not much hope that they would effect a reconceptualization of Uzbek social memory in the near future.[23] Instead, the government of Tajikistan opted to focus its national heritage campaigns around the ninth- and tenth-century Samanids, the first native (Iranian) Muslim dynasty to rule the region from Balkh and Herat in modern Afghanistan to Fergana and Chach in Uzbekistan. An impressive statue of Ismoil Somoni was erected in Dushanbe to serve as a symbol of the chosen "father of the nation" (much like the Amir Timur statue in Tashkent). It could be argued that Tajikistan has gone even further than Uzbekistan in their cult of the golden-age ruler: the government of Tajikistan renamed Communism Peak (the tallest mountain in the Soviet Union) Peak Somoni and even named its currency the somoni (the other Central Asian governments named their currency after a local word related to money). Unfortunately, one of the few remaining architectural monuments from this era, the mausoleum of Ismoil Somoni, is located in Bukhara in Uzbekistan.[24] Thus the divisions caused by borders drawn in the 1920s and 1930s continue to trouble nationalist leaders who seek to unite heritage, territory, and people within a single nation-state.

The third trauma stems from this delimitation and institutionalization process as well. Following the Soviet principle that, in order to develop socially and economically, every nation must have a territory and its own set of national institutions, the Uzbek nation as it is understood to this day was in many ways defined by Soviet ethnographers, demographers, and administrators. Soviet scholars, especially ethnographers, were employed in drawing the borders as well as in institutionalizing the national identity of the new Soviet republics.[25] Soviet scholars created a narrative of Uzbek ethnogenesis and cultural heritage worthy of the heirs of the Silk Road and the Timurid Empire. All of this was done in the name of aiding in the cultural development of the Uzbek nation. Uzbekistan, as is the case with many territories of great empires, was largely brought into existence by the imaginations of its colonizers.[26] The colonial technologies of censuses, maps, and museums created a nation and a people out of an entirely different categorical schema of identities than what had been present before. As Benedict Anderson wrote,

> Interlinked with one another, then, the census, the map and the museum illuminate the late colonial state's style of thinking about its domain . . . a totalizing classificatory grid, which could be applied with endless flexibility to anything under the state's real or contemplated control: peoples, regions, religions, languages, products, monuments, and so forth. The effect of the grid was always to be able to say of anything that it was this, not that; it belonged here, not there. It was bounded, determinate. . . . Map and census thus shaped the grammar which would in due course make possible 'Burma' and 'Burmese', 'Indonesia', and 'Indonesians'. But the concretization of these possibilities —concretizations which have a powerful life today, long after the colonial state has disappeared—owed much to the colonial state's particular imaginings of history and power.[27]

Soviet ethnographers defined various practices as Uzbek (as opposed to Tajik, for example) and noted which regions were "backward" and which were "progressive" according to their historical materialist schemas. Demographers counted the Uzbeks and analyzed their fertility and morbidity, making recommendations for public health policy. And administrators carried out policies, such as ethnic quotas, that gave a new significance to being Uzbek, simply by acting "as if" that identity was significant. Moreover, Soviet authorities "consolidated" local variations of group identities into a single Uzbek nationality.[28] Sart, Muslim, Chaghatay, Xoja, Turk, and other identities faded (but did not disappear) in the wake of what Ingebor Baldauf called "radical Uzbekism," the forcible and rapid development of a Soviet-defined Uzbek national language, literature, and culture.[29] In an attempt to naturalize the idea of the Uzbek nation, the Soviets glossed over these complexities of identity, complexities that persisted in troubling Uzbekistan's contemporary nation-building project in the postindependence period. Particularly salient was the issue of Uzbekistan's claim to a heritage that it shares with many of its contemporary neighbors. The assertion of the right to these eras of the past was one of the keys to Uzbekistan's ability to imagine itself as a nation.

At the same time, the whole conceptual matrix with which these elements of heritage were mapped contained elements of both Russocentrism and Marxist teleology that post-Soviet Uzbek intellectuals challenged, often through a loosely coherent discourse of decolonization. In public discourse, "colonialism" (*mustamlakachilik*) was used as a derogatory term for the unwanted political, economic, and cultural impositions of the Soviet period, but the term came into use only gradually through the 1990s. One of the main elements of the Marxist-Leninist teleology that was challenged as colonialist was the idea that the Uzbeks were not as "advanced" as Russians, and that therefore it was the role of the culturally superior Russians to bring the Uzbeks forward so they could join the modern world. One of my interviewees expressed a common sentiment about the postcolonial push to valorize Uzbek history: "When you know all these things about your history, you evaluate it differently and can take pride in all that. You don't have to think of yourselves as a feudal people brought into the modern era by socialism. You can see how your people were colonized even starting three hundred years ago, not just starting with resettling people during WWII."[30] Thus a major part of the discourse of decolonization in Uzbekistan was the reappropriation of history, the reevaluation of historical events and personages outside of a Marxist theoretical framework, and the definition of the nation's heritage in historical terms that would be recognized by other modern people.

Reappropriating the "Golden Age"

How do people understand their nation's greatness? The idea that the sun never set on the British Empire gave British citizens a sense of proprietorship over the entire globe. The metaphors and technology produced by the space race and the cold war gave citizens of both the United States and the Soviet Union a sense of their own greatness: we are the first, the fastest, the best, the deadliest. Some nations, such as Germany and Japan, demonstrate their self-confidence through economic gestures to support poorer nations, while others, such as Egypt and Greece, are dependent for their confidence on the external validation of their status as cradles of civilization. But what if you're a citizen of one of the many nations that cannot rightfully claim these superlatives? Uzbekistan had little geopolitical influence, a small military, and an even smaller research and development base. It ranked in the bottom half of the world's economies and was not widely recognized for its contributions to world history. Yet the government knew that it needed to link the nation to concepts of greatness and to define its place in the world, both for its citizens and as public relations toward the rest of the global community.

Anthony Smith argues that the appropriation of a worthy and distinctive past is one of the most significant factors in the creation of national identity.[31] Smith claims that "golden ages" perform a number of functions, including satisfying the quest for authentic identity by providing a myth of origin, providing an immemorial existence for the nation through the link with antiquity, rerooting the community in a homeland where the golden age took place, establishing a sense of continuity between the generations, and serving as a reinforcement to the nation's worth through the link to past greatness and a future glorious destiny ("though at present 'we' are oppressed, shortly we shall be restored to our former glory").[32] Golden age heritage as embodied in physical sites that tourists can visit and take home in the form of postcards is especially useful as it allows the state to appear as the guardian of locally based, internationally valued cultural legacies.[33] This process of the Uzbek government's instrumentalization of Central Asian heritage began, not in the independence period, but in the Soviet period, though the cast of villains assembled by Soviet historians as a foil for their teleological analysis has been transformed into the new national heroes.[34]

All around post-Soviet Tashkent, Soviet monuments abounded, but commemorations of seventeenth–nineteenth-century events and personages were much harder to find. There was a dearth of monuments celebrating the prerevolutionary era, with the exception of the few buildings that survived the earthquake. The Soviets and contemporary Uzbeks alike seemed to view that period as backward and characterized by feudal decadence. It is even more interesting to note the absence in public memory of the first Uzbek rulers of the territory, the Shaibani Khans, who were the first Uzbek dynasty to end their nomadic ways when they came to rule over the major oases of Samarkand and Bukhara during the sixteenth century. Given Uzbekistan's nationalist orientation, why was it that they did not commemorate their founders?[35] One reason may be that their claim to the heritage of these great cities allowed them to celebrate a much more glorious dynasty, one that was widely known beyond the borders of Central Asia: the dynasty of Amir Timur (1336–1405), or Tamerlane, as he is known in the West. As Tamerlane scholar Beatriz Manz has argued, "Neither the Samanids nor the [Shaibanid] Uzbeks achieved quite the worldwide prestige and recognition that Temür and his descendants enjoy. It is probably this aspect of Timurid history, more than anything else, which makes Temür suitable for the role he now plays in Uzbekistan. . . . The breadth of Temür's conquests and his reputation are major assets, both because they boost the prestige of Uzbekistan within Central Asia, and because they give it an independent place in world history."[36]

The reticence to valorize the Shaibanids was also related to the legacies of Soviet schemas of historiography. The Uzbeks were originally nomadic, and Subtelny argues that the Shaibanids were ignored because "the Soviets considered nomadic peoples ahistorical and downplayed or ignored their role in cultural development."[37] Ilkhamov describes the neglect of the Shaibanids and the glorification of the Timurids in the post-Soviet era as the result of the legacies of Soviet historiography, which did not allow the discussion of historical conflict between the Soviet nationalities, especially between the Russian and non-Russian nationalities. "By putting forward Tamerlane's and not the Golden Horde's heritage as national symbols Yakubovsky proposed a conflict-free historical background to the relationship between the people of Turkistan and Russia: Tamerlane could be viewed as a natural ally of Moscow Rus in resisting the Golden Horde."[38] Clearly, Soviet ideas about historiography had a large impact on the choices that cultural and political elites made in the early years of nation building in Uzbekistan.

The discourse about Amir Timur became so widespread and ritualized that he was often just referred to as Bobomiz (our grandfather) or Sohib-quron (great leader). His monument adorned the park, Amir Timur Hiyo-boni, at the center of Tashkent's imperial radial street grid, where the statue of Karl Marx used to stand; his likeness appeared in most places previously occupied by Lenin's; his words were dramatized by costumed actors at most holiday presentations; and there was even a local brand of cigarette (Xon) with his likeness on the package. His popularity was due in part to his international recognition and in part to the clever use of symbolism by the Karimov regime to create a cult of personality by proxy.[39] More savvy than his Turkmen counterpart Saparmurat Niyazov who created a Stalinesque cult of his personality that was fodder for international mockery, Islam Karimov promoted himself by association with Timur. Visual and verbal equivalencies were created between Karimov and Timur everywhere in the public realm. For example, in his speeches, Karimov often referred to the policies of Timur in one sentence and current state policies in the next.

Amir Timur was born in 1336 in Shahrisabz, near Samarkand, and he rose to lead the Ulus Chaghatay, one of the sections of the Mongol Empire that had been de facto ruled by settled, Muslim Turkic tribes. Timur went on to conquer parts of India and the Middle East, ruling from his capital city of Samarkand. His descendents, such as his grandson, the illustrious astronomer and king Ulughbek, continued to rule a much contracted territory until they were displaced by the Uzbeks and led off to conquer India by Bobur, Timur's great-grandson. Timur and Ulughbek were widely commemorated throughout Uzbekistan and were used to signify Uzbekistan's desire to achieve greatness in the arts and sciences. The military conquests and brutal violence of Timur were de-emphasized, while his architectural achievements, leadership philosophy, Islamic faith, and patronage of art and science were repeatedly declared.

In the Soviet period, it was impossible to completely ignore Timur, in part because his legacies, such as the Registan architectural complex in Samarkand, were inextricable from the great monuments and cultural achievements that Soviet Uzbekistan wanted to claim as its own. In 1970, during the preparations for the concert to celebrate the 2,500th anniversary of Samarkand (remarkably, the 2,750th anniversary of the city was later celebrated in 2007!), the issue of Timur was a sensitive one, and the conflict over how to depict him, if at all, revealed the tensions between popular memory and official ideology, and between regional and central interpretations of what was permitted in artistic expression. The Samarkand Theatre of Opera and Ballet intended to put on a piece for the show about Bibihanum, Timur's favorite wife. They claimed that the show "presents the figure of Timur as a cruel warrior, a master of court intrigue," and on the advice of the Samarkand City Cultural Directorate, the author and director created a Timur who was "contradictory to the idea of humanism, historical fairness, and idealism." However, a review committee from the republican Ministry of Culture viewed the show shortly before it was to be performed and criticized the producers for not depicting Timur as cruel *enough*. Furthermore, they were divided over whether they should present Timur at all: "It is out of the question to present Timur on stage, but it is also out of the question to present this show without him," worried one of the representatives from the ministry. The people from Samarkand pointed out that the Tashkent officials were making too big a deal out of it. "This is a legend we tell all visiting foreigners, so we decided to make a production of a story the whole world already knows," and some of the representatives from Tashkent agreed that "history is history, and everyone knows it anyway." Other ministry officials worried that canceling the number would cause a controversy that would be more trouble than it was worth, but in the end, Culture Minister Kuchkarov (who held his position from 1953 until 1973!) concluded that it was easier to just avoid history altogether, saying, "Though built by Timur, these monuments belong to the Soviet people now and therefore the show should be contemporary, celebrating what we have spent so much to restore."[40]

In 1996 Uzbekistan celebrated a jubilee for Timur, though the talk of the 660th anniversary of the great leader's birth caused some snickers for its chronological opportunism. Amir Timur's 650th anniversary, unfortunately, had fallen during the Soviet period when Timur was still cast as a villain, and clearly it was too long a wait until Timur's 675th. So, in August 1996, Timur's erstwhile detractors (who were also government leaders) gathered in Samarkand for a spectacle of ancient glory and contemporary grandiosity. A few weeks later, a lavish museum opened in central Tashkent, devoted to the life and empire of Timur. This state museum clearly tried to establish a continuity in the leadership of Uzbekistan that began in the time of Timur and continued to the present day, as President Karimov was clearly alluded to by visual analogies in the halls and displays as the heir to Timur's greatness. Timur was invoked in a variety of contexts as a powerful symbol to legitimate a variety of cultural and political projects. For example, in order to demonstrate the importance of the holiday Navro'z, holiday organizers frequently told me things like "Amir Timur was not so warlike—even he came back from his conquests to celebrate Navro'z."

While the heritage of Timur was used as an analogy for the political situation in Uzbekistan, the Great Silk Road was Uzbekistan's metaphor for their economic legacy and another important trope through which Uzbeks understood their relationship with the rest of the world. Between 100 BCE and 1500 CE, the Great Silk Road allowed the exchange of luxury goods between the Chinese Empire and the kingdoms of Europe, putting Central Asian traders at the center of a global economy. In the independence period, the metaphor of the Great Silk Road proclaimed that Uzbekistan was once a crossroads of civilizations and an important nexus of history, giving people hope that one day the cities of Tashkent, Samarkand, and Bukhara would again be significant to the rest of the world.

In addition to the Great Silk Road being part of the motto of countless tourism and commercial organizations in Uzbekistan, the interest in reviving its promise was also reflected in the cityscape of Tashkent. A broad main boulevard that traversed Tashkent's northeast quadrant was renamed Buyuk Ipak Yo'li Kuchasi, Great Silk Road Street. The Silk Road also appeared as a theme in numerous cultural performances, including the Independence Day extravaganza of 1996 (see chapter 3). The show featured twenty-meter-high inflatable sculptures representing different monuments along the Silk Road as well as a wonderful ensemble of dances and theatrical bits representing various Silk Road cultures, including Chinese, Indian, Turkish, Arabic, and, of course, Uzbek. Since the Silk Road was at its height well before Uzbek tribes sedentarized and began to develop and promote a Turkic high culture, stereotypical elements of classical Persian culture had to stand in for the Uzbeks in this piece. This is another example of the play of heritage and collective memory, as various cultural legacies common to the territory of Uzbekistan can be substituted for an unsuitable Uzbek past.

The other cultures of the Great Silk Road number in the holiday show were represented as something of a hybrid, with synthesized music that was readily available from the radio archives and contemporary versions of "traditional" national costumes. For example, the music and choreography of the Indian number were more representative of Bollywood than classical Indian motifs appropriate to the era of the Silk Road. Somewhat more surprising were the dances representing Germany and France, countries that had little to do with the Silk Road, but who were among Uzbekistan's biggest economic and cultural supporters in Europe. Uzbek boys in lederhosen and Russian girls in dirndls cheerily twirled across the stage in a homage to Uzbekistan's contemporary trading partner. Clearly, the Great Silk Road was a metaphor that linked both social memory and ambitions for the future.

Where Are We Going? Cultural Change and
Institutional Inertia 1988–2003

The quest for cultural revival and nation building in Uzbekistan can be broken down into three periods. First came the late Soviet era and early years of independence, characterized by a new openness in the discussion of Uzbek language, culture, and national identity. Second was the period from about 1992 to 2003, after President Karimov had consolidated his power, but both ideology and institutions were in flux. Third, the period 2003–2007, which was marked by increasing state repression, surveillance, and ideological restrictions. This last period falls outside the time frame during which I was conducting field research on culture and national identity in Uzbekistan, and therefore I will discuss it, and subsequent changes in Karimov's ideology of national independence, in more general terms in the book's conclusion.

The Assertion of Uzbek National Identity, 1988–1992

Shortly before Uzbekistan became independent from the Soviet Union, cultural elites and government officials began a campaign of Uzbek cultural renewal that included expanding the role of Uzbek ethnic themes within socialist culture, the restoration of certain previously banned aspects of Uzbek culture, and the first attempts to reinterpret Uzbek Soviet history, especially the lives and deaths of Jadid writers such as Cho'lpon and Fitrat.[41] These actions were motivated by the concerns of Uzbek nationalist intellectuals, but other forces in other parts of society were working against them. These intellectuals had to be careful, not just because they were challenging years of Communist Party thinking on the role of national culture in the public sphere, but also because of the volatile inter-ethnic atmosphere of Uzbekistan in the late 1980s. In the spring of 1989, a deadly ethnic conflict broke out between Uzbeks and Meskhetian Turks in various towns in the Fergana Valley.[42] Fearing a spread of violent nationalism, the trickle of European outmigration from Uzbekistan turned into a stream, with about 22 percent of Uzbekistan's ethnic Russians emigrating between 1990 and 1996.[43] While these ethnic conflicts had little to do with nationalism per se, nationalist intellectuals were wary of inciting, or being portrayed as inciting, ethnic violence and held themselves back from taking advantage of all the opportunities glasnost offered.

The activities of various intellectuals and students soon developed into social movements that advocated greater political sovereignty and cultural autonomy for Uzbekistan within the framework of the Soviet state, often against the wishes of Uzbekistan's Communist leadership. Birlik (Unity) and Erk (Freedom) were the most prominent of these nationalist movements. Their goals and tactics were relatively mild, focusing on cultural and ecological issues, ranging from the status of the Uzbek language to the desiccation of the Aral Sea.[44] Erk was an offshoot of Birlik that was perceived as more progovernmental, though Erk's founder, Mohammed Solih, made an early move in the national culture game. In 1985 Solih and his colleagues wrote a letter to Mikhail Gorbachev, leader of the Communist Party of the Soviet Union (CPSU), protesting that the government of the Uzbek Soviet Socialist Republic (UZSSR) was undermining national cultural values.[45] In 1988, Solih was rewarded for his bravery, in the spirit of glasnost, by being elected to head of the UZSSR Writer's Union, which for a brief time was an important forum for the nationalist opposition. Solih went on, along with Abdurahim Polat, to be one of the founders of Birlik, which focused on economic and political sovereignty in addition to cultural and environmental issues.

The nationalist movements were short-lived, but saw a limited degree of political success in spite of government repression. Though Birlik and Erk tapped into populist sentiments, they never received widespread support, in part because the government succeeded in linking social movements with ethnic conflict in people's minds. In 1989–1990, even as the legislature discussed the possibilities for the Uzbek SSR's sovereignty within the Soviet Union, they moved against the nationalist movements by cracking down on their activities and curtailing their political rights. By 1991 Birlik had been banned, but Erk actually was allowed to put Solih's candidacy forth against the leader of the Communist Party of Uzbekistan (CPUZ), Islam Karimov, in Uzbekistan's first presidential election. Karimov won with only 86 percent of the vote, in spite of election rigging and the elimination of most opposition parties by restricting access to registration. After Karimov's election and the start of the Tajik civil war in 1992 (which influenced most people to support order at all costs), political freedoms in

Uzbekistan continued to narrow and by 1993, members of Erk and the few other religious and political parties that existed in the early years of independence had been persecuted (including beatings and disappearances). The government refused to register the movements as legal organizations and eventually disbanded them, though Birlik and others have survived abroad.

During the late 1980s, the UZSSR leadership was not so much nationalist as it was eager to grab some of the power that Moscow was giving away. Gregory Gleason argues that Uzbekistan's drive for independence was less far-reaching than that of other Soviet republics and that the nationalistic laws passed by the Uzbek SSR legislature were intended as instruments of negotiation with Moscow, rather than as the foundations for independence.[46] These moves were also designed to co-opt parts of the nationalist movements' agendas by passing language laws giving Uzbek an official status and by declaring national sovereignty in 1990.[47] Kathleen Collins argues that this is a common strategy for authoritarian leaders who lack a coherent ideology or mobilization strategy: "The reference to generic values like patriotism and nationalism, economic development, social justice, and order . . . allow rulers who have gained power without mobilized mass support to neutralize opponents, co-opt a variety of supporters, and decide policies pragmatically."[48] Intellectuals had been publicly raising issues of national culture since about 1988, and eventually the government picked up on the issues that were resonating with the public, supporting the revival of national traditions such as the holiday Navro'z (see below) and in general adopting the rhetoric of national cultural renewal.

Karimov, as well, didn't portray himself as a nationalist until he was forced to, perhaps indicating one of the reasons he wasn't initially interested in developing more extreme ideological and mobilizational institutions. As recently as late 1989, Islam Karimov criticized party leaders in Andijon Oblast' for promoting nationalistic and anti-Soviet ideas.[49] But when a hard-line Communist coup against Gorbachev collapsed in August 1991, Karimov had no choice but to agree with the declaration of Uzbekistan's official independence from the USSR. After the coup, Karimov quickly came around to the nationalist point of view, relearning his native Uzbek tongue and publishing his new, de-Marxified philosophy that "the road of transition to [a] market economy to a decisive extent stems from a comprehensive consideration of national and historical factors, i.e.

traditional way of life of the people, their outlook, thinking, customs and rituals."[50] In this view, the value of the family and the community, the desire to be close to the land, and the syncretism between Islamic and folk practices stood in contrast with the "neocolonialist" centralization of the Soviet system and the "dogmatic ideologies" of socialism and Islamism.[51] His tone became increasingly nationalistic in later works, but it is important to note that it was not markedly anti-Russian.

In 1991, political factions opened up in the elite. Not only were there multiple movements and parties competing for political power, but within the legislature there were splits between the supporters of Karimov and those of his vice-president, Mirsaidov. Additionally, there was the potential for regional splits as *nomenklatura* elites (people approved by the Party for administrative positions) based in Tashkent and elites from the regions jockeyed for political power and economic control.[52] In the end, though, Karimov did a remarkable job of neutralizing his opponents through persecution, co-optation, and pact building, allowing him to consolidate his power in the office of the president. The legislature in the early 1990s gave the president increasing powers and weakened the laws supporting elections, freedom of the press, and freedom of assembly. Karimov came to control appointments for the cabinet of ministers, regional governors (*hokims*), and other powerful positions such as judgeships. He also formed a secretive and influential Presidential Council that does much of the policy work of the government.

As in many of the post-Soviet states, there was very little change in personnel from the old Soviet Uzbek state to the new, independent one. The mantle of the Communist Party (vanguard of the proletariat) simply slipped onto the shoulders of the People's Democratic Party (vanguard of the nation). Karimov made national culture, along with Uzbekistan's so-called "own model" for market transition, the centerpieces of official ideology.[53] Although she dismisses Karimov's ideology as a "nonideology," Collins acknowledges that Karimov "directed enormous state resources into creating the symbols, legends, and history of the united 'Uzbek nation'. . . . In general, the regime's democratic and nationalist agenda amounted to an admission of its desperate need for broader popular legitimacy."[54]

On the one hand, this united Uzbek nation was defined in civic terms, with all persons living in the territory being granted citizenship in 1992. On the other hand, there was a distinct de-Russification that took place, including the already mentioned restoration of old street names, the switch from a Cyrillic alphabet to a Latin one, the emergence of a discourse of decolonization, and the harassment of Russians and other Europeans, ranging from muttered threats on the street to displacement from good jobs. Still, overall the transition from 1989 to 1993 was relatively smooth, both politically and economically. Karimov had ruled out the kind of economic "shock therapy" tried by Poland and other postcommunist countries as an attempt to rapidly move toward a market economy. By 1993, the few political challenges from the nationalist and populist intelligentsia had been crushed, and Karimov's government adopted a course of moderate nationalism. The government actively promoted the renewal of Uzbek traditions and customs, including religious and secular holidays that had been suppressed during the Soviet period.

The most popular religious holidays that Karimov's government brought back were the Ro'za Hayit, the holiday at the end of Ramadan, and the Qurbon Hayit, the holiday that marks the end of the Hajj and commemorates Abraham's willingness to sacrifice his son Ishmael. New holidays the government instituted were obligatory days marking the formal properties of a modern nation such as Independence Day (September 1), Flag Day, and Constitution Day. These holidays were mainly celebrated through public ritual, while religious holidays such as the Hayits and folk holidays like Navro'z (March 21) were celebrated with family and community rituals that were seen as honored traditions. Some holidays were retained from the Soviet period, as well: the International New Year (January 1) and Victory Day (May 9) were also public celebrations with ceremonies and festivities in which all citizens were invited to take part. International Women's Day (March 8) was marked publicly but was mainly celebrated in the workplace and with presents from male family members.

National holidays are commonly used by states as conscious expressions of national identity, and the period after a country becomes independent is often fraught with struggles over the meanings of ritual and festivity.[55] As Kathleen Smith has argued, post-Soviet holidays served as sites of struggle among political and social groups in Russia, who strove to convince the larger public of their interpretation of the holiday's meaning.[56] These interpretations took time to emerge, as leaders struggled to translate the relevance of a Soviet or newly invented holiday for the contemporary context. For example, after the end of the Soviet Union, the anniversary of the

October Revolution (November 7) was marked by both celebration and protest, critique and nostalgia, of the Soviet past. The holiday became the site of discourse production about the Soviet past, about socialist values, and about what it meant to be Russian today, transforming "what had once been a formal, routine display of official power into a vibrant exhibition of popular might and resistance."[57] Over the course of several years, the Communists and liberals consolidated their opposed interpretations of the day's significance. However, in 1996, President Yeltsin tried to neutralize the debate and put forth an official interpretation, renaming November 7 as the Day of Reconciliation and Accord, which would mark the significance of the date without interpreting it. This was a pluralist but "profoundly uncritical" solution, according to Smith, which failed to satisfy anyone outside of the government.[58] In this regard, the difference between public life in Russia and Uzbekistan is that in Russia public dissatisfaction with the government's policies regarding holidays and their social uses is subject to open discussion and debate, whereas I found that in Uzbekistan, even when asking people directly, there seemed to be little understanding or critique of the choices the government had made in terms of which holidays it promoted or demoted. In Uzbekistan, the government decisions about holidays were either broadly popular or unimportant, even to many members of the intelligentsia.

Smith claims that the Russian democrats' "lack of resolution in forging traditions through holiday celebrations may be attributed in part to the crises of identity prevalent across the political spectrum in Russia, as well as to a desire to avoid the heavy-handed manipulation of festivities practiced by the old regime."[59] Uzbekistan's leadership suffered no such qualms, and thus they were able to more successfully seize the opportunity to shape collective memory. Due to the lack of pluralism in Uzbekistan, public debate about post-Soviet national holidays was more subdued than it had been in many other former Soviet republics. First of all, there were no formal organizations representing different political perspectives, such as the Communists and the various types of conservative and liberal democratic parties found in Russia. With no Communist Party to support it, the celebration of the October Revolution was dropped from the new calendar without much of a fuss in Uzbekistan.

Few Soviet holidays had constituencies that the government of Uzbekistan cared about. One exception is the constituency of veterans of the

Second World War, and the evolution of Victory Day (May 9) indicates the continuing importance of certain aspects of Soviet identity to the citizens of Uzbekistan. Rather than being about political identity, the discourse around Uzbekistan's holidays was more oriented toward ethnonational identity, especially the role of Muslim and pre-Muslim traditions in contemporary society. While these holidays (Navro'z, Qurbon Hayit, Ro'za Hayit) aroused passionate discussions about how they should be celebrated, other "invented" holidays (Independence Day, Constitution Day) aroused antipathy or bemusement. For everyone but Uzbek nationalists, independence was a questionable event to celebrate, and the irony of celebrating the much-violated constitution of Uzbekistan grew with each passing year. Other Soviet holidays (New Year, Women's Day) were universally popular and most post-Soviet states have retained these secular, nonpolitical holidays in their commemorative calendars.

The Revival of Navro'z—A Trope of Subordinate Identity

Aside from the revival of Islamic holidays, the most politically and culturally significant holiday in post-Soviet Uzbekistan was Navro'z, and the story of its revival in the late 1980s and early 1990s sheds light on the politics of culture at the time. In part because I was studying holidays, and in part because the celebration of this holiday is an aspect of national culture that is dearly cherished by ordinary Uzbeks, I heard a lot of stories from academics, artists, and acquaintances about the struggle between Tashkent and Moscow over Navro'z during the Soviet period and about why its revival was so important during the period of independence. On my first trip to Uzbekistan in 1995, I was ignorant of the holiday's importance. While I had booked my trip to coincide with the better-known Muslim holidays of Ramadan and Ro'za Hayit (Eid al-Fitr, in Arabic) which fell in February that year, I departed in early March and missed Navro'z, which falls on March 21. My friends and colleagues were appalled that I was not sticking around for the most important holiday of all. The emphasis they put on the holiday led me to make it one of the focal points of my research the following year. Indeed, by examining the history and content of Navro'z as well as how the story of its *revival* was told in the 1990s, we can gain valuable insights into various aspects of Uzbek national identity.

Navro'z is a holiday of the spring equinox that has been celebrated in the territory of today's Uzbekistan since the dominant religion of the region was Zoroastrianism. Even after the majority of the population of the Persian and Turkic world converted to Islam, Zoroastrian practices continued. There are still practicing Zoroastrians in Uzbekistan, though most of them keep their religion a secret. Navro'z, which means "new day" in Persian (*No Ruz* or *Nawruz*), is celebrated throughout contemporary Central Asia, Iran, India, and Turkey, by Muslims as well as Zoroastrians. In Uzbekistan, as in many regions that celebrate Navro'z, the holiday was not a one-day event. Navro'z was more of a season, like Christmas in the United States, and was celebrated in various ways for weeks before and after the day itself. Uzbekistan's main Navro'z celebration fell on the 21st of March every year, and it was considered the most popular holiday, at least among those who are ethnic Uzbeks. The Russian-speaking population knew it as a day off from work and a chance to take in some public entertainment, but they did not know much more about its history and traditions than most Anglo-Americans know about Cinco de Mayo. Several people I talked to, Russians and even some Uzbeks, were not aware of when the holiday was. Many Uzbeks were less familiar with the holiday than their grandparents were since the holiday was deemed religious by the Soviet authorities and consequently banned from being officially celebrated.

According to most sources, Navro'z is a holiday of spring that celebrates the triumph of warmth and light over cold and darkness, the renewal of nature, and the beginning of the agricultural labor cycle. The first aspect, the triumph of light and warmth, is symbolically associated with the equinox and the lengthening of the day, and also with the Zoroastrian symbol of fire, though fire played almost no role in Uzbekistan's Navro'z celebrations, and reference to fire rituals was actively discouraged by the government. Some elites also talked about Navro'z as a time when the forces of evil rise up and must be put down for another year by the forces of good, but these references to the mystical sources of Navro'z were not part of the everyday understanding of Navro'z I encountered among acquaintances and in popular culture.

The celebration of Navro'z was officially banned during most of the Soviet period, though during the Gorbachev era Navro'z's "forces of good" won out over the "evil forces" of Soviet anti-religious campaigns and paranoia about Uzbek religious fundamentalism.

ALISHER AKA: At that time [just prior to independence] there was a lot of discussion about the problem of producing Navro'z. All sorts of cultural and academic figures wrote about what a good tradition Navro'z was, ancient, and how good it would be to reestablish it. And then there was the decree of the president to clear Navro'z's name and make it a day off and to make preparations to celebrate it.

LAURA: Was it dangerous at that time to propose celebrating Navro'z?

ALISHER AKA: Well, some people hadn't interpreted it correctly. For example, people who didn't know or didn't understand Navro'z said it is a religious holiday. Why do you have that green color out there? Are you fundamentalists? etc. Then we came to understand the history of Navro'z before the Islamic period, that this holiday on the territory of Central Asia has a four-thousand-year-old history.[60]

In the 1980s, the issue of Navro'z was a site of contestation between more nationalistic Uzbeks (including many at the Ministry of Cultural Affairs) and those who were loyal to Moscow and saw any ground gained by traditional culture as ground lost to the cause of preserving the Soviet Union. In the 1980s, a holiday called Navbahor ("new spring," to be celebrated on the first Sunday in April) was introduced as a Soviet substitute for Navro'z, but the holiday never had a chance to take root. Its institutionalization coincided with the beginning of perestroika and glasnost, which allowed the debate about Navro'z to be reopened. Had Navbahor been institutionalized in the 1970s, it might have sufficed as a substitute for Navro'z, but coming as it did at the end of a time of Uzbek national humiliation (due to the "cotton affair" of the early 1980s, in which many Uzbek leaders were sacked for corruption), it was received as a slap in the face. In my discussions with scholars and artists about the revival of Navro'z, my interlocutors saw parallels between Moscow's attempt to force Uzbekistan to celebrate Navbahor and the humiliation of the cotton scandal and the subsequent death of the popular Uzbek leader, Sharof Rashidov.[61] The cultural and political were intertwined in this narrative of resistance against Moscow, and, at least among the elite, the revival of Navro'z in the post-Soviet period appeared to be closely tied to the rehabilitation of those tarnished by the cotton scandal.[62] For example, in my interview with Ergash aka, a man who had worked on the Navro'z concert, the conversation turned to Rashidov. Ergash aka had been something of a political bigwig in his younger days and told me that he had been called in to testify against Rashidov, but that all he had said was that "Rashidov did what he had to do and no worse than anyone else." He got fired for his testimony, which included an anecdote that reflected unfavorably on the Communist Party,[63] and more than a decade later, the whole incident still seemed to bother him greatly.

Another narrative about why the Navbahor idea was poorly received was that it was perceived as offensive to Uzbek national culture, an insult to the beloved holiday Navro'z and an example of unwanted interference from Party officials in the burgeoning expression of Uzbek national culture. One of my informants showed me a book he had published in those years where censors literally pasted over the word "Navro'z" with pieces of paper that said "Navbahor." This was apparently a last-ditch attempt on the part of Uzbekistan's Communist hard-liners to neutralize the growing support for the renewal of pre-Soviet traditions, though for most of the late Soviet period Navro'z had merely been refused official sponsorship by the state. This same informant passively resisted calls from his superiors to write scholarly articles about Navbahor and to produce creative material for Navbahor celebrations. He was one of many passionate defenders of Navro'z.

FARHOD AKA: The latest battle against Navro'z took place in the middle-eighties. Navro'z started to be observed as soon as perestroika began. And since here there were certain people who served Moscow directly, they called Moscow and said, "They're reviving a second new year. How on earth can you have two new years?!" So, Moscow listened to them . . . and called the TSK [the Central Committee of the CPUZ]. . . . Abdullaeva [the third secretary] said there was no way there would be a second new year. . . . [But] how can you erase Navro'z? But she tried, and with the help of our toadies [the locals whose loyalty was to Moscow], she came up with the holiday Navbahor. . . . She couldn't destroy Navro'z, so she came up with a different name so she could say to Moscow that she got rid of Navro'z and now we had a new Soviet holiday of spring.[64]

According to Farhod aka, some of Uzbekistan's cultural elites went along with Navbahor, only to find themselves publishing apologies for their betrayal of Navro'z a few years later. During 1986–1987 there were two events where a Navro'z revival was discussed in official forums: at a conference on the nationalities question in Tashkent and at the Writers'

Union conference. At the nationalities conference, Moscow Jews and Uz-bek and Tajik intellectuals all came out in favor of national holidays in general. A letter from the Islamic Directorate (a religious organization officially sponsored by the Soviet state) was presented in rebuttal to argu-ments that Navro'z was a religious holiday, declaring that the Islamic faith did not even recognize the holiday. This latter fact was true, Navro'z is not related to Islam, but the directorate only confused the issue of whether Navro'z was a Muslim holiday or a holiday celebrated by people who hap-pened to be Muslim. In any case, for the vast majority of people in Central Asia today, Navro'z is a cultural holiday that is nearly free of religious associations, not unlike the celebration of Thanksgiving in the United States.[65]

In some ways, the nationalities conference was a turning point in Soviet attitudes toward national culture since even Yuri Bromlei, the architect of Soviet nationality theory, agreed that there was no harm in letting people keep their national holidays. The faction of Uzbek elites who had toed the Communist Party line for so many years suddenly found their behav-ior was unrewarded by Moscow and unsupported by their power base at home. At the conference of the Union of Writers, the Navbahor supporters were dealt a definitive loss.

FARHOD AKA: The head of our section . . . said, "You can't just throw it [Navro'z] out. There was the need for it then as there is now." Everyone listened to him. . . . This was just the beginning of perestroika, you know, and all of a sudden there was this unity, everyone rallied behind this one person, everyone rallied against [Abdullaeva] and there was unity and pride. . . . The whole people felt like victors.

While Farhod aka related to me what he recalled as the history of the struggle for Navro'z, his narrative ties into a broader discourse about the Soviet repression of Navro'z that, I argue, is a trope of subordinate identity. Tropes of subordinate identity narrate the history of a group in a way that pits the wily in-group against the foolish but powerful dominant group, describing the horrible things "they" did to "us" and the clever ways "we" got around "their" rules. They are a way a group can control the objectifica-tion of their culture by self-objectification and project themselves as social equals of the dominant group without having to address actual inequalities between the groups.[66] In this case, the in-group consisted of ethnic Uzbeks who supported national traditions and the dominant group was made up of Soviet loyalists, some of whom were also Uzbeks.

The trope about Navro'z focused on the idiocy of those who opposed the holiday and the perseverance of the holiday's supporters in the face of repression. It also contributed to self-objectification by using the Soviet-modern discourse of national traditions and Soviet forms of celebration. As in the example of the rehabilitation of Amir Timur, the Soviet schemas through which culture and history were understood were simply reversed in the official discourse about Navro'z, so that Navro'z was now good instead of religiously suspect. The fundamental understanding of holidays, heritage, and Uzbek cultural identity as applied to Navro'z remained mostly the same. This reproduction of schemas parallels what others have observed about colonialist discourses that allow "the dominant culture [to obscure] by its homogenizing gesture the historical complexity of our cultural/ideological formations. . . . The dominant ideology attempts to freeze the conflictual and contestatory process of meaning production in order to consolidate its own hegemony."[67] Thus, the triumph of Navro'z trope avoided addressing real inequalities and real oppression by the Soviets by glossing the revival of Navro'z as a victory of the people's ancient history, instead of confronting the actual events of the last century. In the tropes of subordinate identity I encountered in Uzbekistan, only victories were claimed and blame was rarely assigned to anything other than "Soviet power." The following is a typical way elites described the interaction between Soviet power and Uzbek culture:

FARHOD AKA: Now, to understand the criticism of Soviet power, you need to understand the main trend of politics. So what does this consist of? They wanted to quickly create a Soviet people, but how do you do that? So first, you take the characteristics of a people which differentiate them from the others, language, traditions, history, and make them disappear. Navro'z was strongly rooted in our people, and our history has shown that no one can beat Navro'z, it will always come out on top. Because the very idea of Navro'z is the victory over evil!

There are two themes to this story, which were common in Western literature on the Soviet nationalities as well as in the way Uzbek cultural elites talked about cultural history: 1) the Soviets tried to create a Soviet people by eliminating cultural differences, and 2) the strongest of those differences survived because their roots went so deeply into the people. These stories present an uncomplicated, primordialist, and politically innocent picture of the process of cultural change in Uzbekistan. In the late 1980s and early 1990s, the story of the repression of Navro'z had become a trope through which Uzbek-Soviet relations were defined, but one which ignored ways that the Soviet state lent support to the holiday even while undermining its meaning. In this story, which served to legitimate the nationalistic elite's status quo, Navro'z symbolized a triumph of primordial folk culture over the Soviet state's all-out attempt to obliterate it. In reality, the picture was not that simple. The late 1960s and early 1970s saw a more relaxed attitude toward Navro'z, but the fate of the holiday rose and fell with the Brezhnev regime's relative emphasis on the ideology of *sblizhenie*—bringing the ethnic groups of the Soviet Union closer together.

In the 1990s, Uzbeks tended to explain the survival of Navro'z in terms that ignored its presence even during Soviet times. Several informants said things to me like, "For many years they repressed Navro'z, but since it was a true folk holiday, the people carried it in their hearts." However, people celebrated Navro'z at home with their families during the Soviet period, and there were also newspaper accounts of Navro'z festivities in various locales during the 1970s, as well as films made in Moscow that were created to educate all Soviet peoples about the colorful Central Asian folk holiday Navro'z. In 1971, the Ministry of Culture and the Tashkent Department of Culture began sponsoring an official Navro'z in the same park where the extravaganza was staged in the 1990s. The official plan filed for the 1974 celebration shows a marked contrast with the materials from the 1980s in that in 1974, Soviet socialist symbolism was incorporated along with folkloric symbolism.[68] For example, in the staging area, along with a Navro'z background panel, there was a panel with a picture of Lenin and one dedicated to the ninth five-year plan.[69] The celebration itself was similar to contemporary Navro'zes in that it involved a *sayil* (street fair) in the same park and a show, but it was different in that it was held on April 28 (an even more spring-like time of year than March 21)—obviously an attempt to emphasize the holiday's folkloric aspects over its ritual meaning. Still, the point of the holiday was to focus on "picking out the best and most valuable customs and rituals of the people. . . . With the victory of socialism in our homeland, the best traditions of our national culture have been developed."[70]

As we will see in later chapters, when artists talk about the renaissance of folk culture, they claim that culture was repressed while at the same time admitting that it has always existed. This seeming paradox suggests that the meaning of folk culture and rituals such as those associated with Navro'z has changed in important ways. For example, in newspaper articles, the activities of an Uzbek circus troupe were referred to as "entertainment" in the Soviet period, but came to be referred to as "Uzbekistan's ancient arts" in the post-Soviet period.[71] Thus whether or not there was an actual revival of folk arts or an increase in ethnic Uzbek cultural activities in the post-Soviet period, the significance of these activities changed, as did the way that they were seen retrospectively. These new perspectives were commonly used to make sense of cultural nation-building in the 1990s.

The most interesting aspect of the history of Soviet Navro'z is that my informants' discussions of repression had little to do with terror or censorship. Rather, repression for them more often meant the refusal of state support for something they wanted to legitimate as part of Uzbek national culture. In a state socialist society, the lack of state support for something was just as damning as actual negative sanctions such as censorship or punishment because without state support, it was difficult for culture producers to conceive of, let alone execute, a project.[72] Sometimes, especially in the Stalin period and during times of special campaigns designed to root out a particular social evil, repression took the form of negative sanctions such as purges, violence, and intimidation. For the most part, however, the Brezhnev period was one of stability and self-censorship, where the state discouraged unapproved cultural phenomena by giving them no institutional support. The Soviets were good at the game of giving with one hand while taking away with the other. In addition to repressing undesirable aspects of national cultures, the Soviet state supported other aspects, thereby institutionalizing a particular understanding of culture and nationality.

While it is true that people were not allowed to celebrate Navro'z just any way they wanted during the Soviet period, it is also true that the Soviets did not behave as if they intended to eliminate the holiday altogether. After the Navbahor controversy in 1987, the socialist content of Navro'z was increasingly replaced with national content, while the form of the holiday's celebration increasingly relied on modern standards of mass celebration. The story people in Uzbekistan told each other about the repression of

Navro'z served to support the status quo by portraying Soviet injustices in relatively harmless terms and by avoiding finger pointing at the people responsible for carrying out these injustices (many of whom were still in power). The story's theme was that, in the end, "the people" were victorious.

Though the spirit of Navro'z may indeed be indomitable, this victory of the people over the Soviets did not correlate to a victory of tradition over modernity because the spirit of how Navro'z was celebrated had been thoroughly modernized according to Soviet sensibilities. Navro'z traditionally was celebrated in the marketplaces, city squares, and main streets, not unlike contemporary sayils. The entertainment consisted of clowns, musicians, storytellers, and games such as *ko'pkari*, a game of horsemanship.[73] In most post-Soviet celebrations throughout the country, the clowns, musicians, and storytellers entertained from an elevated stage in a carefully planned and rehearsed performance, and Uzbeks saw ko'pkari *performed* more often than they saw it *played*. The triumph of the Navro'z trope told people that finally they were participating in an authentic experience that is rightfully theirs by tradition. However, it was the spectacular state and its cultural elites who monopolized the public sphere's definition of the holiday's authenticity and its meaning as tradition.

The Evolution of Karimov's "Ideology of National Independence"
1992–2003

After Islam Karimov had consolidated his power and achieved a consensus with rival groups about power sharing and ideological priorities, Uzbekistan's roadmap to the future was largely dictated by the president and his closest advisors. Karimov wrote books on Uzbekistan's unique path to independence and progress, a path that combined traditional features of Uzbek culture and society with the best practices of modern nation states. In 1992, he wrote:

> The source of inspiration for independent Uzbekistan is our people's commitment to universal human values. Our people have managed to keep alive the sparks of justice, equality, good-neighborliness and humanism through centuries of adversity. The highest objective of reformation in Uzbekistan is to revive those traditions, fill them with new

content, and set up the necessary conditions for achieving peace and democracy, prosperity, cultural advancement, freedom of conscience and intellectual maturity for every person on earth. . . . Special attention must be given to the renaissance of our traditional natural culture. However, such a revival of national self-awareness cannot depart from the ideals of the humanistic world culture, universal human values and the traditions of our multinational society.[74]

Karimov's cultural ideals were not so different from those of his Soviet predecessors, except for their lack of emphasis on a Marxist dialectic. The interest in the renewal of traditions and in increasing the use of the Uzbek language were officially recognized by the Uzbek SSR's Ministry of Culture in 1988, and many programs promoting Uzbek national identity, such as those encouraging the exploration of folklore and the professionalization of Uzbek dance, go back to the earliest decades of the Soviet era. Karimov's "ideology of national independence" and the official national identity promoted by cultural elites were crafted with global cultural norms in mind, but these norms were actually a part of a Soviet legacy that persisted in the cultural institutions of Uzbekistan and facilitated the nation's transition into a globalized world, a point I will come back to in chapter 2.

Scholarship on culture in late Soviet Uzbekistan tends to focus on points of conflict: Russification, language policies, the suppression of history, and "underground" Islam.[75] In many cases, this came from the lack of access to data that would contradict preexisting stereotypes, and in other cases, it was because of a desire on the part of Western scholars and Soviet émigrés to portray all aspects of the Soviet system in a negative light (who knew the religious fanatics they praised for being anti-Soviet in 1989 would become the terrorists they feared in 1999?) Certainly, in my research, echoes could be found of all the criticisms of the Soviet system made by Sovietologists, pan-Turkists, and pan-Islamists.[76] However, the lived experience of Uzbekistan's cultural elites was filled with both humiliation and jubilation, repression and creativity. The price of independence was high, and like many former Soviet citizens, they expressed nostalgia for some features of the past. This ambivalence toward the Soviet legacy is one of the keys to understanding the continuity between Soviet and post-Soviet culture in Uzbekistan.

For about a decade after independence, the regime's ideology remained rather vaguely elaborated. It was primarily a valorization of contemporary stereotypes about Uzbek culture and heritage and avoided directly addressing tricky questions such as "What kinds of Muslims are we?" and "How are we to relate to Russians, both here and abroad?" There was also a demobilization of society, with key organizations such as Kamolot, the successor to the Soviet youth organization Komsomol, nearly going extinct in 1996. In an interview with a staff member of the (formerly Komsomol) Central Committee (which was in the process of being partially dismantled as it was turned into "the Youth Fund 'Kamolot'," a transition from which it fully recovered only in 2004), I asked what the differences were between Komsomol and Kamolot, and my interviewee, Ulughbek, admitted that they took a lot from Komsomol. "Like our president says, don't tear down your old house before building a new one. . . . Basically, we organize free-time activities for young people to keep them off the street and away from alcohol. We sponsor contests, and we are trying to give away better prizes these days so more people will participate, and make the activities genuinely interesting."[77] I asked him what the ideological agenda of Kamolot was, and he repeated to me the phrases that I had already read in President Karimov's works: peaceful, friendly relations with other countries; common Turkestan culture and heritage, and hopefully economic ties; Uzbekistan's finding its own path with no turning back; and no political integration with other countries. Thus the official ideology in the early 1990s related very much to blanket policy guidelines and had little to say about what the content of these policies should be.

In the mid- to late 1990s, Karimov managed to perpetually extend his term through referenda. Political competition took place largely behind closed doors, and economic reforms failed to take hold as Soviet-era leading families consolidated their power through the appropriation of state resources.[78] Meanwhile, the government made it increasingly difficult for small and medium enterprises to operate, both through tax and tariff laws and through strong-arm tactics on the part of businesses tied to the government. The press saw its already limited freedoms decline, though those with access to the internet were able to engage in the exchange of information with relatively little fear of repercussions. During most of the 1990s, Uzbekistan was quite open to the outside world, celebrating its new place at the table. Uzbekistan joined numerous intergovernmental organizations and signed on to scores of international treaties, many of which it did not intend to implement. Television broadcasts from many different countries were available via satellite and cable, and travel was relatively unrestricted.

Thus a number of outside influences made their way into Uzbekistan, challenging the government to modify its Soviet habits. The most notable challenge came from religion, specifically Islam. One of the most important answers to the question of "who are we?" in Uzbek national identity is "we are Muslims." Most Uzbeks, including members of the government, identify themselves as Muslim, yet the belief in Allah and the practice of Islam were problematic issues both personally and politically. Many elites identified as both Muslim and atheist: "I am an atheist, but I don't want to be. I believe in time I will be able to ask God's forgiveness," said one former member of the Communist Party.[79] An official at the Ministry of Culture related the following story about the difference that independence made to one hard-line atheist official:

AHMADJON AKA: We were putting on [a play by an Uzbek author during the Soviet period] and there was a phrase, "Oh God, I hope I miss!" An ideological leader of the Party came to review it, and he asked why the character called on God. Of course, it's just a saying, a habit. It doesn't mean someone believes, but of course we all had to be atheists, and the director said it was a necessary phrase, but in the end this guy said, "If you don't get rid of that phrase, I'll close you down! Even if you've already invested so much in the production, I don't care."

LAURA: And he was an Uzbek, yes?

AHMADJON AKA: Yes, he was the kind of guy who would go to a funeral and when everyone else was praying or doing the *omin*, he was such a tough guy he'd just stand there like a ramrod, not moving. He was from the department of agitprop. He's still alive in Termez, and I hear he's practically a religious fanatic now![80]

The post-Soviet government of Uzbekistan backed itself into a tricky corner, attempting to control the blossoming of a national identity that did not depend on either of its most immediate sources: its recent Communist identity or its persistent Muslim identity. Though government officials had no problem with Muslim culture, they were ambivalent about promoting religious practice. During the Hayit in 1995 and 1996, the state television

Figure 6. The Kukaldosh Medresse complex, located near the Chorsu Bazaar and the Old City. Tashkent's Juma Mosque is to the right. PHOTO BY AUTHOR.

paid more attention to the local cultural rituals and their meaning than to the religious aspects of the holiday. It was clear that by teaching about the holiday, the state wasn't trying to make people into good Muslims, but rather into good Uzbeks. Comparing the Hayit to Navro'z makes it clear that the state places a much larger emphasis on Navro'z and its subtle combination of folkloric, Zoroastrian, and animistic elements. However, in the early to mid-1990s, before the state began to restrict the production and dissemination of religious literature, Uzbekistan's citizens had access to new experiences and sources of information that shaped their national identities, including coming to see Uzbekistan not just as a post-Soviet state but as part of a broader Muslim world. For many Uzbeks, the revival of national culture was inextricably linked with the revival of Islam, and over the course of the 1990s the government had to adapt itself to the changing religious dynamics among its population.[81]

In 1995, I lived with an Uzbek family that was interested in learning how to be better Muslims. The Rahmanov family had formerly been well-off and had a spacious apartment in the center of Tashkent that belied their now-impoverished state (while I was there, the mother and sole provider was laid off from her already low-paying job). They were not an exceptionally traditional family: they wore stylish, European clothing, spoke a mixture of Russian and Uzbek at home, and in part perhaps because the father of the family died several years before, the daughters were allowed a good deal of freedom, and they all married for love. During the Soviet period, the family observed very few Muslim rituals (most Uzbeks, for example, continued to observe at least some aspects of Muslim death rituals), but in 1995, the mother, Dildora opa, and the oldest daughter, Nargiza opa (who lived in another apartment with her husband and two children), had decided to learn how to be more observant. They agreed to fast during Ramadan and learn how to pray from a booklet for children distributed by a Turkish missionary organization. They did not attempt to pray five times a day, but while I was living there, they did the morning and the evening prayers, booklet in hand. Other members of the extended family took some interest in Dildora opa's project, especially in learning how to pray properly, and some of them also took on fasting during Ramadan, but the others were not as strict about it and would admit over dinner, for example, that they had had a snack or something to drink during the day. I visited with the Rahmanov family regularly over the next eleven years, and Dildora opa and Nargiza opa continued to pray in the evenings together, though the rest of the family took less interest in being regularly observant. Nargiza, especially, seemed to really take comfort from her religious practice and became more devout over time, though she changed very little else about her outward appearance or demeanor.

The Rahmanovs were a fairly typical Tashkent family when it came to exercising their freedom of conscience in post-Soviet Uzbekistan. They went the route of self-study, and each practiced religion as it made sense to him or her, but most of the family members would agree that they were more religious than they had been before the end of the Soviet Union. Their religious activities had the added advantage of falling in line with the kind of spiritual revival that the government approved of: moderate, individual, religious observance that was accompanied by Uzbek cultural practices, such as the local ways of celebrating Ro'za Hayit (Eid al-Fitr) and the wearing of headscarves tied behind the head (when they wore headscarves at all). Though the Rahmanov women learned to pray from a Turkish booklet, they did not copy Turkish-style dress, and they learned about

Muslim theology primarily from books and articles published in Russia or Uzbekistan, rather than studying more fundamentalist texts from Pakistan or Saudi Arabia (which were banned by the late 1990s, in any case).

Another family that I was close to for more than ten years, the Habibullaevs, took a different path, one that brought them close to the limits of what the government would allow in terms of religious expression. Usman Habibullaev was a well-educated man, gentle and serious, who worked in a white-collar profession and lived in a European-style apartment building. But he was more traditional than Dildora opa and lived by a firm moral code that eventually cost him his job due to his refusal to participate in the corruption that was becoming ever more widespread after 2000. He and his wife arranged the marriages of their children and encouraged their children to take an interest in Islam, even during the Soviet period. Nodira, the family's oldest daughter, had studied Arabic at one of the three Tashkent elementary schools to offer Arabic as part of the curriculum in the 1970s, and her mother encouraged her to try to recite the Koran at home. Nodira was already married and living apart from the family when I got to know her and her family in 1996, and though she was a believer and dressed modestly by Tashkent standards, she was not affected by the transformation her natal family was about to undergo.

Over the next two years, the Habibullaev family began observing the pillars of Islam fairly strictly, and Nodira's younger brothers studied the Koran in a small group class that broke up after the government began to crack down on private study of Islam. Furthermore, the brothers persuaded their mother and younger sisters to wear hijab that included a headscarf that fastened in front and covered their upper bodies except for their faces. In 1997 the government passed laws against wearing this kind of religious garb in public, and some women were harassed or expelled from universities for wearing too much or the wrong kind of covering, but the law was not often enforced, and the Habibullaev girls apparently never got in trouble for wearing what they wanted in public.[82] Occasionally a teacher of theirs at the institute where they studied would ask them to take off the scarf or to tie it in back rather than fastening it in the front, but Usmon aka would go each year to speak to the teachers and assure them that his girls were just modest and that their style of dress had nothing to do with Hizb-ut-Tahrir or any other unofficial religious group. The Habibullaev daughters also pushed the limits of what was allowed when they enrolled in Arabic classes offered by the Egyptian Embassy after they graduated from high school. Learning Arabic, meeting in any group that might be construed as a private religious study group, and wearing more than usually modest clothing were all activities that various government officials labeled as "Wahhabist," or possibly dangerous activities that had the potential to cast the Habibullaev family under suspicion as terrorists, especially as the government increasingly cracked down on "alien" forms of religious expression in the early 2000s. In 2006, the Habibullaev family's younger children were all married, the men worked mainly in white-collar professions, and the women were well educated. The family continued to be devout in both their personal and public religious practices, but like many families in Tashkent, their enthusiasm for religion had settled down into manageable daily routines.

However, among the cultural elites of Tashkent with whom I worked most closely, in the 1990s the interest in folk culture was much higher than the interest in religion. Those that were interested in their religion were motivated by a desire to recover part of the ethnic culture they felt they had lost, not just because they wanted to be good Muslims. Certainly this was not true of many Uzbeks, but this orientation toward cultural or secular Islam seemed to be fairly widespread in Tashkent at the time.

In addressing the question I mentioned earlier, "Where are we going?" the government of Uzbekistan was confronted with the universal paradox of tradition and modernity in the realm of religious observance as well as in the realms of economic policy, political institutions, and cultural practices. The official government discourse reflected a broader global trend of modern concepts of identity and heritage superseding the revival of actual cultural values of the past. As David Lowenthal has argued, in many nations, "the Westernized identities deployed by non-Western collectivities are perhaps more crucial to their self-images than are attempts to resuscitate pride in their antecedent 'native' cultures."[83] In its nation-building program, the government of Uzbekistan sought ways to recover popular traditions that were suppressed during the Soviet period, but it was mainly interested in those that did not endanger its image as a modern, secular state in line with international norms.

Mikhail, a theater director, told me about a stage designer he knew who tried to use the "wrong" heritage when he participated in a fashion festival. His work was based on Oriental themes such as the baccha, the dancing boys who were part of the urban culture of sexual relations between men and boys in prerevolutionary Turkistan. "It is, after all, an authentic part of local historical culture, and there's no denying it was exploited in the past with postcards and the like, before the Soviet period. But the government doesn't want to see bacchas as part of their heritage," Mikhail said.[84] The country's elites aspired to see Uzbekistan as a "normal" nation with a normal economy and political culture, but at the same time they wanted to preserve a unique cultural identity that felt authentic to them. The elite's concern with these issues was reflected in every realm of culture, from the repertoire of the Uzbek National Academic Theater, to the articles in monthly journals, as well as in the content of national holiday spectacles.

When I asked cultural elites about the importance of tradition and modernity in Uzbekistan's culture, I often received the explanation "our culture is a combination of national traditions and universal human values." Uzbek elites saw that there were cultural elements peculiar to the history of the Uzbeks, as well as other elements that all nations seemed to share. This dichotomy divided the content of culture in a way that paired the idea of Uzbek tradition with the idea of the "particular," as opposed to the "universal." Values that were seen by Uzbek elites as particularly Uzbek were such things as hospitality, the desire for a large extended family, and respect for elders. These values can be contrasted with the elite's perception of Western cultures, which were often seen as on the opposite end of these values: private instead of welcoming, individualistic instead of family oriented, admiring youth rather than wisdom. But when Uzbek elites spoke of universal human values, they were referring to things such as peace, love of one's homeland, and scientific progress.

Modernity in Uzbekistan was associated with Russification and Europeanization (not so much with Americanization) as well as with the vigorous economies and glamorous lifestyles of non-Western urban centers such as Kuala Lumpur, Mumbai, and Singapore, which were visited frequently on the "trading holidays" taken by Tashkent's middle-class citizens. The shiny new buildings in Tashkent more closely resembled the modernity seen in the metropoles of Iraq or India than in the architecture of the United States or France. Again, for their ideology of national independence, officials in Uzbekistan were heavily dependent on Soviet legacies, but they also gained independence in an era of intense globalization, which gave them many options in deciding what models to follow.

In this chapter I have given a broad overview of the historical and political influences on the reconstruction of official national identity in Uzbekistan during the 1990s, and I have provided some specific examples about how the debates about national identity drew on existing schemas of culture that helped the discourse of national identity find broad acceptance. In the reworking of an official national identity for Uzbeks, the issue of linking heritage to territory was plagued by problems related to the division of Uzbeks as a distinct ethnic group from their neighboring peoples, especially the Tajiks. The Soviet past, and the discourse about culture in particular, was unproblematically incorporated into national identity: much of that era's political history was taboo in the public realm while at the same time, most of the era's assumptions about Uzbek national identity were unquestioned in the post-Soviet period. The exceptions to both of these generalizations were the revival of interest in Islam, occasional explorations of Russian and Soviet repression, and the widespread negation of the "Russian elder brother" trope that portrayed Uzbeks as culturally inferior to Russians. The following chapters will exemplify these basic themes of Uzbek national identity, as well as the key points of tension in the debates surrounding the renewal of national culture, by looking in detail at the form, content, and production of culture, and in particular, of national holiday concerts in Tashkent.

Chapter Two

|||

CULTURAL FORM:
GLOBALIZATION AND THE
SPECTACULAR STATE

|||

The specialized role played by the spectacle is that of spokesman
of all other activities, a sort of diplomatic representative of hierarchical
society at its own court, and the source of the only discourse which
that society allows itself to hear.

| Guy Debord, *The Society of the Spectacle* |

On 12 February 1996 I attended my first meeting of the "creative
group" responsible for the production of the show (Rus. *spektakl'*;
Uzb. *tomosha*) to take place on Navro'z, the Zoroastrian spring
equinox holiday that is one of Uzbekistan's two major national
holidays. For their command center, the organizers had taken over
a large hall in the fortuitously named Navro'z Wedding Palace
adjacent to the square where the spectacle was to be performed,
located between the Alisher Navoiy National Garden and the Palace of People's Friendship (a concert hall) near the center of Tashkent. The rental of the hall for the month of planning meetings as
well as the financing for the entire holiday (from paying the state
theater organization's costume workshop to providing meals for
children during rehearsals) involved a complicated transfer of
funds between ministerial, quasi-governmental, and city government offices, all mediated by the Ministry of Finance.

The staff was headed by Rustam Hamidov,[1] a well-known actor who had risen to the position of director of the Hamza The-

ater (Tashkent's main Uzbek-language drama theater) during the Soviet period. In the postindependence period, President Karimov had granted Hamidov control over all of the national holiday spectacles (except for the 1995 Navro'z, the direction of which had been given to Hamidov's long-time rival, Baxtiyor Yo'ldoshev), and the Mayor of Tashkent was about to promote Hamidov to a position heading up the Tashkent City Cultural Directorate. Second in command was Shuxrat Jalilov, the deputy mayor of Tashkent who played the role of staid bureaucrat to Hamidov's visionary artist. Jalilov had the power to pull strings and to intimidate people when things went less than smoothly (as he put it to the staff one day, "If you have any problems leaning on anyone to do their job, come tell me about it, and I will get a memo with Jurabekov's [the First Deputy Prime Minister] name on it"). In attendance at the staff meeting every day were a number of the nation's most prominent choreographers and theater directors, charged with making the holiday extravaganza beautiful, interesting, and edifying. Also present was Hamidov's coscenarist, Yo'ldosh Muqimov, an octogenarian who had been a journalist, a historian, and eventually something of a minor dissident during the Soviet period. More recently, Muqimov had begun publishing volumes of folktales that he had written and then hidden away many years before, some of which dealt with the "true" stories and traditions associated with Navro'z, which he had recorded based on memories of the tales his grandmother told.

During the next several weeks, I got to know these people as well as many more choreographers, seamstresses, artists, puppeteers, school superintendents, composers, factory representatives, employees of the Ministry of Cultural Affairs, secretaries, dancers, actors, musicians, accountants, and academic consultants. All these people were induced to put in time on top of their regular jobs by the promise of much needed bonus money, the rewards of participating in the renewal of Uzbekistan's national culture after a long period of Soviet control, and the threat of repercussions should they refuse. However, the continuity with Soviet methods of cultural production was striking, from the way the financing was handled to the frequently audible threats of Jalilov: "Are you going to be a help or a hindrance? Do you want the prime minister to hear about this?!"

Continuities with the Soviet period were apparent to me not just in methods of organization but also in the way that Soviet definitions of Uzbek national identity set the discursive limits on content, in spite of an explicitly anti-Soviet rhetoric about the overall project of holiday production. Spectacle producers took pride in improving the cultural level of the people by "teaching them about their own ancient traditions which were forgotten during the Soviet period." However, by observing these events as they unfolded, I was able to see the tensions between those who wanted to use the holiday shows as a forum for "forgotten culture" and those who saw the holidays as political communication. For example, though Muqimov had been brought in because of the authenticity of his folktales, in the course of rehearsals, the flavor of Muqimov's folklore was sacrificed to special effects, the requirements of "massness" (hundreds of performers on stage at once), and the desire of the producers to get a message across instead of "just" entertaining. And sometimes color and detail lost out to plain disorganization. Later, during previews of the extravaganza for representatives of the literary elite and Cabinet of Ministers, cultural history was overruled by foreign policy concerns and ideological dictates. Hundreds of hours of creative work devoted to dramatizing Zoroastrian legends went to waste in the interest of keeping the exploration of "Uzbek national history" within the limits already established by Soviet historians and contemporary ideologists. It appeared that Soviet ideas about what culture is and how it should be produced were hanging on a lot longer than socialist symbolism had.

Another interesting thing about the way that extravaganza producers went about this cultural renewal campaign was that they did not raise the question of the renewal of cultural forms, only of cultural content. While the content of legends was debated, the choice to present these legends in the form of a mass spectacle was not discussed (the only question I heard raised about the manner of presentation had to do with the size of the live audience). This is not entirely surprising because the "renewal" of traditional cultural forms would require that the renewers, in this case political and cultural elites, saw some sort of utility in decentralization, deprofessionalization, and a return to premodern tastes and sensibilities. Modern cultural forms such as the mass spectacle were seen by the holiday directors as a natural vehicle for the expression of revived traditional culture, even though such modern cultural forms served to further distance cultural practices from the way they were experienced in everyday life. As Handler and Linnekin point out, in any spectacular preservation of tradition, the performers and spectators "do not so much participate in a preserved past as they invent a new one. . . . Those elements of the past selected to represent traditional culture are placed in contexts utterly different from their prior, unmarked settings. . . . Traditions thought to be preserved are created out of the conceptual needs of the present."[2]

But what conceptual needs of the present were met by the mass spectacle form? Within the broader framework of the discourse about cultural renewal and national holidays in the 1990s, I analyze the choice of Olympics-style spectacle as the main event in Uzbekistan's new national holidays.[3] I argue that the preference for this mass spectacle form was a kind of cultural globalization grounded in Soviet internationalism. Cultural elites favored mass spectacle because it demonstrated their proficiency in producing "international" culture while at the same time providing them with an impressive vehicle for the display of national and local culture. The decision to move away from Soviet-style military parades had both an ideological component (related to a desire to be more like a "normal" country) and a contingent component (related to the creative team chosen to direct the events). I conclude by analyzing the properties of this particular cultural form that make it advantageous to a spectacular state.

The Formal Structure of Holiday Spectacles

Of all Uzbekistan's national holidays, Navro'z and Independence Day (Mustaqillik Kuni) were celebrated on the largest scale in terms of state spending ($1–2 million per holiday just for the televised concert) and had the greatest significance for the public representation of national identity. Navro'z was like a holiday season lasting several weeks, with an outdoor extravaganza celebrated on the morning of March 21. Independence Day was celebrated on September 1, but the holiday began with an outdoor spectacle on the evening of August 31. While there were many other ways these holidays were celebrated, including private or community celebrations and urban street fairs, the Tashkent extravaganza was the focus of most of the state's time and money.

The Navro'z spectacle took place every year in the Alisher Navoiy National Garden, located in Tashkent's central district. Framing the staging area were five dramatic backdrops: three impressive modern buildings (a "wedding palace," a concert hall, and the parliament building); a two-hundred-year-old religious building that served as a museum of atheism during the Soviet period; and a hill, upon which a wide staircase led to a large, blue-domed gazebo housing a statue of the fifteenth-century poet, Alisher Navoiy. Along with the president, prominent political and religious figures, and the international diplomatic community, the seating area held ten thousand audience members who had the right connections to obtain an invitation to the event (tickets were not for sale). The seats were in a U shape around the staging area, and those seated in the center section had the ideal position for viewing the backdrop of the hill.

In addition to the consistency in the physical characteristics of the staging area, there were other formal similarities from year to year. The crest of the hill was always lined with young men holding colorful banners that blew in the breeze. Streaming down the staircases on the hill were young women in whimsical costumes—some in rainbow-colored hoop skirts and others dressed to look like red tulips. Off in the distance, from behind the hill, hot air balloons were launched, sending off a series of rockets that produced trails of colorful smoke as they rose slowly into the air.

Taking an example from the 1996 show, during one dance the center stage was crowded with young female dancers in diaphanous green costumes, designed in the style of women in Persian miniatures, the typical costume for professional women's dance ensembles.[4] The dance style, however, was modern with "oriental" flourishes: geometric patterns embellished with stylistic elements of Central Asian hand and head movements. On the outskirts of the stage was the Uzbek National Chorus: middle-aged men wearing tuxedos and middle-aged women, some of whom were wearing European chiffon dresses, others wearing long, Central Asian velvet robes. The chorus was mouthing words to a majestic-sounding song celebrating the coming of Navro'z, which had been recorded for the spectacle's soundtrack a week or two before. Although in similar kinds of concerts elsewhere it is expected that the microphones are transmitting the actual voices of the performers, in fact there were no live performances in Uzbekistan's holiday extravaganzas; everything was lip-synched, which contributed to the rather formulaic feeling of the shows. The song itself, blasting from the loudspeakers, was of the genre known as national orchestral music: European-style music played by Uzbek national instruments, accompanied by the choir, which is also an imported music genre.

Surrounding the central stage were four smaller stages that were also occupied by dancing girls in beautiful costumes. Between the stages were lanes through which performers could enter and exit the main stage, and visible in the background were the puppets and costumed performers waiting to take the stage for the next number. The lanes were lined with artificial flowers (March 21 is too early in the season for real flowers) donated by the local Italian-Uzbekistan joint-venture plastic factory. These lanes became part of the staging area later in the show when residents from each of Tashkent's neighborhood districts paraded through, as in a Brazilian carnival, dressed in all sorts of costumes, only some of which played on the official theme of animals from the "Chinese" zodiac (which is a symbolic system common to many parts of Central Asia). Also still to come were more background effects that constantly drew the viewers' attention to something new and interesting: high-wire acts; fountains; twenty-meter-tall, brightly colored balloons that were in the shape of horses, bulls, and roosters; kites flying; children on roller skates zooming through the staging area; young men dressed as Timurid-era soldiers marching or doing tricks on horses; expensive clusters of Mylar balloons, imported from Moscow, being set free to decorate the sky with a snaky rainbow trail.

The concert on Navro'z usually ran sixty to ninety minutes, and the one on Independence Day ran up to two hours. The entire program was pre-recorded, and there was usually no interaction between the performers and members of the audience. Typically, there was a prologue, followed by the president's speech, and then the main part of the show began. There were two important visual elements of these spectacles. First there was "massness" (Rus. *massnost'*), which implies both a large scale and popular appeal. Concretely, it meant involving a lot of people in the spectacle. There were literally thousands of extras in these holiday extravaganzas, many of whom were employed as part of the background effects, rather than as featured performers. The other element was a sense of overwhelming activity: in addition to the main stage there were often side stages where dancers performed generic dances; during the show, props such as twenty-meter-high inflatable animals suddenly popped up along the sides of the main stage; every so often balloons rose up or fireworks went off in the far background; there were hundreds of people sitting in bleachers in the nearer background holding up colored cards that formed pictures or words; young men carrying banners and young women in whimsical costumes cycled through the area behind the stage, forming patterns and giving a sense of fluidity to the background; circus performers walked the tight rope off to the side; and during the 1996 Navro'z spectacle, a folkloric parade took place literally in front of the main stage, threading through the entire staging area. It would be impossible to find a dull moment in one of Uzbekistan's holiday extravaganzas, and apart from Olympics opening ceremonies, few events anywhere in the world approach the scale, the extravagance, and the visual chaos of holiday concerts in Uzbekistan.

The shows were divided up into blocks, thematically unified sets of song and dance numbers. One block found in every spectacle was the Regions Block where amateur and professional ensembles from each province of Uzbekistan performed a snapshot of culture representing their region. The elements of these snapshots included distinctive costume, musical and dance styles, patriotic lyrics that mentioned the region's accomplishments, and bits of theatrical "business"[5] representing the way of life in the region, such as baking bread, embroidering, or churning butter. Another obligatory block was the International Block, which featured similar cultural snapshots of various cultures around the world. Usually each continent was represented by one culture. As in the Regions Block, the styles of music, costume, and dance were highly stereotyped and easily recognizable, but it is interesting to note that the international numbers did not contain staged folklife rituals. The regional and International Blocks appeared in both Navro'z and Independence Day spectacles.

The Children's Blocks featured child performers. Their costume was modernized traditional, that is, it used traditional fabrics in ways that copy more European designs. The music was bouncy, synthesized pop, and the lyrics of the songs focused on hope, the future, and love for the country. The last block of either spectacle was usually the Pop Block (Rus. *estradnyi blok*), a series of song excerpts sung by the most popular stars, culminating in a patriotic ensemble piece. The styles of music and costume in this block were as diverse as the stars themselves, and dance was incorporated only in the background of the performances.

Other blocks were found more often in the Independence Day show. Independence Day always featured a Friendship Block, with representations of the cultures of the peoples who live in Uzbekistan. In 1995 and 1996, the cultures of the peoples of "Turkistan," that is, the other formerly Soviet Central Asian nations, were also represented. During the Sport Block, young athletes demonstrated their skills on stage, and individuals or teams who had won competitions that year were honored. The Military Block was much more light hearted than its Soviet counterpart. Military hardware was usually not displayed; instead the focus was on precision drill routines and newly composed patriotic music. Both the Sport and Military Blocks featured costume typical of athletes or armies anywhere in the world, and no special ethnic color was expected to be displayed during these blocks.

There were also narrative blocks recounting stories that varied from year to year. Navro'z had the most variation in composition, with most of its blocks being narrative blocks that illustrated folk tales, legends, and rituals. Independence Day had narrative blocks, too, representing one of the main ideological themes of that year. In 1996 it was the idea of the "Great Silk Road," which linked Uzbekistan to both a past and a future of economic prosperity. In 1995 one narrative block was about patriotism and portrayed the important elements of "traditional" Uzbek national identity.

Attendance at these concerts was by invitation only, and the seating was limited to ten thousand, making a ticket a very precious thing indeed. For the masses, the main event on these holidays was the street fair (though many people watched the broadcast of the extravaganzas on television), while the holiday spectacle was a show first and foremost for the elite. The people I knew in Uzbekistan had a different television-watching style than do people in the United States: usually the television was on in the background, but rarely was it attended to. Nearly everyone I knew said that they turned the television on especially to watch holiday extravaganzas, but when I asked them what they thought about specific details of the spectacles, often they had not been paying close enough attention to recall anything but the performances of the pop stars. I strongly suspect that holiday spectacles, aside from the draw of the performances of the pop stars, do not have much import for the average citizen of Uzbekistan. They were seen not as opportunities for learning about ancient traditions or for celebrating new patriotic values, but rather as a waste of money on "more of the same 'bumburra bumburra' *doira* (drum) beat" (as one acquaintance put it) and repetitious dances seen on state television. Another said, "All those dancing girls all the time—I don't even watch Uzbek programming anymore, except maybe the news." Upon seeing costumes for one of the Independence Day numbers, which were decorated with long neon glowstick tubes, even one of the holiday organizers commented, "This is good.

Everyone has had it with *atlas* [the "national" silk fabric] twirling around the stage. This is fresh." So while these holiday spectacles were important to cultural elites financially and philosophically, the same cannot be said for many ordinary citizens of Uzbekistan.

So if the public is rather indifferent to these holiday spectacles, why does the state devote so much time and money to these extravaganzas, and why have they taken the form of mass spectacles in the first place, instead of parades or concerts? My answer is that universal cultural forms such as this kind of mass spectacle allow cultural elites a means of communicating their culture's uniqueness and normalcy to their peers internationally. Spectacle producers are oriented toward not just their actual audience but also toward an imagined audience, and broader processes of the globalization of culture can be seen in their orientation toward global significant others. Additionally, the mass spectacle form provides the government with control over both the work of culture producers and the meaning of the cultural product.

The Importance of Universalism to Cultural Elites

Anthony Giddens's work on modernity discusses how in modern societies, time and space interact in ways they previously had not. The result of these changes is that distant social influences have an increasing reach across time and space (through print, communications technology, rapid transportation, and so forth). Time and space have both distanciated and disembedded from local context through the mechanical clock, the Julian calendar, and so on, and social interaction often takes place without physical copresence.[6] Building on these concepts, as well as Max Weber's concept of social action (the way our choices are shaped by our anticipation of others' reactions to them), Roland Robertson sees globalization as distanciated social action. He argues that in the era of globalization, social action is marked by an increasing consciousness of the world as a single place.[7]

When we extend this idea to the globalization of culture and the arts, we see that culture producers increasingly strive for international recognition of their own culture and compete for status as an artist of "international quality." This desire for international recognition is not just vanity, as might be the case with an individual artist's desire to be internationally famous; it is not simply about individual virtuosity. It is grounded in the perception that international recognition enhances the legitimacy of local cultural practices at the level of a local or national collectivity. The claims of "international quality" or "state-of-the-art" are based on assumptions about how globalized others would judge the work, but the value of these judgments rests in the local impression these claims create. A particular work may never reach its imagined global audience, but if the claim to "international quality" is believed by the audience or the work's sponsors, it works to enhance the artist's prestige and is a valuable form of cultural capital.

These claims about the evaluation by a global audience are claims about the level of quality, not the content of the production. This theory of cultural globalization does not necessarily entail homogenization on the level of content. Culture producers may find it satisfying to put on a world-class production of a Shakespearean play, or to imitate Michael Jackson's costumes and dance moves in a stage show, but frequently these global forms will be used as vehicles for local content. This kind of finesse in combining local content with a global form is given greater value locally than the wholesale imitation of someone else's culture, and in many cases, the culture producers themselves are seeking to convey local content to their international peers through a mutually intelligible global cultural form.

However, the intelligibility of these cultural forms was undoubtedly mediated by Russian culture. For many years, artists in Uzbekistan were encouraged to become proficient in European and, specifically, Russian cultural forms. In post-Soviet Uzbekistan, culture producers had to wrestle with the question of to what extent they were still interested in perpetuating Russian culture in particular.[8] But what cultural forms were "Russian"? While some Sovietologists see the development of genres such as ballet and opera as Russification, many Uzbeks I spoke to did not see it in those terms, depending on the context of the conversation. If the conversation's context was "the Russians and what they did to us," then certainly cultural changes were framed discursively in terms of Russification, colonialism, and repression. On the other hand, if the context was neutral ("What is Uzbek culture?") or positive ("Ours is a glorious civilization"), then these same changes were framed in terms of moving up to international standards. Sometimes Uzbekistan's imported cultural forms were referred to as European, but more often they were discussed in the Soviet idiom as "international" culture. The acceptance of these changes as part of a natural process of global cultural development was a large part of the reason the Soviet version of Uzbek culture remained hegemonic in the post-Soviet period.

Much of the cultural development process in Uzbekistan fits under the Soviet rhetoric of "the internationalization of national cultures." As part of its cultural development, every union republic had to have its own drama, opera, and ballet theaters. The last two generations of Soviet Uzbeks were brought up to take pride in these artistic forms as representing the accomplishments of their "internationalist" nation in the arts. Every union republic also had its own professional and folk ensembles that distilled the "ethnic" culture of their nation in order to preserve the best parts of their tradition and to enrich the cultures of the other peoples of the USSR. I argue that this internationalization is comparable to the larger forces of modernization and cultural imperialism that we see bringing about Europeanization in non-Soviet countries. The development of national culture also has its parallel in the global trend toward the idealization and objectification of folk cultures, which David Guss explicitly connects with state power: "At the heart of all traditionalizing processes is the desire to mask over real issues of power and domination. By classifying popular forms as 'traditions,' they are effectively neutralized and removed from real time— or at least that is the hope of ruling elites who wish to manipulate them as part of a much larger legitimizing enterprise. Promoted as natural entities with ties to both land and origin, they become important supports for broader claims to national authority."[9] These similarities in the patterns of cultural change point to ways that Soviet ideology and policy were part of a larger global modernization of culture that had its roots in nation building as well as in romantic nationalism.

Another key element of development was cultural exchange, thus linking "progress" to cultural syncretism. During the Soviet period, cultural exchanges were a way for choreographers to learn new moves, for musicians to experiment with new techniques, and for critics to be exposed to a range of theatrical styles. The Soviet system of arts education also allowed Central Asians to study in Europe, most often in Moscow. In theater, promising students from Uzbekistan were sent to study at the Uzbek Drama Department of the Moscow Studio Theater School. Afterward, they returned to Tashkent to perform Russian classics such as Gogol's *The Inspector General* and world classics such as *Hamlet*.[10] In addition, the state paved the way for frequent international travel, especially to other socialist countries. These opportunities for travel not only enhanced the "artistic arsenal" of Uzbekistan's artists by exposing them to new styles and techniques, but it gave them the prestige of international travel and the opportunity to obtain foreign material goods. These exchanges took many forms: the best artists from a republic were sent to train in Moscow, professional ensembles went on yearly tours nationwide, ten-day festivals of the culture of fellow republics were held annually in republic capitals, and contests of national and folk cultures were held throughout the Union.

However, this kind of travel became very rare in the post-Soviet period, greatly reducing the actual participation of Uzbek artists in global cultural fields.[11] In the 1990s, travel abroad was still seen as a major stimulus for creativity and innovation in cultural production. One choreographer was called to the Presidential Council to give his input on what policies should be pursued. When I asked him what he told them, he said, "I told them to send festival producers abroad so we can see how other countries do it, so we can give it that real *mass* appeal."[12] Others worried that without exposure to progressive, international art, their art world might settle into provincialism. The Alisher Navoiy Opera and Ballet Theater, the Gorkii Russian Language Theater, and Uzbekistan's classical music ensembles rarely get paid invitations to tour abroad anymore. Interestingly, Uzbekistan's amateur ensembles have more opportunities to tour than before because they provide what the world market wants to pay for: ethnic color. One Ministry of Cultural Affairs official said that he thought that now the development of amateur folk art is more important than the development of professional art because the amateurs are the ones who get invited abroad; they are what audiences want to see. Some elites say this trend is good, that Uzbekistan should let go of what was always a second-rate imitation of European high culture and get back to Uzbek culture's roots. However, few artists in the straightjacket of the state culture production bureaucracy are able to do more than commodify the already existing Soviet version of Uzbek folk culture. Ironically, culture producers with exposure to, and support from, international organizations such as UNESCO are doing the most work in recovering the indigenous roots of Uzbek culture.

Thus, a simple model of imposed changes and native resistance does not capture my interviewees' sense of their own agency in the "development" of Uzbek national culture. The story that the majority of them told was one of Soviet institutions empowering the overall development of Uzbek culture, even as relations of domination and repression on the part of the *Soviet* state (*not* just Russian culture) prevented culture producers from exercising a full range of creative expression. The narrative given by this theater critic is typical:

ODIL AKA: the Soviets came and right away established theaters in all the regions, usually right across the square from the party building and the Lenin statue. There was nothing in the way of culture except for these repertory theaters. This had its good side as well as its bad side. On the one hand, it was just politics, but on the other hand, it gave people the opportunity to express their talents in a new way. Any people has the full range of artistic talents in their genes, but until European theater came to Central Asia, these talents were latent and wasted. *Masxara* was the local form of theater, but it was only a limited art form. So the first generation of actors was like an explosion of pent-up energy, and they were immensely talented.[13]

Other elites took a more extreme position, referring to the cultural imperialism of the Russians as "slavery." Most, however, took a pragmatic view:

HAMID AKA: I do not want to disparage the Soviet system, no, there were a lot of good things in it, and thanks to it, I was able to study in Moscow for free. There were a lot of plusses and good sides to it, but all of the nations that were not Russian were gradually becoming Russian. . . . There was a process of Russianization taking place. We did not even understand it was happening, that we were losing our national pride. But now we are thinking about this consciously, we understand now that "I am an Uzbek after all! Not a Kazakh or a Ukrainian, but an Uzbek! I have beautiful traditions of my own which need to be recovered."[14]

Interestingly, the assimilative goal of Soviet cultural exchanges was not criticized or even commented on, even by the more nationalistic elites I interviewed. The majority of people I spoke to seemed to feel that very little assimilation had taken place, and that cross-cultural exchanges had improved Uzbek national culture. It turns out that cultural exchanges with other republics of equivalent national-territorial status had an unintended consequence: they strengthened the artists' sense of the importance and place of *their* national culture in the Soviet hierarchy of nations. This is one of the important dimensions of the modernization of culture, according to Roland Robertson: the universalization of particularism.[15] The modernization of Uzbek culture provided a framework for its validation relative to other national cultures. One choreographer felt that internationalism allowed him to better appreciate his own culture:

> HAMID AKA: When we had the Union, our repertoire contained a lot of folk dances of the peoples of the USSR. Now everyone stays within their own borders except when there is some sort of diplomatic event, and maybe one time you perform a different kind of dance. . . . Maybe it's like eating different kinds of food, but all the same when you eat *palov* [the Uzbeks' favorite rice dish] again, you realize that it's the best. Only then can you evaluate the value of your own national art.[16]

This is an important point: national identity is relational. Without other nations for comparison, the identifying characteristics of one's own nation go unnoticed. The contests and tours of "national" culture ensembles reinforced the Soviet hierarchy of nationality in which Uzbek high art was accorded an equal place with the high culture of (most) other union republics.

Of course, some cultures were more equal than others, as the saying goes, and the Soviets often treated Russian culture as equivalent to a universal culture. This practice of treating the Russian as universal and the Uzbek as specific was offensive to artists in Uzbekistan, many of whom saw this as a hypocritical betrayal of the official Soviet doctrine of internationalism.

> HAMID AKA: When we were called to Moscow for one of those big concerts with participants from all the republics, for a session of the party or Komsomol or whatever, each republic got, say, three minutes on stage. But the Russians had a ballet performance, and one from [another] ensemble, and also the Beriozka [Russian folklore] ensemble. No one would cast aspersions on these ensembles, I admire them, but it was written in the old constitution that all the republics were equal. We understood what was going on, and we were insulted and fought over

every second [of stage time]. . . . And another thing was that in these concerts only Russian pop groups performed, even though there were pop groups in all the republics.

LAURA: So only folk groups performed in Moscow?

HAMID AKA: Basically. Rarely someone from Ukraine or the Baltics would perform [pop music]. Ballet was always represented by the Bolshoi even though the republics also have their ballet companies.[17]

Thus it was not just the Russification of Uzbek culture that my informants objected to. The de facto marginalization of Uzbek culture on the Union level belied the glorious "development" of Uzbek high culture and the advanced "assimilation" of Uzbek and European culture. Outside of the Uzbek SSR, Uzbek high culture was still seen as colorful and folksy, and Uzbek versions of ballet and pop music were seen as pale copies of the European originals.

In most countries, a particular cultural form becomes emblematic of the nation: Welsh bardic poetry, Scottish clan costume, and so on, but often these beloved national traditions were invented and propagated in the modern era by an individual or a small group of intellectuals or philanthropists.[18] In Uzbekistan, national dance (which, as Mary Masayo Doi has argued, was basically invented in the 1920s by a local woman of Armenian heritage, Tamaraxonim, and an Uzbek man, Muxitdin Kari-Yakubov)[19] is the cultural form that the nation is most invested in, so the issue of invention and Russification in national dance was an especially sensitive one that many people discussed with me (see the discussions with Farida opa and Ghulom aka in chapter 3). The assertion that a particular element of culture was authentically Uzbek (and not Russian or European) came up rarely, as most artists felt free to admit the syncretism of Uzbek culture. However, even Hamid aka, the internationalist choreographer I quoted above, reacted indignantly to an East German newspaper's review of his company's performance of Uzbek national dances in the 1980s:

HAMID AKA: When the translator told us what they said, I laughed until I cried. It said: the costumes were beautiful, the dancing was beautiful, but—the dances had Russian elements. They weren't criticizing, it was the GDR after all, but they said, 'they used Russian elements!' You've seen how there isn't a single Russian element in our dances! When the translator said that, I just couldn't believe it. I laughed so hard! Because they just wanted to emphasize that we were so close to the Russians, that they're our brothers, and we were drawing on them. We laughed but we were also indignant that in general what stood out were Russian elements.[20]

I did not admit to Hamid aka that I probably would have written the same thing had I been the reviewer, so strongly did I see the influence of ballet and masculine styles of Russian folk dance on his company's contemporary performances. The difference in our perceptions may have to do with our differing interpretations of what cultural forms were ethnically marked or unmarked, particular or universal. This was one of the main places my analysis diverged from that of my informants because I was looking at elements of form and content, while many of them looked mainly to content for meaning while ignoring the meanings I saw in cultural forms. For Uzbeks such as Hamid aka, authenticity came down not to an opposition between Russian and Uzbek cultural elements, but between elements that they understood to be Russian or Uzbek "national" versus elements that they understood as being normal, progressive, or simply colorful. Form was important when it was marked as national, but not when it was marked as universal. For example, ballet's influence on the form of ensemble national dance appeared to be neutralized by Uzbek ethnic content, but actual ballet was seen as a progressive cultural form that was marked as "European," and therefore "not ours," according to several of my interviewees, even when the ballet was by an Uzbek on themes from Uzbek history or folklore. "Ballet" as a form is more distinctly marked as European in Uzbekistan, whereas "the national dance ensemble" is seen as a universal, and therefore culturally neutral, form that authentically and unproblematically bears particular ethnic content.

This contrast between "European" and "ours" showed up in relation to holidays, as well. Nodir aka commented, "It's interesting that we still celebrate the [international] New Year, but we don't say that it's European, not our holiday. Kids have a holiday at that time, and we do shows for them here [at our theater]. We get to have two new year celebrations! All our nations and nationalities celebrate these holidays together."[21] Similarly, mass holiday spectacles were seen as an unmarked (universal) container for true national cultural content. Other default modern cultural forms such as choral singing and uniform ethnic costume, when filled with Uzbek national content, were even seen as "traditional" culture.

Thus my attention to cultural form is justified not only in terms of an empirical interest in mass spectacle but because of the theoretical importance of the ways these forms are marked or unmarked and the effects that unmarked forms have on local culture production. Through their mass holiday spectacles, Uzbekistan's cultural elites tried to craft a vision of national identity that adequately communicated who they were to an imagined audience of global society. This globalized imagined community is a symptom of a broader globalization process, which Arjun Appadurai characterizes as "a complex transnational construction of imaginary landscapes. The world we live in today is characterized by a new role for the imagination in social life."[22] However, the process I am examining is somewhat more specific and more restrictive than what Appadurai and other globalization theorists term "hybridization" or "indigenization." Like Richard Wilk, I am focusing on the way that local choices are "tied to a series of different sources of social power inside and outside of [national] society . . . [creating] local identity on a global stage."[23] What is important to the culture producers in my study is that the myriad content they wish to create be expressed through a "universal" cultural form that provides a means through which they can effectively communicate cultural and professional equivalence (even if the similarity is premised on the comparability of their cultural differences!) to their international peers.

The Olympics—A Paragon of Unmarked Universalism

The Olympics ("a festival of human unity," as Coubertin called his venture) are the quintessential universal cultural form, and the genre of performance seen in their opening and closing ceremonies is unmarked by any specific national culture, making it ideal for the purposes of Uzbekistan's cultural elite. The Olympics are a tightly controlled, seemingly depoliticized arena for the competition of nation-states, and the Uzbek government's choice of Olympics-style spectacle relates both to the state's need for control over cultural expression and to its desire to appear as if it was conforming to international models of nationhood. Scholars of the Olympic movement have shown that the Olympics serve as an important element in a country's orientation toward global society.[24] Olympics-style ceremonies, like rock music and other global cultural forms, are seen by culture producers around the world as proper frames within which a modern nation celebrates and propagates its unique identity.[25]

The genre of Olympics-style spectacle came to Uzbekistan on the initiative of elites working through Soviet-level institutions to create Soviet versions of global culture. The 1980 Olympics in Moscow and the subsequent "Hollywood" Olympics in Los Angeles in 1984 set new standards for the level of spectacle in the opening and closing ceremonies (especially since the Los Angeles organizing committee was determined not to be out-done in these tit-for-tat boycotted games). In addition to the usual ceremonial entry of the athletes, lighting of the torch, and bidding farewell to the athletes, the Moscow ceremonies included mass gymnastic displays, fireworks, entire sections of the stadium holding colored cards to form animated pictures, and Misha (the games' mascot) in the form of a huge inflatable bear who waved goodbye to the crowds before floating wistfully away. By staging their national holidays as Olympics-style spectacles, Uzbekistan's cultural elites were able to demonstrate (both domestically and abroad) world-class technical proficiency while at the same time showcasing state-sanctioned elements of the ideology and culture of Uzbekistan.

In order for distanciated social action to affect the choices that culture producers make, the agents in question must have at least a subjective perception that they are somehow interacting with other participants in a global field of culture. The Moscow Olympics served as the direct link between global cultural forms and contemporary mass spectacle in Uzbekistan when this spectacular way of orchestrating live performance was imported to Uzbekistan from Moscow by the director of the 1980 Olympic ceremonies, who was also in charge of Tashkent's two-thousand-year anniversary celebration in 1983. He worked with a team of local directors that included Rustam Hamidov, the lead director of Uzbekistan's contemporary national holiday extravaganzas. Hamidov was chosen as director precisely because of his experience with this genre, which was apparently seen by cultural and political elites as the ideal cultural form to express Uzbekistan's new national identity (see below).

Hamidov, in fact, was able to actively participate in Uzbekistan's learning from global models. From the very first meeting of the creative group, Hamidov discussed how the 1996 Olympics in Atlanta served as a model for international friendship and cooperation and gave Uzbekistan a chance to demonstrate its athletic accomplishments and its place in the world community of nations. During the preparation for Uzbekistan's fifth anniversary in 1996, right in the middle of the most intensive rehearsal period, the holiday's organizational committee sent Hamidov to Atlanta while the summer Olympic Games were taking place in order for him to get ideas about how to make Uzbekistan's Independence Day celebration more closely resemble its role model. The impact was not dramatic, but it provides a concrete example of the more mundane aspect of the particularization of universalism: the mastery of technology. The most notable change Hamidov made in the 1996 Independence Day show because of this visit to Atlanta was the use of "torches" made of jaggedly cut fabric in the colors of the Olympic rings and "fueled" by fans from below. Hamidov also pointed out how some of the kinds of things they were doing (combining "theatricalization" with choreography) was similar to the Aboriginal number in the closing ceremony that previewed the spectacle that Sydney would put on four years later. "In the Olympic ceremony, everything was movement," he said, "nobody just walked. It was carnival."

Nonetheless, Hamidov was interacting passively with the Atlanta ceremonies from which he drew inspiration and legitimation for his own artistic vision. In Uzbekistan, concrete *participation* in global cultural fields played a much smaller part in shaping holiday extravaganzas than the *imagination* of a global audience. This showed up in a variety of ways during the production process. For example, in 1996 the holiday spectacle's directors would regularly admonish performers to work harder since the whole world would be watching them (though, in reality the broadcast probably reached few households outside of Uzbekistan's borders). During the staff meeting for Navro'z 1996, when the creative team reviewed the complete program for the first time, one of the organizers ended by reminding everyone that this holiday has an international aspect, that there would be guests in the audience from other countries, and that it was important to portray the "multinational Uzbekistan" as united. Another holiday producer, Karim aka, said, "[This year's Independence Day spectacle] had a lot more about ties with other countries, in the audience and in the performance. Now Uzbekistan has this status. Earlier it was very difficult for us to have such international connections. And our dancers are performing all these dances from around the world. The arts are the best way to communicate with other nations because it's understood right away."[26]

In some cases, this imagination of a global audience could be directly linked to the kinds of effects that world polity theorists see as evidence of global culture, of the standardization of the way that elites craft their nationhood.[27] In an informal planning meeting for Independence Day 1996, one of the lead directors of the holiday talked about how the organizers didn't need to reinvent the wheel with this holiday since all countries have their independence day. He also said explicitly that he looked to France, the United States, and to the Olympics for his models of how to do a spectacular holiday celebration.

Imagining a world audience for the extravaganza also affected what content was deemed acceptable by the government. Spectacle producers were extremely self-conscious about the image of Uzbekistan that they were projecting in the world, and this also resulted in a degree of homogenization of content, but to a set of standards consciously chosen by them, and not necessarily the standards of Russian or Western culture. For example, other "Muslim countries" were sometimes mentioned by culture producers as their imagined interlocutors. The imagining of not just a generalized global audience, but a more narrow "significant other" demonstrated the way that multiple fields at the supranational level shaped the choices of the spectacle producers. One director talked about how a dance he worked on for the Navro'z holiday extravaganza was artistically interesting for him, but it had to be cut because of concerns about how it would play in different countries. However, he said he understood why the dance dramatizing pre-Muslim Zoroastrian rituals was cut after the government's review of the extravaganza:

> MANSUR AKA: [The dance] was interesting in and of itself, but since different viewers would see it, since it would be transmitted by television and tapes would go to different countries, it was an issue of Uzbekistan being a Muslim country, a Muslim state . . . There are these political nuances. "What are they worshipping? Where are they going with this?" So that we don't give the wrong impression to our neighboring countries, to Muslim governments.[28]

The producers of Uzbekistan's national holiday spectacles treated them as if they were what Roche calls "mega-events," large-scale cultural events that have a dramatic character, mass appeal, and international signifi-cance.[29] Although Uzbekistan's national holidays are not actually of inter-national significance, this is not how they were perceived by the people producing them. For their creators, these holiday events were, like mega-events, "key occasions in which nations . . . construct and present images of themselves for recognition in relation to other nations and 'in the eyes of the world,' . . . in which national 'tradition' and 'community' . . . [are] invented and imagined not just by and for leaders and citizens . . . but also by and for the publics of other nations."[30] The participation of Uz-bekistan's cultural elites in Olympics-style productions legitimated their nation-building project within the terms of the global cultural field. Inter-nationally recognizable global cultural forms such as Olympics-style spec-tacle are useful to elites who wish to demonstrate their culture's univer-sality as well as its uniqueness.

Changes in Form—from Parades to Spectacles

Although the mass spectacle form was used throughout the Soviet Union for nonholiday occasions, for many years, Kazakhstan, Kyrgyzstan, and Tajikistan all continued the tradition of celebrating their Independence Day with the universal cultural form of the military parade, sometimes fol-lowed by a "festive procession" or a concert afterwards. In Kazakhstan, Re-public Day and Navro'z were celebrated with modest outdoor concerts to which the general public was invited. These shows contained both "friend-ship of the peoples" folk dancing and pop music, with little or no dra-matization of thematic content. In spite of Turkmenistan's official foreign policy of neutrality, Turkmenistan's 2006 Independence Day parade also displayed tanks, artillery, and fighter aircraft, after which troops took an oath of loyalty to the president and chanted a popular slogan, "Nation, Homeland, the Great Leader of the Turkmen (Turkmenbashi the Great)!" Following the parade was a display of horsemanship (a particular point of pride for the Turkmen) and a concert.[31] So why did elites in Uzbekistan reject the variety show concert format and military parades in favor of the mass spectacle?

During the Soviet era, Uzbekistan had its share of military parades. In the 1970s and 1980s, the major Soviet national holidays (May Day, Vic-tory Day, Anniversary of the Revolution) were all celebrated in the Uzbek ssr with military parades on Tashkent's Revolution (now Independence) Square. May Day also had a "festive procession" component, with civilians in colorful costumes, and Victory Day in the 1980s also had a more spectacle-like event in a stadium. The main background visual elements to these holidays were the republic's leadership standing on a central podium, "flags of the ussr and the brotherly union republics, [and] portraits of the founders of Marxism-Leninism and members . . . of the Politburo."[32] In the foreground was the parade, consisting of floats (such as a cotton harvester from the Tashselmash farm equipment factory) and ordinary citizens dressed in national costume or dressy (European) clothing, carrying things such as banners, posters, or branches of cotton symbolizing the harvest (Great October—the anniversary of the revolution), or flowers (May Day) symbolizing the coming of spring. The posters and banners read (in Russian and Uzbek): "Tashkent, city of peace and friendship," "Our labor is for you, our homeland," "Under the leadership of the cpsu— toward a new victory," "We are for perestroika!" "70 years of Great October," "May, peace, labor," "Friendship, May, labor," and "Long live May 1!" There were also posters without words: a picture of a mushroom cloud with a red X over it and posters of Party leaders, literary figures, and military heroes.

Prior to the holiday, schools and workplaces would gear up by sponsoring contests and elaborating on the theme of the holiday. On the eve of the celebration, the republic's elite would gather for an oratory or cultural presentation in a major hall while the ordinary citizen was bombarded with holiday programming on television. The day of the holiday, many thousands of people were involved in the parade, marching across the plaza under the banner of their school, workplace, or collective farm. Some Tashkenters who were not part of the parade gathered around the square to be a part of the excitement but most watched the parades on tv at home. Afterward or on the following day, everyone participated in the street fairs and in private gatherings. Other holidays such as Lenin's Birthday, Women's Day, and Army Day, were celebrated with activities and contests in schools and workplaces, sometimes accompanied by public events. The New Year (European) was not built up in the same way as an ideological event, but it was celebrated publicly with bonfires or fireworks (as well as privately, of course).

The most relevant Soviet holidays for comparison with the festivities of the 1990s are the major holidays such as May Day (a parallel in some ways to Navro'z) and "Great October/November seventh," (parallel in many ways to Independence Day). Both May Day and Great October were celebrated with a *demonstratsiia*, a parade featuring military hardware, colorful banners, and citizens marching with their co-workers or fellow students. Even late in the Soviet period, the newspaper reported that on May 1 in Tashkent's Lenin Square,

> the sound of a fanfare rings out. . . . The demonstration begins with a moving column of standard-bearers, and behind them march the firm steps of Tashkent's working vanguard: veterans of the party, of war, and of labor. Their numerous medals shine in the brilliant May sun. . . . Then floats bearing the words "May" and "Tashkent" enter the square, and behind them are the representatives of the workers' collectives of Uzbekistan's capital. . . . Then comes a column of demonstrators from the 50 Years of the Uzbek SSR and Communist Party of Uzbekistan Sewing Factory . . . [who], since the beginning of this year, have put out 270,000 items of clothing . . . [and have] generated about three million rubles in profit.[33]

Another important holiday, Victory Day, was celebrated in Tashkent with an "artistic military-athletic celebration" in a stadium. This form of celebration, not the military parade, was the precursor to independent Uzbekistan's spectacle form (see below). Another example of a mass spectacle celebration was the Tashkent two-thousand-year jubilee, celebrated in 1983 and produced by a team of spectacle experts from around the Soviet Union.

> In the prologue . . . Uzbek national musical instruments, the *karnay* and *surnay*, sounded a greeting as singers, storytellers, and musicians in national costume, with old instruments, entered and enacted a traditional Eastern improvisational-folkloric scene. . . . In the episode called "Eastern Legend," which, in the mind of the authors, was to portray the deliverance of the people of the republic from oppression . . . the main activity was a portrayal of the revolutionary ritual of burning the *paranja* [veil]. . . . The episode "Harvest Festival" was also based mainly on national traditions and folklore. . . . Accompanied by the music of karnays and surnays, elders in national costumes entered in columns,

representing the provinces of Uzbekistan. . . . To the sounds of a contest between *doiras* [drums] was added the cries of young men and ululating girls, and the sound of a surnay. Then began the national games: young men on horseback, tightrope walkers, clowns, acrobats, and puppeteers. The episode concluded with an enactment of a wedding.[34]

This kind of theatrical spectacle, involving a cast of thousands in a staged music and dance performance, as well as the elements of the spectacle itself, is very similar to how holidays were celebrated in Uzbekistan in the 1990s. But the main spectacular element of Soviet national holidays was a parade, not an outdoor theatrical show. There were some similarities between Soviet parades and Uzbekistan's spectacles, such as both being performed outdoors on a huge square, being broadcast on television, and incorporating thousands of people in the holiday display. There were also many differences.

How did this change come about, from disciplined formations marching across a square to a bright and colorful extravaganza? And what does this drastic change in form mean for the examination of the hegemony of Soviet forms in independent Uzbekistan? One answer to the former question is that spectacles were what President Karimov wanted. Often when I asked why something was the way it was, be it how a holiday is celebrated or what dance was cut from a performance, people would reply, "because that is what the president wanted." There is no doubt some truth to this. In the early 1990s, Karimov signed a decree on how holidays were to be celebrated, so perhaps it was his own personal preference. However, the invocation of Karimov's will was a common claim to legitimize a particular course of action, so we should not put too much stock in the holiday being the result of a particular, conscious choice on his part.[35]

Another explanation that recognizes both the importance of the Soviet internationalist legacy and the role of contingent events has to do with the people who were chosen to produce the holiday. During the Soviet period, Party leaders and military commanders were in charge of the holiday parade, and since the artistic dimension of it was small and the overall production changed little from year to year, there was not much for them to do except tell people when and where to show up and make sure there was enough security to keep the crowds under control. However, as I mentioned above, holidays in the post-Soviet period were given over to theatrical types: during the 1980s, Hamidov (coming from a background in theater) and Kolosovskii (a sports administrator) had worked together on mass theatrical presentations (*massovye teatral'nye predstavleniia*), or MTPS, as well as on "artistic military-athletic celebrations" like those on Victory Day. MTPS were a Soviet cultural form that was employed, not on holidays, but for other kinds of celebrations, such as the two-thousand-year jubilee of Tashkent, the International Youth Festivals in Moscow, and the 1980 Moscow Olympics.[36] In one handbook on the orchestration of outdoor performances, the author explains that MTPS have to be unsubtle, closer to the style of a caricature than a life sketch, and they have to be simple in order to appeal to a broad audience.[37] "To put on an MTP is to create a specific formal world: a world of poetic structure, of symbols and allegory, of hyperbole and the grotesque, of metaphor and association."[38] The cultural form of the MTP is well suited to the spectacular state's desire to monopolize meaning while creating an illusion of participation since it is, according to one of its Soviet theorists "one of the most effective forms of agitation and propaganda for the political, aesthetic, and ethic education of the population. Here we find the combination of the forms of political meetings and collective recreation, the enlightenment functions of agitation and entertainment, the synthesis of a staged show and the amateur masses, and the mixture of ritual and improvisation."[39]

During the late 1980s, when Navro'z began to be officially celebrated again, Hamidov was in charge of organizing what resembled a folk festival more than an MTP, but each year Hamidov made the celebration bigger, more elaborate, and after independence the Navro'z spectacle took the form it had throughout the rest of the decade, if on a smaller scale. Throughout the 1990s, Hamidov and his team were in charge of nearly every Navro'z and Independence Day and brought their own style to the performance, with an emphasis on massive scale, special effects (many forms of balloons and lighting effects, most notably), and a breakdown of the show into annually repeated thematic blocks. While Karimov may have preferred an outdoor spectacle to a parade, the details of this now-institutionalized holiday form were largely due to Hamidov's influence. Thus the form of Uzbekistan's holidays had their roots in the Soviet era but were transferred from one realm of celebration to another.

The transfer of the form of spectacle associated with one-time events to semiannual holiday celebrations entailed a lot of effort and cost for the state that Soviet holidays did not require, but the MTP had its advantages, too. The benefits of this kind of celebration were a distancing from the association with Soviet culture that the military parade entails and a rhetorical advantage in the claim that these holidays were "closer to the people." Another reason people gave for the switch from parades to mass spectacles concerns having celebrations that resembled those of a "normal" country. Soviet holidays were seen by some of my interviewees as overly politicized, as uninteresting and alienating, and as exercises in which they were not invested. In my interview with Nodir aka, a theater director, I asked about his participation in these events and asked him to contrast the way things were done now with the way they were during the Soviet period.

LAURA: Did you participate in holidays before independence?

NODIR AKA: [sarcastically] What holidays? There was May Day, November 7, and the New Year. The local party called us and said come to the square at 9:00. That's all. We carried a poster of Lenin or Gorbachev or whoever, got our flags, and went there. Stood there. At 9:00 [someone] would give a speech. Then we marched in front of the tribune.

LAURA: So there wasn't a show?

NODIR AKA: No, what show? . . . Only after the parade, in our own neighborhoods, there would be a concert of some sort. It was service. . . . We'd just march past and say "long live, long live, long live." What the heck? What ever came of those "long lives?!" Now the viewer comes and sees the show we've put on and afterward continues that celebration. They're a participant in the holiday. If they want to dance, they dance, sing. The outdoor festivities begin. People do what they want. Things are more free now, nobody's going to question what you're doing. Of course, it should be orderly. You get all those people together in one place and still everything's peaceful, everyone is happy.

LAURA: Why were the Soviet holidays so boring?

NODIR AKA: Again, it was a command. Every school, factory, firm was ordered to come. The slogans in Russian and Uzbek, the "long lives" that we lived with for so many years. Now . . . the viewers don't just stand and watch, everyone participates. That's the way it used to be with us, our grandfathers told us before the Soviet Union, that's how they used to celebrate Navro'z and other holidays. But we are improving our holidays every year. We still have a way to go; we've only begun to show a part of it, but it will all come back.[40]

The claim was persistently advanced by the spectacle producers that contemporary holidays were more participatory, though it is clear that they were not strictly so. They involved fewer people overall, and the live audiences were even more restricted than they were during the both the Soviet period and the first few years of independence before formal invitations were required to be admitted to view the show. The live audiences were also more restricted than those attending similar celebrations in neighboring countries such as Kazakhstan. Navro'z especially was referred to by my interviewees as a popular (*xalq*) as opposed to a political (*siyosiy*) holiday such as Independence Day, and indeed, between 1988 and 1994 the celebration was much more informal, involving people milling about Friendship of the Peoples Square watching performances. Though the audiences now had to obtain invitations and sit in rows, the spectacle producers still seemed to feel that the main characteristics of these holidays (their location in the open air and their massness) were somehow more faithful to ancient folk tradition than military parades. As Mansur aka expressed, "[The switch to open-air holiday spectacles is] a very big change. First of all, it is a rebirth of our own ancient traditions. . . . Second, the outdoor square permits "massness" and since Navro'z is a people's [*narodnyi*] holiday, why should it be limited by a stage?"[41]

While the elements of the spectacles were indeed more narodnyi (that is, xalq, involving song, dance, colorful costume, a smattering of pop stars —versus factory after factory, float after float), the control over content and participation was as tight as or tighter than ever, allowing even less room for spontaneity and creativity. During the Soviet period, theatrical spectacles of the kind Uzbekistan now favors were held in stadiums, sometimes over the course of several days, so that hundreds of thousands of people could attend. Several people mentioned that the reason these spectacles were not in stadiums anymore was because "our president wants it that way." Perhaps this was in part out of security concerns, but it was also due to the willingness of the government-led Organizational Committee (the "Orgkom," see chapter 4) to produce holiday spectacles in a way that the elite imagined was traditional and perhaps due also to the desire of Karimov and his advisors for a more elitist form of performance to dramatize new political boundaries. Uzbekistan was no longer a workers' state, the people and "Party" were no longer one. The spectacular state used even the staging of holidays to clearly communicate these new boundaries to the people.

Mass Spectacle and the Spectacular State

A spectacular state is one that strategically appropriates ritual, ceremony, and expressive culture as one of the *primary* means of communication with the citizenry. All states are spectacular to some degree, employing ritual in governmental proceedings, ceremony in transitions such as inaugurations, and performance in celebrating national values. As Clifford Geertz argued, the governing elites of any complex society "justify their existence and order their actions in terms of a collection of stories [and] ceremonies . . . that mark the center as center and give what goes on there its aura of being not merely important but in some odd fashion connected to the way the world is built."[42]

But some states more than others rely on these oblique forms of communication, which they perceive give them more control over meaning than more direct but diffuse forms of communication such as the mass media or face-to-face contact. For example, Mabel Berezin has shown that in Mussolini's Italy, public spectacle was the fascists' preferred means of cultural communication.[43] According to Christel Lane, in the Soviet Union mass public ritual was an important means of glossing over conflicting social relationships caused by the lack of political differentiation and the gap between ideology and reality. For example, during the Brezhnev era, officials were concerned that the alienation and apathy of youth belied the "unity of the people and the party" and consequently increased the efforts to institutionalize a socialist ceremonial system.[44] In societies where the state wants to monopolize the public sphere, spectacular forms of political participation allow the state to mobilize citizens in ways that create an illusion of participation, without allowing any actual citizen input into the process. The success of this monopoly on communication shows up in the coherence with which official documents, people on the streets, national holidays, and so forth all express a similar set of ideas, what Alexei Yurchak calls a "performative shift," the replication of textual forms from one context to the next as part of normal life. Yurchak argues that it is not the literal meaning of these discourses that are important, but rather that their significance lies in the increasingly normative participation in their reproduction.[45]

Political spectacle in any society reflects particular relations of power. Michel Foucault argued that the spectacle of the sovereign was an expression of potency related to triumph, a political ceremony that manifested the power of the monarch. Contemporary relations of power do not center on the sovereign, however, but on the discipline of populations. The disciplinary regime of power, therefore, has its own type of ceremony: "It was not the triumph, but the review, the 'parade,' an ostentatious form of the examination. In it the 'subjects' were presented as 'objects' to the observation of a power that was manifested only by its gaze."[46] However, the kinds of spectacle we are discussing here combine this disciplinary power with a more specific form of sovereign power, in that the power is manifested by the gaze of the *president* and high government officials, not simply through the categorization of state subjects and their normative participation in the reproduction of ideology.

Spectacle is usually used as a positive form of power, one that produces and includes, rather than repressing and punishing. George Ritzer, for example, explores how spectacle is used in capitalist societies to enchant a world disenchanted by rationalization, in much the same way that Uzbekistan's cultural elites overcome the disenchantment of Soviet politicization with spectacular nationalism.[47] Guy Debord's view is more cynical when he attempts to bridge the apparent gap between state-socialist societies and western capitalist societies by asserting that they are all sectors of an overarching global capitalist system, "differing forms of a single alienation," all using spectacle to mask the reality of the material and historical conditions under which we live.[48] Both authors argue that in societies with an abundance of commodities and pluralism in the public sphere, the form of spectacle is more diffuse than it is in what I call spectacular states. In more pluralistic societies, spectacle is enacted as the pursuit of material goods that we fantasize will ease our alienation. In societies dominated by bureaucracies (whether they have a market or a planned economy), there is a more "concentrated form of the spectacle [that] imposes an image of the good which is a résumé of everything that exists officially."[49]

This "image of the good," this ideology, when cloaked in spectacle, takes on a vibrant quality of democratic participation, even though there is nothing democratic or participatory about it. Spectacle produces a hum of excitement and physiological arousal that, as Durkheim noted, binds us more closely to the group sharing the experience and fixes in our minds the ideas and symbols portrayed therein.[50] Of everyone involved, this excitement and intensity is most keenly felt by the spectacle producers themselves. Thus their solidarity with the nation-state is cemented, regardless of the lasting effects of the spectacle on the masses. In chapter 4, I will explore the details about how the production of holiday spectacles was organized and will analyze the effects of the spectacle form on its participants.

Spectacular states may imagine that they can lower the cost of maintaining their power by engaging in expensive but occasional spectacles rather than engaging in extensive mobilizational or surveillance and punishment activities.[51] However, the states I have characterized as "spectacular" usually rely heavily on repression or mobilization *in addition to* using the positive power of spectacle. What distinguishes Uzbekistan from these other states is that in its attempt to "normalize" its public culture in accordance with global norms, it relied at first quite heavily on spectacle rather than its repressive forms of power to produce public compliance with the state. Only after the "colored revolutions" of 2003 did the government of Uzbekistan, perhaps realizing that its positive propaganda was not sufficient to keep itself in power, increasingly rely on surveillance and repression.

In post-Soviet Uzbekistan, the state was coercive in its relationships with cultural elites in that it set the parameters of acceptable discourse, exercised censorship, and punished open dissent. However, the choice of celebrating holidays through Olympics-style spectacles was not primarily related to the demands of Uzbekistan's spectacular state. Soviet-style military parades could have easily been perpetuated, as they were in other Central Asian states. Instead, the political and cultural elites involved in holiday production first took the step of "depoliticizing" and "normalizing" holidays (making them less like Soviet holidays) by celebrating the revived folk holiday Navro'z in the form of a folk festival that took place yearly from 1988 to 1991. Then, in 1992, they took a step toward a more mass-spectacular form that, by 1994, bore a direct and deliberate resemblance to the opening and closing ceremonies of the Olympics. The Presidential Council chose Hamidov as the lead director, and this choice reflected the desire among many elites for Uzbekistan to represent itself not just as a "normal" nation but as one that could compete "on the level of world culture." The choice of this particular cultural form itself gave meaning to Uzbekistan's national identity: it said that Uzbekistan was now an equal in the global community.

Chapter Three

|||

CULTURAL CONTENT
AND POSTCOLONIAL CIVIC
NATIONALISM

|||

When the stick has been bent in one direction for so long,
one must bend it back the other way in order to straighten it out.

| Nikolai Chernyshevsky |

In August 1996, the government of Uzbekistan held the first annual musical competition called O'zbekiston Vatanim Manim, Uzbekistan My Homeland, in order to increase the country's "arsenal
of patriotic songs." Certainly there were many songs about Uzbekistan dating from the Soviet period, but many of them had lyrics
that, although perhaps not alluding directly to socialism or the
Communist Party, had unavoidable associations with that period,
such as the word *o'rtaq* (comrade). The government wanted to
encourage composers to come up with new songs that incorporated the current threads of national ideology. Some of the win-
ning songs were showcased just a week before the celebration of
Uzbekistan's fifth anniversary of independence at a concert where
winners of the regional competitions went up against artists of
international fame such as Sherali Juraev, who stole the show
with one of the few performances that wasn't lip-synched: an elo-
quently sung version of a patriotic poem by Abdulla Oripov calling
on Uzbeks to be aware of the greatness of their historical legacies.

The musical styles of the songs encompassed everything from
folk to opera (and what does it say about my schema of culture that

I think the reader will see these genres as the extremes?). The themes of the songs centered around Uzbekistan's natural environment (rivers, mountains, flowers) and nature metaphors (for example, Uzbekistan blossoming); national heritage (the words *oltin meros*, golden heritage, were mentioned frequently as were the names of famous "ancestors" such as Timur and Ulughbek); wishing the country blessings (both through the secular wish for success, *"omon bo'ling,"* and through the invocation of Allah); and independence, expressed fairly often as the Uzbek value of hospitality, as in welcoming the world to independent Uzbekistan.

Most of the singers were Uzbeks, and all of the songs had at least some lyrics in Uzbek. This ethnolinguistic dominance even showed up in this contest's portrayal of Uzbekistan's multiethnic nationhood. One song was performed by a pop group from Navoi province, famous for having a Russian singer who sang well in Uzbek, and a Korean university student sang a pop song entirely in Uzbek. The third-place winner of the competition was a Russian opera singer from Tashkent who sang a song called "I love you, Uzbekistan." The musical accompaniment was "Russian," that is balalaika and accordion, but the song had a verse each in Russian, Uzbek, and English. The English verse was:

My Uzbekistan, may your flowers bloom forever.
Cherish [the] native land and care for all your children.
Uzbekistan, we love you.
Long may you bloom, Uzbekistan.
Ancient caravans, from you we draw our proud traditions.
The golden bird of happiness has spread its wings above you.
I love you, Uzbekistan.

Many of the competitors in this contest were already scheduled to participate in Independence Day concerts around the country, but apparently government officials were so taken with this song that, at the last minute, they slotted the singer to perform the song's Russian verse during the Independence Day concert, just to reinforce the already cosmopolitan, internationalist message they hoped to convey with the content of the spectacle. Awarding a prize to a song that was both international and patriotic and to a singer who was both Russian and Uzbekistani fit with the messages Uzbekistan's elites wanted to send about national identity in the new Uzbekistan.

This kind of multiethnic national identity is one that most of the post-Soviet Central Asian governments want to project in order to demonstrate that they are normal, modern nation-states. However, this image is in tension with the very real core of ethnic nationalism embraced by each of these countries. In general, the Central Asian states have adopted fairly open citizenship and language laws, though in each of these states there is a widespread perception of ethnic discrimination in jobs and employment that favors the titular nationality. Scholars examining nationalism in post-Soviet Central Asia tend to focus on the relationships between the titular nationality of a country (for example, Kazakhs in Kazakhstan) and the largely Russian minority population.[1] There were three main interpretations of Central Asian nationalism in the 1990s: one emphasized the potential for ethnic conflict in the region, another focused on the policies of the governments as being characteristic of "nationalizing regimes," and a third examined the ways that the Central Asian governments pursued civic, as opposed to ethnic, nationalism. Each of these interpretations touched on important issues, but looking back over the period, the questions of ethnic and civic nationalism seem to have been answered more by demographics than by deliberate policy decisions. In Uzbekistan, the fact that Uzbeks constituted a much larger proportion of the population than in Kazakhstan and Kyrgyzstan, for example, meant that the ethnic component of national identity played a very strong role, though not one that completely overwhelmed the civic component. What took place in Uzbekistan is best characterized as postcolonial civic nationalism, a point I will argue shortly.

Toward the end of the Soviet era, it looked as though Central Asia might face the same sorts of bloody ethnic conflicts that were overtaking the Caucasus. The interethnic violence of 1989 and 1990 in the Fergana Valley led many experts to forecast clashes based on ethnic or religious differences,[2] and for a while it seemed that the Central Asian states had the potential for extreme nationalism. However, the countries of Central Asia were relatively peaceful in the years after the collapse of the Soviet Union, and the bloody conflicts that arose in Tajikistan and Andijan cannot be accurately characterized as religious or ethnic intercommunal violence. Many authors' analyses were based on an unwarranted assumption that the presence of ethnic diversity in Central Asia was itself a threat to stability, or worse, assumed that the fear of interethnic violence on the part of

Russians and other ethnic minorities was a valid indicator of the probability of violence.[3] As Nick Megoran argues, the scholars who reasoned that the probability of ethnic conflict in the region was high tended to suffer from a lack of perspective about whether the nationalistic practices they observed were intense or mild compared to similar situations in the peaceful, stable parts of the world such as Western Europe, where, in fact, the conditions for conflict may be more severe.[4]

Over time, many scholars came to agree that ethnic conflict was less likely than regional conflict, and the violent conflicts of the 1990s and early 2000s bore out this analysis.[5] But were the Central Asian states "nationalizing regimes," pursuing policies that had the goal of assimilating, marginalizing, or expelling nontitular groups?[6] There was still disagreement about whether to characterize the Central Asian states as having primarily "nationalizing nationalisms," (in Rogers Brubaker's terms) that make policies "in the name of a 'core nation' or nationality, defined in ethnocultural terms, and sharply distinguished from the citizenry as a whole."[7] Alternatively, the Central Asian states could be understood as "national, but not nationalizing" states, where rights for certain minorities are guaranteed and with elements of a civic state, which is "the state of and for all of its citizens, irrespective of their ethnicity."[8] In Kazakhstan and Kyrgyzstan, the Russian language was granted a special status, while the titular languages grew in usage, though as Bhavna Dave argues, "state leaders cared more about the symbolic significance of the language than its actual use or survival."[9] In both these countries, a wave of nationalization was followed by a growing concern with civic identity and minority rights.[10] Because of violent incidents in both Kyrgyzstan and Tajikistan, members of the Uzbek minority feared further destabilizing ethnic relations, withdrawing from politics when they weren't shut out already. However, in both countries, Matteo Fumagalli argues, Uzbeks considered themselves indigenous citizens of their respective countries and saw Presidents Akaev and Rakhmanov as less nationalistic than the alternatives they feared.[11]

In this chapter, I will explore the ways that nationalism was expressed through cultural content in Uzbekistan between 1995 and 2004 and argue that despite the foreshadowing of explosive ethnic conflict and "nationalizing nationalisms" that took place in the late Soviet period, the government of Uzbekistan aspired to emulate a secular, civic-national model of statehood. This aspiration in part is related to Soviet legacies of internationalism and the pressures of international norms. However, my perspective on some of these issues is based on the research I did with cultural elites, who were arguably more cosmopolitan and less chauvinistic than political elites. It would be naïve to think that just because the intelligentsia still retains Soviet ideologies of tolerance, everyone in the society must share those same ideas. In any society, there is a split between the ideas of the elite, which tend to be grounded in a more cosmopolitan outlook, and the ideas of the masses, which are grounded in more local concerns. Cosmopolitans identify with universal values, and their identity is based on having things in common with people who are from different countries, making cosmopolitan ideologies inherently tolerant of difference. Thus I would like to stress that much of what I analyze in this chapter is an image of the nation that the cultural elite would like to project to the rest of the world. It would be a mistake to assume that the ideals expressed in official culture unproblematically reflect or influence public opinion, but it is not an exaggeration to say that at least the Soviet-era ideology of "friendship of the peoples" continued to have an impact on interethnic relations into the 2000s, at least among the generation in power. Other, more representative research has shown that the middle-aged generation that grew up under the conditions of "mature socialism" showed the highest levels of ethnic tolerance.[12]

In everyday life, the biggest obstacles to the government's civic-national ideals were not just ethnic chauvinism but also the government's own postcolonial nationalizing policies and the ethnic nature of the networks that control political and economic power in the country. Thus there was a conflict between the ideal and the reality of nationalism in post-Soviet Uzbekistan. In officially produced culture, this ideal was expressed as what I characterize as postcolonial civic nationalism. I use the term "postcolonial" with caution because the colonial nature of the Soviet Union has been the subject of considerable debate among scholars.[13] While clearly a different kind of empire than the British or French Empires, the emerging consensus, which my analysis supports, is that the Soviet Union was a modernizing colonial empire that was quite comparable to other European imperial states,[14] especially in ethnocultural terms. However, there has been little discussion of whether the paradigm of "postcolonialism" therefore also applies to post-Soviet Central Asia.[15]

Part of the problem with applying "postcolonial theory" to the Soviet case is that it is not so much a theory in the scientific sense as a set of contextually situated critiques of a particular kind of domination, usually a discourse and its attendant practices (such as Orientalism), that constructs a hierarchy that privileges the culture of the center over that of the periphery.[16] Postcolonial theory has yet to develop within Central Asia, in part because postcolonial critique is generally the result of intellectual hybridity, as individuals from the periphery use the intellectual devices of the center to construct their critique, though there is also a strong tradition in postcolonial theory of grassroots critique.[17] In addition to the differences between Soviet colonialism and other colonialisms, Central Asia is different from other cases of postcolonialism because its independence was delivered without a struggle. The lack of anticolonial movements and the near absence of anticolonial critiques among Soviet Central Asians is undoubtedly hindering, not just the emergence of such critiques since independence, but also the formulation of *any* critique of domination.

Thus my argument about postcolonial civic nationalism is not grounded in indigenous postcolonial critiques but is rather my interpretation of what messages the government intended to convey through cultural content. On the one hand, the content of official culture in Uzbekistan was a reaction against Russian cultural imperialism, but, on the other hand, it was an affirmation of both Soviet nation building and modernist internationalism in Uzbekistan. Soviet institutions, far from destroying traditional culture, acted to preserve traditional culture even as they transformed it, not just in a socialist-state way, but also by participating in the establishment of international cultural norms that provide legitimation for the practices of Uzbekistan's cultural elites today.[18]

While global cultural norms are one legitimate frame of reference for culture producers in post-Soviet space, the other main frame of reference is "the past." As authors writing about postcommunist cultural studies have also pointed out, cultural change in post-Soviet space is often related to the desire to become "normal" again by leaving the experiments of communism and returning to what is familiar from the past.[19] Both frames of reference, "the world" and "the past," are the product of Soviet definitions that relied on Russian cultural norms, leading to a hierarchy of cultures characteristic of colonialism, but with additional subtleties that are the result of the Soviet Union's brand of nonexploitative, modernizing colonialism.[20] First, I will explore the way that cultural elites participate in a postcolonial discourse about nationhood and culture. My analysis breaks this discourse into two main components: one is a debate about cultural "renewal," (*vosstanovlenie*) and the other is a process of de-Sovietization that is talked about as "depoliticization" (*depolitisizatsiia*). Then I will go into an in-depth content analysis of the civic and ethnic elements of Uzbekistani national identity as they showed up in national holiday spectacles.

Bending the Stick and the Discourse of Cultural Renewal

I mentioned before that a major critique of colonialism in Soviet Uzbekistan had to do with the valorization of Russian culture and the denigration of Uzbek culture. A little background may be necessary to show how this hierarchy of cultures was established. As was the case in other empires, Soviet historians and ethnographers played a large role in defining national cultures when they selected which elements of traditional culture were progressive and worthy of a "democratic" nation and which were backward and should be eliminated.[21] After independence, Uzbeks continued to take pride in the parts of their heritage that were esteemed by Russia as progressive, ranging from their traditionally sedentary lifestyle (which was more evolved than the nomadic lifestyle of their neighbors, according to Marxism), to literary and scholarly luminaries such as Alisher Navoiy (1441–1501, a member of the Timurid court and considered to be the founder of Uzbek literature), Mirzo Ulughbek (1393/94–1449, grandson of Timur, ruler of Samarkand, and the astronomer who compiled the most comprehensive catalog of stars in the world at that time), and Ibn Sino (also known as Avicenna, 981–1037, who was born near Bukhara and wrote world-famous medical books).[22]

"Backward" aspects of traditional Uzbek culture, however, were often replaced with "progressive" Russian standards, especially in the realm of material culture: Russian-style houses, clothing, food, and so forth were held to be self-evidently more healthy and rational than native ways of life. The "internationalization of national cultures" was seen as a means of development, enriching national culture through the adoption of new forms and genres of culture. In Soviet discourse, the enrichment and development of a national culture was best achieved by the adoption of the progressive aspects of other national cultures, specifically Russian national culture.[23] According to the point of view prevalent in the Brezhnev era, the

Russian presence in Central Asia was beneficial in that it acquainted the native urban population with classics of Russian literature and with other achievements in science, technology, painting, theater, and music.[24] Other progressive social changes were less concrete but nonetheless brought the Asian nationalities closer to Europeans in terms of their cultural habits: rising levels of education, printing books in native languages, the opening of museums and libraries, participation in clubs, and participation in folklore groups.[25]

An example of this ideal of the internationalization of culture, as well as its problematic implementation, comes from the uncataloged archives of the Ministry of Cultural Affairs. Professional theater organizations located in the outlying regions of Uzbekistan were regularly inspected by the Union of Theatrical Workers, who reported their findings to the ministry. In 1986, a theater in the Karakalpak Autonomous Region was criticized for not devoting enough attention to the classics of Russian and foreign theater. Evidently its repertoire consisted entirely of works by Soviet Central Asian writers. The lack of progress in Russification in Karakalpakistan is clear in the theater director's response to the critics' demands that more Russian classics be performed: "But our actors don't speak Russian well!"[26]

This example highlights both the campaigns to import European culture and the attempt to internationalize indigenous high culture. The Karakalpak theater's repertoire was scrutinized to ensure that it was properly internationalized through the importation of European culture, but the existence of the theater and its locally produced repertoire was itself evidence of the transformation of indigenous culture to something resembling European high culture. Some of these cases were not viewed as cultural imperialism by Uzbekistan's cultural elites, who saw this type of transformation as the progressive development of national culture. While the transformation is fairly obvious to outside observers, often it was accepted as part of authentic culture by Uzbeks (and Karakalpaks).

Not only were international forms imported to Uzbekistan (in the form of European-style, scripted, proscenium theater, for example), but national forms (such as the Shosh Maqam) were also internationalized through changes in instrumentation and the fixing of tones to a Western scale.[27] The Soviet ideal was not that all national cultures should be homogenous but rather that the methods of production be modernized and that international forms be adorned with local color: "The unification of the progressive elements of national traditions and folklore with the progressive possibilities of theatrical methods of an international character . . . has two interconnected aspects: the transformation of traditional-folk forms of festivity already existing in the republic by the inclusion of techniques and elements of international artistic culture . . . [and] the enrichment of borrowed forms and genres . . . [with] the folk traditions, arts, and folklore of a particular region."[28]

Ghulom aka, a professional composer, described in our interview how the Soviets pretty much invented the ensemble style of Uzbek dance by creating a women's dance ensemble in Uzbekistan initially modeled on Moscow's Russian folk dance troupe, Beriozka.[29] The elements of the dance and costume came from traditional Uzbek courtyard dancing, but the style of ensemble dancing that was one of the most distinctive markers of Uzbek culture and national identity (given its extensive use in holidays, diplomatic events, and television performances) was an invention that internationalized the form of national cultural expression. Farida opa, a choreographer, also pointed out that the masculine style of Uzbek dance was almost entirely a Soviet invention; she claimed that men just did not dance in the old days (except when dressed as women).[30] In the area of music, famous musicians from around Uzbekistan were invited to Tashkent to record, notate, arrange, harmonize, and research traditional music and, significantly, to study European music. The relationship of traditional music to the music of contemporary European-style composers was problematic, but the state's main priority in the development of music in Uzbekistan was "the assimilation of so-called European professional music. In general, this priority was preserved right down to the beginning of the 1990s."[31]

The elites I interviewed in the 1990s commonly characterized the process of cultural change they were going through as balancing renewed traditional culture and universal human values. They did not talk about the process as decolonization, retraditionalization, or nationalization. They, as well as the mass media, would talk about the renewal/revival/recovery (vosstanovlenie) of traditional Uzbek culture, but most of what Tashkent's cultural elites were actually producing combined the revival of traditional cultural content with modern messages of international cooperation, and, as I argued in chapter 2, these messages were presented through cultural forms that remained intact from the Soviet period. For example, the content of the holiday Navro'z combined traditional folklore with popular culture.

But in addition to "traditional" local celebrations of Navro'z in each region, the state organized an outdoor theatrical spectacle for television broadcast and a Soviet-style sayil (street fair) in Tashkent with amusements for the people. The state also attempted to impose uniformity on regional celebrations through "training seminars" and monitoring in the form of television footage showing the standardized public celebrations in the regions.

Independence provided an opportunity for culture producers to explore aspects of their culture that were repressed or neglected during the Soviet period. But in Uzbekistan, as in other postcolonial countries, there was a certain ambivalence about tradition, which is always implicitly contrasted with modernity. There were quite a few elites who passionately advocated a revival of traditions and a smaller number who were interested only in producing culture "of an international standard." The majority had mixed feelings or strove for a syncretic blend of traditional and modern that would ring true in the contemporary milieu.[32] Whatever their goals, nearly everyone pursued these goals by employing the resources of the state.

In the production of the Navro'z holiday spectacle, for example, there was continual and ongoing tension between those who strove for some sort of historical or cultural authenticity and those who simply wanted to put on a good show. Furthermore, everyone agreed that repetition needed to be avoided, but while those more interested in the renewal of national culture advocated "going back" to rediscover old stories and symbols, others situated the renewal of culture firmly in a contemporary framework. The lead directors of the show, for example, were primarily concerned with entertaining and ease of communication with the audience rather than authenticity, and one of the ethnic Europeans who worked on the production didn't even give lip service to authenticity and claimed his colleagues did not really care about authenticity either:

LAURA: So what were your goals?

IVAN: We had the goal . . .

LAURA: I mean your own goals.

IVAN: No, we worked on this together. The problem [with the Navro'z spectacle] was that there weren't enough special effects. The thing is that when you have a mass holiday like this, the more special effects you have, the more the people go "ooh, aah!"

LAURA: So that was your goal, to make the people go "Ah!"?

IVAN: Only that. It was like we were just watching a concert, a bunch of dances. These folk traditions have always been around, and everyone knows them. So we need to inject some life into them. Add some effects, smoke or something, and it would be a different story . . .

LAURA [later in the conversation]: Some say Navro'z should be even more folk. You don't agree?

IVAN: Well, you see, this is a folk holiday and in its own time, a thousand years ago, it was completely new. There needs to be some kind of progress, development. This is and always has been a folk holiday, it's not going to stop being folk if we add something new! They gave the viewer a concert, that's all. It needs to be more interesting. The TV viewer sees, say, the dance of spring—he's already seen it a hundred times! But every new production has something new about it, and I wanted that new thing to be technical effects.[33]

Ivan, as a non-Uzbek and as someone with a background that wasn't in the arts or academia, was clearly more invested in the spectacle's ability to grab the viewer's attention than in any message conveyed by its content. For him, the message of Navro'z was important because people cared about it and would respond to it positively if it were presented in an engaging way. For Ivan, cultural renewal wasn't necessary, authenticity wasn't necessary. All that was necessary was that the viewer be engaged, and for that, he thought that novelty was more important than adherence to tradition.

Very few ethnic Uzbek elites I spoke with shared this open disregard for the authenticity of national culture or dismissed the cultural renewal debate entirely. One exception was Olim aka, an official in the Ministry of Higher Education, who wanted only to look forward: "A lot of people talk about renewal, renewal, but I think it is more correct to talk not about renewal but about construction of a new state on a market basis."[34] More common was a sense that what was most important was a kind of cultural renewal that included cultural *development* and that this process should be quite openly fostered and manipulated by the state. Those elites whose occupation was not directly related to Uzbek ethnic cultural forms, such as Karim aka, a composer of European-style music and an administrator at the Professional Musicians' Association, were especially concerned with keeping up with contemporary and international styles in music as well as global practices in the music business (as in international marketing and so on):

KARIM AKA: As for contemporary music, maybe in some areas we're repeating ourselves, maybe, but in other areas we're moving ahead. Here you go, we have [groups like] these kids who are showing up now [he gestures to the hip-hop group rehearsing outside], as you can hear. . . . In the genre of light music, we're sort of standing still because we don't have the schools for it. . . . We need to establish schools here, and it is happening through a decree of the cabinet of ministers, that O'znavo should establish a college, above and beyond the music school we already have, to train our kids in *estrada* [light popular music]. . . . We have our own singers, but they're mostly modeled on the Tom Jones or Elvis Presley style, and we have some other performers that maybe we need to learn how to promote more. That is very important, we don't have a strong promotional infrastructure for estrada and jazz.[35]

Cultural elites who had a bureaucratic (as opposed to creative) career also tended to be more blasé about cultural renewal and more in favor of modern and European cultural forms, and they did not feel at all self-conscious about the idea that culture should serve the state.

OLIM AKA: These holidays, especially Independence Day, aren't just about art. . . . We'll see in the concert the main points of propaganda about the government's reforms that you can read about in any newspaper. It is going to be about ideology, just as it always was. We have to propagandize our joint ventures and industry. . . . So that is why we have to show the accomplishments of the government because Uzbekistan didn't exist before to be revived. . . . In the sphere of culture, no one is trying to wipe out classic culture, ballet, or choir music just because they're trying to revive something else. . . . Along these same lines you can't develop only that which was forgotten. People talk about the re-birth of national culture, music, choreography, but . . . these festivals first and foremost serve the development of the arts.[36]

There was also, among practicing artists at least, a desire to develop the non–folk arts through a kind of syncretism that blends tradition with contemporary tastes. Mansur aka, a theatrical director, expressed this idea as well:

MANSUR AKA: A folk holiday should [interruption] . . . without atmosphere, without a taste of the contemporary, none of the ancient, historical, folk elements [of the holiday] will evoke the interest they should, you see. If you limit it to only what was in ancient times, the rites and rituals, art, folklore, ethnography, it will be like a mere illustration. This is why I think that Navro'z of 1996, based on history of the ancient holiday Navro'z, but at the same time relating to today's life and attitudes to folk holidays, to mass holidays, was a more relevant reflection of today's audience. . . . Of course without the past there is no present. It has to carry traces, through ballet, choreography, drama, costumes, masks, mass participation, it all underlines its ancient national path, while at the same time reflecting contemporary attitudes about the holiday.[37]

Sherali aka, a choreographer, said that he wanted to start a dance school that would help revive traditional dance movements authentic to the various regions of Uzbekistan. This stemmed in part from a nostalgic desire to preserve a culture in its wholeness, derived from a romanticism that sees nationalities as bounded entities with an essence that can be distilled. There was a belief, not just in Uzbekistan, that there is something inherently good and beautiful about the "intact" culture of a region as it existed before Russian and Western influences corrupted it. But when I pressed Sherali aka on this issue, he talked about how it is also good to have as wide a variety of movements to draw on as possible, that the primary reason to rediscover "traditional" Fergana dance is not to objectify a pure cultural form and put it in stasis but to enrich the repertoire of movements available to today's choreographers. "We must take ideas from the people, add technical skill, and develop them."[38]

Many Uzbek elites feared that "the people" had forgotten their history and culture. I was repeatedly told "we have to know our past in order to know who we are and where we are going." Those who saw their work as part of a rebirth of Uzbek ethnic culture were fully aware that they were not part of a grassroots movement, but rather one that was sponsored officially ever since Uzbeks began to assert themselves against Soviet power in the late 1980s.[39] "Yes, I feel I'm part of a larger movement toward cultural renewal," said Sherali aka, "but it all comes from the top, really, you know. Because of the money. None of it is possible without the money."[40] Given this realism, there was little naiveté among my interviewees about restoring "pure" traditional culture.

However, some people who were strong advocates of cultural renewal were also critical of syncretism and the development of folk culture, and these people also tended to see the state, or at least the Soviet state and its modernizing policies, as part of the problem. These people felt that syncretism leads to the degradation of pure cultural objects while "development" leads to standardization. One of the main influences that artists felt led to a standardization of culture during the Soviet period was professionalization. Farida opa was a choreographer from one of the regional centers of Uzbekistan whom I met in Tashkent. During the course of our interview, she explained the difference between what she called "Uzbek dance" and "Soviet Uzbek dance:" the former was dance the way it was performed in everyday life, and the latter was altered because of the requirements of performing for an audience.[41] Interestingly, she did not use Uzbek dance as her example of the way the Soviets subtly transformed folk culture but instead used the example of the Chukchi, a Siberian people who were often the butt of Soviet jokes and were generally viewed as among the most "primitive" of the Soviet peoples. Perhaps being a choreographer herself, she felt too much a part of the culture to separate its "Soviet" strands from its "Uzbek" strands. Perhaps in her attempt to demonstrate the Orientalizing effect of Soviet colonialism on her culture, she became the Orientalizer through what was, to her, a more clear-cut example: the superexotic Chukchi.

Farida opa demonstrated for me a "shaman dance" of the Chukchi: she stood up and performed her version of an "authentic" Chukchi shaman dance, her head bent, her arms waving at her sides, her back hunched. "And what the Soviet choreographer would do," she said, "was to make the dancers face the audience, 'raise your head!' they would say, 'it looks better that way.' They cleaned up the movements, standardized them." Then she did her imitation of a stylized Soviet Chukchi dance, with the same moves but with the front of the torso more opened up, more oriented toward the audience. "They did the same thing with Khorezm dance, for example," she said. "The real Khorezm movement might be like this," she said, her arms arcing in front of her, fingers pointing down, "but the Soviets would want them to throw back their shoulders, or something, so that it's no longer the way the people would do it at home, but for the audience. They thought it looked better that way, and now that's how everyone does it because that's how they've seen it done."[42]

Ghulom aka, a composer, and others pointed out the role the media, especially television, play in propagating these standardized versions. The media not only teach people how to differentiate regional styles one from another, they also influence a blending of styles as the entire country is exposed to the elements of a particular regional style. This was seen as a harmful phenomenon by many of the people I interviewed, who opposed any syncretism in the folk arts, seeing "development" (as opposed to recovery) almost like destroying a historical artifact.

> GHULOM AKA: We shouldn't mix them [styles] because every region has its own very rich traditions and culture. Earlier, every region had its own music that people could tell apart but since radio came along, we hear music from all over the world and it is easier to mix up the styles, but I wanted them [the regional ensembles] to each use its own style which is beautiful in its own way.

> LAURA: Why is that important?

> GHULOM AKA: So they don't lose their own folklore, their own history, which would be an easy thing to do. When Khorezm music and dance is performed, it should be obvious it's Khorezm. We shouldn't lose these differences because it is richness, it is history. Mixing it up just isn't as interesting. Every region should guard its own traditions because that is the richness of history.[43]

This process of standardization through "development" continues today. One example of this and of the ways that the ideas of authorities at the center get transmitted to the periphery was the seminar I attended in Tashkent in February 1996, "The Director's Role in Organizing Mass and Open-Air Performances and the Steps of Producing a Scenario." The seminar was put on by the Republican Center for Public Creative Activity and Cultural-Educational Affairs, a division of the Uzbekistan Ministry of Cultural Affairs. Although not specifically about Navro'z, the timing of the seminar and the concrete examples used in the lectures indicated that this was an opportunity for Tashkent-based experts to shape the way Navro'z would be officially celebrated in the regions. The lectures tended to focus on the correct and incorrect way to do things, but it wasn't just the cultural meanings (such as what should be emphasized in a Navro'z festival versus one on Independence Day) that were conveyed by the speakers, but also the importance of professionalism, of doing the best and liveliest show they could with limited resources and talent. Lastly, both universalism and particularism were to play a part in local festivities: speakers likened Uzbek holidays to those in China and India and seemed especially enamored of incorporating more of a feel of Latin American carnival into Navro'z; but at the same time, they encouraged local directors to keep local color prominent in the performance.

Farida opa pointed out that another influence on standardization during the Soviet period was "the plan." Art was produced according to the plan, and you had to make up a certain number of dances each year, so people just used the moves they already knew, leading to stagnation, she said. Baxriddin aka, from the Ministry of Cultural Affairs, also pointed out that standardization was related to large-scale production. With Soviet industrialization, many master craftsmen were forced to stop operating since all production was to be carried out in artels or factories.[44] Of course, having factories produce items that were once made by hand results in a large degree of homogenization of available styles, but Baxriddin aka, a painter, also noted in our interview that this had an effect on what were considered to be "regional" styles. "Before, there were many different craftsmen, each working in his own style. After industrialization, maybe only one man was left in an entire region doing ceramics or wood carving, and by default his style became known as the style of the entire region! These things were taught in the central schools, of course, but the information was very sketchy, more theoretical."[45] The propagation of theoretical (that is, comparative, universalizing) knowledge about a formerly living craft is another example of the Soviet modernization of culture.

Most of the cultural changes I discussed with my interviewees related to changes that modernization brought, for better or worse. Change as "imperialism" was implied, if not openly referred to as such, in terms of the valorization of Russian culture and the denigration of Uzbek culture. There was one other variant of this perspective on cultural imperialism that stressed the dependency on central planning that was cultivated by the Soviet system:

BAXRIDDIN AKA: There is a missing link in the chain, a missing bridge between the ages. . . . Renewal is inadequate because the gap was too big, the cultural ecology was violated, polluted . . . there need to be renewals on a local scale but they will be incomplete. There are thousands of things lost, and you just can't recover them all. . . . There is a lot of damage to make up for, and we can't recover everything all at once. Russian culture was also damaged by the Soviets.[46]

Baxriddin aka argued that so much was lost during the Soviet period that direct continuity with the past would be impossible. His perspective was that for reasons of practicality it was important to return to indigenous technology in order not to be dependent on Russia.

Thus there was a lot of ambivalence within Tashkent's cultural elite about the Soviet legacies of colonialism, modernization, and cultural development and a diversity of opinion about what role the newly independent state should play in the renewal of ethnic Uzbek culture. A few elites I spoke to were very dubious about any change at all, be it renewal or development. They saw state involvement in culture as a source of insurmountable inertia and found it difficult to conceive of radical changes. Jamshid aka, an instructor at the Institute of Culture, was the most pessimistic of my informants. "Nothing has changed," he said. "Uzbekistan is like a dog that lived all its life inside the courtyard and suddenly the door to the street is opened and it won't go out. The elite are just puppets. Puppets and parrots."[47]

But to what extent was the renewal of Uzbek culture part of a nationalizing process that worked to the detriment of Uzbekistan's civic national goals? In fact, many non-Uzbeks felt that the "bowed stick" was being bent too far in the other direction. They saw what we might call a process of reverse discrimination building up speed. Grisha, a music critic, commented, "Now there is a reversal, and there is more attention to national culture, the priorities have changed. European culture is being neglected." He said it is understandable from a historic point of view, that this is just what people do when there is a revolution or change in governments. I asked him for concrete examples of how he knows there is less attention to European culture, and he answered, "When you try to put on an event featuring European culture, such as the festival of contemporary music, sometimes there is resistance, passive or active. All the new schools and institutions being created are for national culture. In public discourse there is no discussion of, say, European painting, but only about Eastern miniatures. The roads are being closed to Russophone authors." He called it "the Soviet syndrome, neo-Bolshevism. Destroy the old to create the new."[48]

The Depoliticization of Culture

The campaigns for cultural renewal were one of the main elements in the discussion about decolonizing the content of public culture in Uzbekistan, but another of the main changes from the Soviet era that was often mentioned by cultural elites was the depoliticization of culture. This, then, relates to another discourse about the cultural imperialism of the Soviet period: depoliticization was used in this context to describe the shift from socialist to nationalist content in culture production, with Soviet and Communist Party symbols being recast in the minds of culture producers as impositions from Moscow that distorted the "normal development" of Uzbek national symbols.

The most noticeable change in terms of content was of course the elimination of socialist and explicitly Soviet symbolism. When I asked one of the holiday directors whether Soviet holidays in Uzbekistan had Uzbek characteristics, he replied,

> ALISHER AKA: I'd have to say that in any case, there wasn't anything particularly Uzbek about them. Because when we saw the holiday broadcasts on television from Baku, Moscow, Leningrad, Yerevan, Frunze, Alma Ata, they all had the same marches and festivals. They were all the same, you know? The exact same enterprises, the exact same factories— the only difference was in the show the people in an ensemble wore their own national costumes and did their own dances. This kind of national orientation didn't exist. The Soviets stole that. In short, they were very much alike. The national element was small.[49]

Depoliticization also showed up when holiday producers told me that they had a greater sense of artistic freedom than they did during the Soviet period, and I found this sentiment to be shared by artists more broadly in Uzbekistan, with the exception that their freedom was limited much more by economics than by the state. Culture producers told me that their work had changed since the Soviet period in that not every play or work of art had to be justified ideologically; sometimes art could be just for fun. However, in interviews with artists not involved in holiday performances, a somewhat different sentiment emerged: a share of their work still had to go to state ideological work, and then they would be allowed to have "fun." But at least that share was smaller than it had been in the Soviet period when, as one theater director put it, the rule was "five [plays] for them [the state] and one for us [the artists]."[50] As another director explained, at the flagship Uzbek-language theater, the Hamza, the rule was more like "you can do one of 'yours' for every one of 'theirs'."[51]

Another director stressed not freedom but artistic merit as one of the ways culture has been depoliticized:

ALISHER AKA: [Soviet holidays] had what we might call an academic character. For fifteen minutes on May 1 [there] was an artistic-athletic festival on the square, then the march began. That of course was also very interesting, and there was something artistic to it; every region, organization, factory, showing off their achievements and products in the form of props; the people who produced these things marched, and the people enjoyed it. So that is how the march was organized, and after that the street fair began. I would say that today's holidays have become more artistic, they have lost their officiousness and are more elevated in their artistic level, their level of culture. They're not so academic and official, but rather they are aimed at making people happy, at being spectacular.[52]

For the holiday workers, the important difference was that though Uzbekistan's holiday spectacles were still highly ideological, they were so in a national-patriotic way. The artists seemed to feel they had a lot more room for creativity when they were restricted to patriotic sentiments than when they were restricted to socialist sentiments. This may have been true, if only until they exhausted their own interest in exploring their newly sanctioned national identity. As I continued to visit Uzbekistan through 2006, I was able to see that indeed, after fifteen years of nationalist kitsch, even the most ideologically motivated artists were burning out on the limited range of materials allowed to them by the official state symbolism. During the 2000s, there was more room for the exploration of certain aspects of heritage, such as Naqshbandi Sufism, and a wider repertoire of cultural and historical heroes to draw on, but the holiday concerts in particular were described to me as "the usual," with little innovation in form or content.

While Uzbekistan's culture and public life still seemed very politicized to me, this is largely because we in the United States do not make the distinction between politics and ideology that Uzbeks do. The fact that culture remains highly ideological did not surprise or disturb many of Tashkent's cultural elite—ideological tints were a part of public life for them. The difference in their eyes was that the political part of life (that is, what was associated with the Party, with economic plans and decrees from Moscow) had greatly receded. Slogans such as "Uzbekistan will be self-sufficient in gold, oil, cotton, and wheat" were echoed in the media so often that you would hear them coming up in everyday conversation, but these were goals set by Karimov, not by Gorbachev. Some slogans became perennial favorites in the postindependence period, such as "Uzbekistan is a future great state," and "Don't tear down your old home before building a new one." Other campaigns changed and developed over the years. Some, like "Amir Timur 660," the 1996 jubilee of Timur's birth, were themes for just one year, while others, like "Turkistan, Our Common Home," were themes for several years running. Artists who worked on the holiday spectacles always used these ideological campaigns as a stimulus for their creativity and incorporated these themes into the holiday performances, not because they were told to, but because that was part of their job as artists working on this particular project.

A final example of the depoliticization of holidays since the Soviet period was seen in the dramatic shift to nonverbal visual elements in Uzbekistan's holiday spectacles. The pedagogical mission of Soviet holidays was literally spelled out in their main events. Marchers carried banners and placards with familiar slogans ("Glory to Labor, Glory to the Party," "Soviet Power Is People's Power," "Peace, Labor, May") that declared the explicitly political basis for the holiday. Words played a much smaller part in new holidays and conveyed information more subtly, through sparse narration, usually in the form of poetry in Uzbek. While the meaning of the words was clearly ideological, the poetry was viewed by holiday organizers as both less political and more artistic. An example from the 1996 Independence Day script (by poet Erkin Vohidov, my translation) illustrates the "Turkistan, our common home" ideological campaign designed to build a supranational identification with the territory that became the five republics of Soviet Central Asia:

Mother Earth of Old
Turkistan is one—the homeland is one.
Dearest of all to our soul
Turkistan is one—the homeland is one.

To Mother Earth attend
Her voice's echo will not end.
Souls will speak, the Fatherland
Turkistan is one—the homeland is one.

However, there was a split between the poets and scholars working on the scenarios and the lead directors. One of the directors asserted that the "purpose of the text in these sorts of performances is to serve as a guide to the action." In selecting prerecorded music for the prologue in the Independence Day holiday program, the lead director acknowledged that the lyrics weren't that important as long as the word homeland (*vatan*) was in the song somewhere: "Nobody's going to hear [the words] anyway. What matters is the emotional impact of the music. The prologue should be grand, it should move people, leave a strong impression, get the idea across—show what is the vatan." Words in mass spectacle productions were secondary to sounds and visual impressions.

Nearly all visual information in these holiday extravaganzas was communicated through symbols, lights, and colors. Instead of hoisting a banner that quoted President Karimov's slogan, "Our Goal is Self-sufficiency in Oil, Gold, Cotton, and Wheat," the Independence Day spectacle participants in 1995 dressed up as an oil well, a brick of gold, a branch of cotton, and a stalk of wheat. Everyone knew what the importance of these items was without having it spelled out as part of a Party plan. Instead of the perception that the *apparat* was directing everything, there was a perception (among the elites, at least) that Karimov and his advisors were doing their best to guide the country in the right direction and that it was everyone's pride and duty to achieve increased production levels in these essential industries. Though these sentiments changed later on, in the mid-1990s they were quite strong and fairly widespread, according to opinion polls.[53]

What is interesting from my position as an outsider is that the kitschy style that I associated with Soviet symbolism was not part of this depoliticization process: the aesthetics of Uzbekistan's holiday spectacles were not so different from Soviet holiday aesthetics. Instead of dancing workers, one found dancing oil wells or sheaves of wheat; instead of quoting the words of Marx or Lenin in the scenario, the words of Amir Timur or Karimov were quoted. What cultural elites had changed were specific elements of content, not the political uses of culture. These changes, from floats representing industry and banners echoing Party policies to staged entertainment by professional artists and dramatic scenes enacting significant events from Uzbekistan's history, were seen by cultural elites as signs of the depoliticization of culture in Uzbekistan since Independence.

Perhaps the switch from the infamous Soviet form of the slogan to the form of the colorful illustration was enough to make an ideological campaign seem less political than its Soviet counterpart. Slogans were still used by the government, but to a lesser degree and in a different way. The slogan "Uzbekistan is a Future Great State" adorned a building on Independence Square, and before 1996 part of the sign attributed the saying to President Karimov. In 1996 his name was taken off the sign, indicating what I believe the Uzbeks saw as a depoliticization of ideology. Many of the other slogans on state-owned billboards throughout the city had Karimov's sayings on them, but the ones dedicated to holidays were usually nonpolitical, and often even lacking an explicit ideological message. As one theater director commented, "Now, thank God, at my theater we have one slogan on Navro'z: have a happy holiday. That's it. That's enough! We had it with excerpts from Gorbachev's speech, Lenin's works. That's the kind of era it was, but it's not that way now."

Not everyone involved in the production of holiday spectacles perceived that his culture had been depoliticized, however. Some people, especially ethnic Europeans, had a very different take on how much (or little) had changed since independence:

> IVAN: May First, for example, in its time was about the unity of the people, the party, and the government, etc. etc., and we shouted "hooray, hooray." Now we just shout a different hooray. I'm saying too much! . . . Earlier they forced us to shout. I'm sorry, but [in Navro'z] we had people from the different regions in the procession with their own slogans; it's

just that they were folk slogans instead of political slogans. All the same there were slogans. How can you live without slogans? . . . We have to strive toward something.[54]

The Uzbek elites I talked to were invested in projecting an image of their national culture as free, as developing "naturally" after years of "distortions." Their attitude about how much everything had changed may have reflected somewhat wishful thinking on their part, but more than that, indicated that they felt they had a stake in the distinct identity the government of Uzbekistan wanted to project as being independent of the Soviet past. European elites did not share this investment in the new national identity and more frequently stated that they retained a more ethnically neutral Soviet identity that no longer had any kind of institutional support from Moscow or elsewhere. This distance allowed them, and me, to perceive greater continuity with Soviet cultural production.

In Weberian terms, we can see the spectacular elements of Soviet holidays, the scale and the color, as an attempt to overcome the disenchantment of a Soviet rationality that permeated even festive occasions with a sense of officiousness. The spontaneity and creativity of contemporary Uzbekistan's holiday extravaganzas were more like the spectacular culture of a theme park: a simulation carefully controlled by its creators. Holidays may have seemed less political and the public may have enjoyed them, but in this the spectacle's creators were only more clever than their Soviet predecessors in creating a plausible simulation of festivity.

The Content of National Holiday Spectacles

The production of national holidays performances was a concrete site of convergence for these concerns about recovery and depoliticization, syncretism and modernization. As I argued in chapter 2, after independence, Uzbekistan's cultural elites turned to an "ethnically unmarked" international cultural form, the mass spectacle, as a way to demonstrate that Uzbek culture can compete on a world level given the right technology, personnel, and inspiration. Though one of the most important agenda items in cultural nation-building in post-Soviet Uzbekistan was de-Sovietization and the renewed expression of national culture, what exactly counted as Soviet, as national, or as international/modern for that matter?

The production of holiday spectacles gives us a window on a world of concepts and categories that were shared and disputed between cultural elites. In the discussions about the content of national holiday concerts, as well as in the final products, even a hint of interethnic animosity was to be avoided at all costs, and while the ethnic core of the nation was to be highlighted as part of a postcolonial response to Soviet-era downplaying of Uzbek national culture, civic elements of national identity were extremely important as part of the image these concerts projected.

The empirical basis for the rest of this chapter comes from my ethnographic fieldwork as well as a content analysis of the themes addressed in holiday spectacles. In the previous chapter, I mentioned that the main structural unit of these holiday extravaganzas was the "block." Blocks were composed of one or more thematically coherent song and dance numbers. The individual numbers, most of which last from one to three minutes, had very different styles of costume, music, and movement, but all of the numbers in a block were linked by a particular theme. Using videotapes of seven holiday extravaganzas (Navro'z 1995, 1996, and 1998; Independence Day 1993, and 1995–1997),[55] I coded each block in terms of its thematic content. This was done based on the overall impression the block conveyed, though some blocks were so heterogeneous that they had to be split and counted separately. If the words were intelligible (some vocal styles made it difficult to understand the Uzbek lyrics, and some blocks had songs with lyrics that were not Russian or Uzbek), I gave those the first priority in determining up to five content keywords for each block. I also assigned keywords based on the visual symbols in the scene and on what the spectacle producers told me each block was supposed to convey. The coding scheme was simplified after I analyzed which themes tended to go together in the same blocks and combined similar keywords into one aspect of content. I ended up with five main themes, which I will refer to later (from most to least prevalent): heritage (for example, references to history and legends); patriotism (formulaic expressions of love for the homeland that might touch on the other themes but focused mainly on ideas of independence and new-found freedom); nature (for example, excitement about spring flowers blooming); nationhood (which included all sorts of expressions of culture particular to Uzbekistan, ranging from folkways to interethnic harmony, and also included lessons about Uzbekistan's place in the world); and family (for example, references to children or mothers).

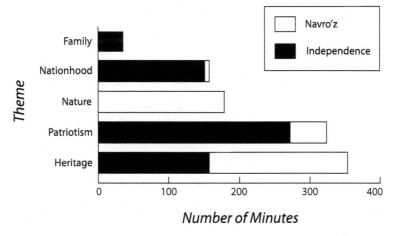

Figure 7. The differing thematic content of the Navro'z and Independence Day holiday concerts.

As figure 7 shows, Navro'z and Independence Day had thematically different concerts, with a greater emphasis on folkloristic themes of nature and ethnic heritage in Navro'z and more attention paid to patriotism and features of the nation-state during Independence Day. The content of the concerts reflected different emphases on civic and ethnic versions of the official national identity. During staff meetings of Navro'z 1996, the directors would repeat instructions (for example, to those who would like to simply reuse a number from last Independence Day) that this holiday was *milliy* (national), xalq (folk), and *ommaviy* (mass, popular), unlike Independence Day, which was a siyosiy (political) holiday for the vatan (homeland). This distinction between Navro'z as a holiday of the Uzbek people and Independence Day as a holiday of the civic nation was present, not just in the discourse about the holiday, but also in the practice of language use among spectacle producers. In the organizational meetings for both holidays, Russian was the dominant language, but during the Navro'z meetings, Uzbek was spoken much more frequently than it was during Independence Day meetings. Since the group of people who were working on the extravaganzas was largely the same, with the same proportion of monolingual Russophones, the difference in language use clearly indicates the spectacle producers' understanding of the ethnic exclusivity of Navro'z, contrasted with the inclusivity of Independence Day. The marginalization of Russophones in the staff meetings was seen by some as yet more evidence of the "stick being bent too far back in the other direction." As Ivan expressed, "My honest opinion, again, is that I don't take sides, but here were Russians and, I'm sorry, Russian is the language of international communication here. If you want to know my personal opinion, there should have been bilingual explanation of the text. Maybe in English! But Russian is the language everyone understands. Maybe we've gone a little overboard with it."[56]

The distinctions holiday producers saw between the ethnic and civic emphases of the holidays were nicely summarized by one choreographer who said that Navro'z should be a folk holiday focusing on (Uzbek, ethnic) national culture, while Independence Day should focus on the universal elements of Uzbekistan's culture in addition to showcasing ethnic culture.

> HAMID AKA: Independence Day is an entirely different matter. During Independence Day, we should show what we have gained in the past year. In agriculture, in sports, culture, military technology, art, literature, etc. There we should say, here is what we are, Uzbekistan. Orchestral music is also part of our achievements, classical ballet is an achievement, our young military men, these are our achievements, but they don't belong in Navro'z. That's why I didn't like last year's Navro'z [in 1995]. It was so full of orchestral music you couldn't even get the sense of the holiday. This year was the most interesting one we've had so far. And it was also of the highest quality so far.[57]

There were two important qualities Hamid aka commented on that differentiate Navro'z from Independence Day: the first was the type of culture that the holiday featured (defined in terms of the genre, for example, folk or contemporary culture) and the second was the themes highlighted in the extravaganza (defined in terms of the content). Navro'z was a holiday to celebrate Uzbekistan's traditions, and since part of the state's legitimacy rested on staking a claim to a certain heritage, there was an ideological component to Navro'z. Likewise, there was a heritage component to Independence Day that expressed the traditional/ethnic component of the country's national identity. As Alisher aka explained at the first staff meeting for Independence Day 1996, "All countries have their independence day. The focus is on *contemporary* Uzbekistan and its accomplishments: the regions showing their color, pride in sport, etc." The differences in emphasis between Navro'z and Independence Day can be seen in figure 8.

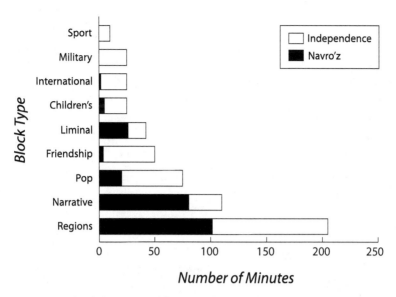

Figure 8. The differing structural content of the Navro'z and Independence Day holiday concerts.

The details of these particular blocks will be discussed below, but what figure 8 calls our attention to is the fact that the themes of the Independence Day concerts tended to be internationalist ones, focusing on universal aspects of nationhood such as sport (usually defined in these performances as events in which Uzbekistan competes in the Olympics), the military (in this case, a military band instead of the Soviet parade of military hardware), the cultures of other nation-states (the international blocks), interethnic harmony within Uzbekistan (the friendship blocks), and contemporary popular culture. Navro'z, on the other hand, spent its more limited minutes (the concerts were usually twenty to thirty minutes shorter than the Independence Day concerts) focusing on the performances of groups from Uzbekistan's regions and on narrative blocks that related folk tales and so on. In the following section I will give an overview of the content of these blocks and discuss the way their themes were expressed through certain types of culture corresponding to the universal/ particular dichotomy in the schemas of culture producers. Then I will explain the specific content of the holiday spectacles and analyze how these themes relate to the ethnic and civic aspects of national identity in Uzbekistan.

Overview: Universalism and Particularism in Spectacle Themes

I have already mentioned that Uzbeks would often tell me "our culture is a combination of national traditions and universal human values." Holiday concerts expressed both particular and universal values, but the way that these different values were expressed demonstrates that when universal values were performed, they were not culturally neutral. It turns out that in holiday spectacles, universal values were expressed mainly through Western-influenced culture (for example, European classical or pop music), while particularistic values were more frequently expressed through national and folk culture. The analysis of the content of Uzbekistan's holiday extravaganzas allows us to address the broader question of the colonial inculcation of modern cultural schemas.[58] These holiday concerts provide evidence of how a colonial hierarchy of cultures continued to be enacted among culture producers, reproducing a schema that placed Western culture above Eastern, and the culture of the cosmopolitan center over the culture of the backward periphery.

The way the Soviets institutionalized culture created contradictions, which meant that the cultural elites I studied could perceive that Soviet policies had distorted authentic culture, while simultaneously apprehending the object "authentic Uzbek culture" through a Soviet lens. Thus even though they had a desire to restore traditional culture, they also believed that traditional culture was in some ways backward and unenlightened. This hierarchy of cultures was illustrated by the way elites talked about different types of culture as well as the way they used the different types of culture to express different ideas in holiday spectacles. This hierarchy reflected a bias in favor of Western culture and a simultaneous denigration/romanticizing of folk culture. This aesthetic paradigm privileges what was seen as "developed" culture over everyday-life culture, Western over Eastern culture, and the culture of the center over the culture of the periphery.

In addition to a highbrow/lowbrow typology, Soviet culture was also divided by imperial hierarchies.[59] The high culture/popular culture split reflects the importance of class distinction in the West, whereas the Soviet typology emphasizes cultural "development" and differences between the culture of the center and the culture of the periphery. In Uzbekistan, there were four main terms that encompassed most of the cultural production people discussed with me. High prestige culture of European origin was usually referred to as international culture (Uzb. *jahon madaniyati*; Rus. *mezhdunarodnaia/internatsional'naia kul'tura*). Middle- to highbrow culture associated with a particular geographic entity was referred to as national culture (Uzb. *milliy madaniyat*; Rus. *natsional'naia kul'tura*). Syncretic middle- to lowbrow culture not necessarily associated with a particular nation was usually referred to as popular culture (Uzb. *ommaviy madaniyat*; Rus. *massovaia/popularnaia kul'tura*). Folk culture (Uzb. *xalq madaniyati*; Rus. *narodnaia kul'tura*) was the term used to refer to geographically specific, middle- to lowbrow culture. International culture was associated with progress (toward a modern or European ideal, toward a better standard of living), while national culture was associated with tradition in the form of homogenized, objectified, charming, and colorful ethnic cultural forms that represented the unchanging essence of a nation. Popular culture was a syncretic blend of local and international contemporary influences, enjoyed by people of all ages, but thought of as "light" entertainment, lacking the edifying qualities of the first two types. Folk culture was literally culture produced by the people themselves (as opposed to by professionals) and was associated with backwardness (the culture of the village and of the unsophisticated masses), as well as with a romantic ideal of the authenticity of the simple person.

Figure 9 further emphasizes the differences between the particularistic ethnic content of the Navro'z concerts versus the more universalistic content of the Independence Day concerts. Folk culture took up twice as much time in Navro'z as it did in Independence Day, and the proportion of the concert devoted to the universal genres (international and popular) went from 29 percent of the Navro'z concerts to 44 percent of the Independence Day concerts. Examples of international culture in a holiday extravaganza would be European classical music and dance, such as Tchaikovsky and ballet, as well as international costume such as gymnastic or military uniform. National culture differed from nation to nation, but to take the example of Germany from the 1996 Independence Day spectacle, the national culture was symbolized by means of male dancers in lederhosen and female dancers in ruffled frocks, doing a somewhat raucous and athletic dance to the stereotypically German tune of the song known in English as "Roll Out the Barrel."[60] Thus even a European national culture represented something less refined than classical European ("international") culture. Popular culture used electronic instruments in its music, the

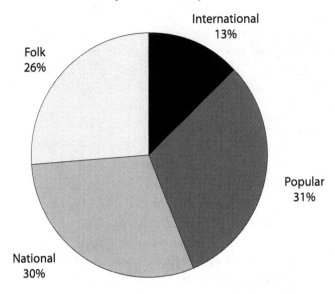

Independence Day

International
13%

Folk
26%

Popular
31%

National
30%

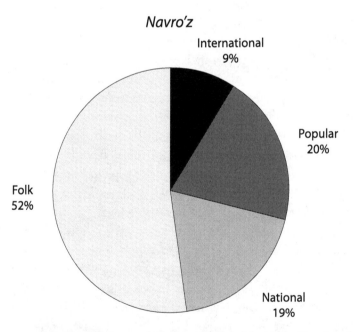

Navro'z

International
9%

Popular
20%

Folk
52%

National
19%

Figure 9. The differing types of culture presented during the Navro'z and Independence Day holiday concerts as expressed by the percentage of time devoted to each type of culture.

costumes were flashier and sexier, and the dance moves were extremely syncretic, drawing on Uzbek classical dance as well as American hiphop. Finally, folk culture featured acoustic, not electronic, music, colorful costumes with minute regional variations, and, in addition to dance, it included other kinds of movement such as game playing or daily life activities.

The organization of the show into thematic blocks allowed culture producers to create an illusion of the purity of tradition by expressing traditional values and universal values in different blocks. For example, even though the Andijon region had a new, state-of-the-art Daewoo auto plant, we did not see dancers from Andijon dressed up as auto workers welding joints to the sound of rock music during Andijon's dance number in the folksy Regions Block. Instead, we saw colorful traditional dress and folk music. According to the schemas of culture producers, those kinds of modern accomplishments should certainly be portrayed in holiday extravaganzas, but in a block more appropriate for expressing international values such as technological progress. The image of a modern worker juxtaposed with traditional music and dance did not fit into the schema of Uzbekistan's culture producers. These universal versus particular aspects of Uzbekistan's contemporary national culture were expressed in different ways in holiday spectacles, with content relating to national traditions being expressed more than half the time through folk culture, and never through international culture (see the column for the Regions Block in figure 10). Conversely, universal values were never expressed through folk culture, but most often through international and popular culture (see the columns for the Sport and Military Blocks in figure 10).

A concrete illustration of how these schemas worked in practice came out in the way that certain numbers in the holiday extravaganzas were crafted. In each show there were certain "liminal" numbers that didn't belong to a particular block but were prologues or finales, or otherwise served to make a transition between blocks. As liminal numbers, they could have had just about any style with just about any content, but in practice the style of music and dance in the liminal blocks was most often national or international, and never folk. The content of liminal numbers was usually focused on the main theme of the holiday: patriotism for Independence Day and nature for Navro'z. In terms of style, these numbers usually had either riotous pop or majestic European music. During

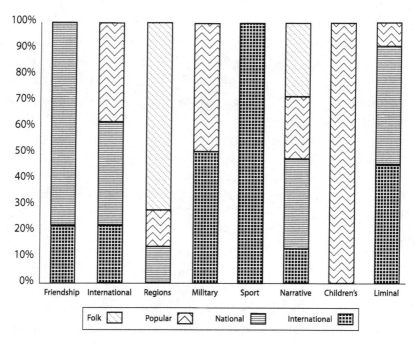

Figure 10. How different blocks linked universal and particular values through the type of culture being performed.

the preparations for Independence Day 1996, the directors toyed with the idea of getting experimental with the prologue/national anthem, but censored themselves on the basis of the conservatism of their audience. Alisher aka actually suggested doing something innovative with the national anthem, referring to how the Atlanta Olympics organizer had "The Star Spangled Banner" performed in an unconventional manner. He said he wanted "something that will move people. . . . Something using surrealism or unusual elements," but he talked himself out if it, saying, "Our public probably isn't ready for that. We have some people who understand art [but not everyone]."

Another interesting thing I observed during the process of picking out a prologue for Independence Day 1996 was the way the directors' aesthetics matched up with different kinds of music, giving further evidence for the hierarchy of cultures element of the Soviet schema. One director said he wanted something majestic, "with a full orchestra, a choir, and a soloist with a fresh, new voice." The kinds of pieces he considered fitting for a *majestic* prologue were all musically very European sounding. The traditional prologue for an Uzbek event such as a wedding or a festival would be sounded by the cacophonous karnay and surnay, reedy and bellowing horns played during holiday spectacles only as the introduction to the Regions Block, which features Uzbek folk music. These traditional instruments were used in spectacles to signal folk, festive, and inviting themes, similar to how they were used in more traditional weddings. However, to signal lofty, majestic, and solemn themes, European-style orchestral and choir music was selected by extravaganza producers.

Now that I have addressed some of the fundamental divisions in the way that cultural elites map out different types of culture with different kinds of themes, I will provide a qualitative analysis of the content of these blocks and discuss, where possible, the planning and background discussions that went into these blocks. First I will provide an interpretive analysis of the blocks that emphasized mainly universal values and themes of civic nationhood, though in places the discussion also touches on the tensions between ethnic and civic nationhood. The last section discusses the themes of the concerts that were the most clear-cut examples of ethnic nationalism and interprets what the meaning of ethnic particularism is in Uzbek national culture today.

Universalism and Themes of Civic Nationhood

Much of Uzbekistan's political ideology related to the country's new role as an equal among nations, which I am categorizing as an aspect of universalism. The theme of Uzbekistan's place in the world was one of the ideological themes that dominated those blocks that emphasized Uzbekistan as one among other similar nations and peoples, such as the Friendship and the International Blocks. Often the narration of blocks such as the Military and Sports Block contained the phrase *O'zbekiston turmushga*, which literally means "Uzbekistan to life," and was sometimes followed by a verb indicating that Uzbekistan was coming out of isolation and joining the "real world," as opposed to the aberrations of socialism and colonialism. It is also an idiom that is used to talk about someone marrying, that is, coming of age and starting a new, independent life.

While slogans like "Uzbekistan is a future great state" were attempts at inspiring confidence in the state's transition programs, many of the ideological themes in holiday spectacles reflected a more external orientation in nation building. The theme of Uzbekistan's place in the world came up repeatedly in various blocks, especially those I have called "narrative blocks." In the years following independence, Uzbekistan's government worked on all fronts, from the diplomatic to the artistic, to make Uzbekistan look like a normal nation-state, just as good as any other in the world community. In holiday extravaganzas, this was evidenced by the presence of the Military and Sport Blocks, and it appeared thematically in International Blocks featuring dances from various countries, including Uzbekistan, and in narrative blocks such as "The Great Silk Road," which I discuss below.

THE MILITARY BLOCK—The Military Block was entirely under the direction of military officials and the only control the extravaganza producers had over this block was deciding how long it was going to be and where it would fit into the ninety-minute Independence Day program. The Military Block never had a place in the Navro'z show. The format of the block was pretty standard from year to year, as was its content. The block began with soldiers marching in formation onto the stage with brass marching band musical accompaniment. Then there were a series of patriotic songs sung by people in uniform. The songs were either set to marching band or pop music, and the words always focused on love of the homeland, and often mentioned historical legacies, such as the military strength of Amir Timur. As far as I could tell, the lyrics did not mention the legacies of the Soviet Army, such as defeating the Nazis, as they would have during the Soviet period.[61] Generally the metaphors focused on history, love of the natural beauty of the homeland, and the burning desire of youth to help their country become great.

THE SPORT BLOCK—The Sport Block was another block that was presented only in Independence Day spectacles, though occasionally Navro'z featured a brief promenade of prominent athletes wearing their various medals from international competitions. The Sport Block was not featured every year, though it was especially important in 1996 because the Olympic games that summer in Atlanta were the first summer games where athletes were competing under the flag of Uzbekistan. The spectacle producers intended the Sport Block to explicitly evoke the Olympics and the ideals it represents, and they did this by copying visual effects (such as Atlanta's Olympic-ring-colored "torches" made of fabric blown upward by a large fan) and even music. "Every Olympics has a theme song. Ghulom aka, tape this year's song and redo it with our singers, in Uzbek if we can," said one director at a planning meeting. This suggestion wasn't followed through, but it adds to the examples in chapter 2 of the concrete ways that globalization influences local culture production.

The Sport Block had two main visual elements: gymnastics (for girls) and martial arts (for boys) performed all over the stage by individuals and groups, and the promenade of Olympic contestants and other famous athletes. The audio component consisted of the names of the athletes read on the soundtrack and a musical accompaniment that was a recording of a piece of European classical music. Other than commenting on Uzbekistan's new role as an equal nation under Olympic guidelines and the country's athletic achievements (a boxer from Uzbekistan took a bronze medal in the 1996 Olympics), there was not much content to this block.

THE POP BLOCK—The estrada (popular music) blocks almost always consisted of a series of famous singers and bands who sang a song, or part of a song, at center stage. Then, at the end, all came together to sing as a group. Sometimes the musicians wrote a song appropriate for the occasion (emphasizing nature or patriotism depending on the holiday), other times they adapted the lyrics of one of their hits to the theme of the holiday. Only occasionally did a group perform one of its hits that had nothing to do with the holiday's theme; thus all of the Pop Blocks for Navro'z concerts tended to have a theme of nature and those of the Independence Day concerts focused on patriotic themes.

ELEMENTS (NAVRO'Z '95) AND SEASONS (NAVRO'Z '98)—The dominant theme in both these blocks was the celebration of nature, but it's not entirely clear whether this theme should be categorized as universal or particular. Nature was portrayed many ways in the Navro'z spectacle, but always in a positive, almost sacred, light that may be indicative of Uzbek ethnic identity. On the other hand, the theme of nature was clearly seen by the holiday organizers as a universal theme, and they used mainly international or popular costume and music in these blocks. Also, nature was often portrayed schematically, with each season or each of the four elements getting a musical number of its own, rather than as some interpretation indigenous to Uzbekistan. On the other hand, various culturally specific rituals associated with the coming of spring, such as planting seeds, were also portrayed frequently. In the pop-style musical numbers, blooming flowers, budding trees, greening landscape, and spring in general were praised. In Uzbekistan, all kinds of music tend to focus more on themes of nature than does music in the United States, so holiday producers had a wealth of material to draw on for blocks with a nature theme.

In both of these blocks, the elements or seasons were represented symbolically on stage through costume and props, while music (mostly European classical music) played in the background and a narrator read poems in Uzbek that related to the element or season being portrayed. In the case of the Elements Block, I found out from the producers that their intention was to create an abstract conceptual piece depicting the stages of the formation of the universe and the earth. This high concept contrasts with the straightforward representation of the seasons a few years later: summer's heat, autumn's bounty, winter's harsh trials, and spring's restoration of vitality. President Karimov allegedly criticized the 1995 production for being too European in style (Navro'z, after all, was supposed to be devoted to Uzbek tradition), too abstract and incomprehensible to ordinary people, which explains the directors' focus on simplicity and iconicity in the narrative blocks of subsequent years.

INTERNATIONAL BLOCKS—The structure of most International Blocks was a series of dances from around the world, plus an Uzbek dance. The International Blocks were visually very similar to the Friendship Blocks, except that they usually featured nations that did not have coethnics living in the territory of Uzbekistan. One exception was the Germans, and during the 1996 Independence Day spectacle, the producers debated whether they should include a German number in the Friendship Block or in the Silk Road Block. For diplomatic reasons, the German number was eventually included in the Silk Road Block. (Though the Silk Road Block was an example of an International Block, it also had significant narrative content and is included below for separate discussion.) Other examples of International Blocks included a group number featuring people, decked out in every kind of "national costume" imaginable, dancing in a group to a syntho-country-western tune during the 1995 Navro'z spectacle, and an Independence Day number in 1993 featuring a representative nation from each continent.

Every International Block had ideological content, sending messages (through the choices made by the creative team) about which countries were diplomatically important to Uzbekistan. There was also a heritage component in that Uzbek classical music and dance was structurally placed on the same level as the national culture of these other states. The message was basically twofold: 1) if your country is friendly to us, you will be rewarded with a dance (this was what happened with Turkey, France, and Germany in the 1996 Silk Road number discussed below), and 2) we are all on the same level, politically as well as culturally.

As for the way these other countries were represented, sometimes the extravaganza producers traded accuracy for convenience. The costumes were designed rather hastily, and the music was drawn from a very limited archive at the State Tele-radio Company. The results were sometimes less than politic, as some costume designers found out when they were taken to task by someone from the Foreign Ministry, who had received a complaint from the Egyptian Embassy about how much skin had been showing in an "Arab" belly dance number one year. The following year the "Arabs" wore black, spangled body stockings under their costumes. The details of national costume got worked out by memory and favored variety over authenticity, as I observed during a staff meeting: when a costume designer argued with a choreographer about the authenticity of a detail, the choreographer actually dismissed the designer's concerns by saying "I remember from seeing all those dances on TV; the costumes were like this." The choreographers had to oversee the production of entire blocks and didn't want to get bogged down with the details.

Another example of the "facing outward" of national identity was the Turkistan Block, which was linked to the slogan "Turkistan, Our Common Home," which was employed by the Akaev government in Kyrgyzstan as well. In the Turkistan block, Kyrgyzstan, Kazakhstan, Tajikistan, and Turkmenistan were represented through short numbers. The content of this block did not vary much from spectacle to spectacle, nor did the music and the costume. The only thing that varied was the one or two lines of introduction that emphasized that all the peoples of Central Asia belong to a larger historical entity, Turkistan, and continue to have common cultural, political, and economic interests. This block corresponded to an idea that President Karimov reiterated in public forums in the mid-1990s: that the countries of Central Asia should unite in an economic union with Tashkent as its capital. This block usually ended with an Uzbek dance, or there was some structural element of Uzbek culture uniting the various blocks, emphasizing Uzbekistan's leading role in such a federation.

THE GREAT SILK ROAD (INDEPENDENCE DAY 1996) — The Great Silk Road Block consisted of a series of dances interspersed with narration about how each trade embassy was traveling through Uzbekistan along the Great Silk Road. In the background were huge balloons, inflatable models of classical architecture from Uzbekistan and neighboring countries, and crowds of extras milled about on the sidelines to simulate a busy marketplace. Actors dramatized the ambassadors from each country meeting with, and receiving the hospitality of, the local (Uzbek?)[62] leader. In the final block, numbers were staged that represented (in order of appearance) China, India, Arabia, Turkey, Germany, and France. The final number of the block had all of the people of the marketplace united in a swirling dance under a canopy made to look like a traditional Uzbek wall hanging (Uzb. *so'zani*).

The Great Silk Road was a political as well as a cultural metaphor that was often used in Uzbekistan (and in other Central Asian countries) to link the country to its glorious past as well as to other neighboring countries in the contemporary world. The metaphor of the phrase "Great Silk Road" as it was used in the discourse of holiday producers invoked a certain kind of idealism. The idea of the Great Silk Road was that nations can be united peacefully through mutual economic cooperation. More concretely, it was used to indicate that since Uzbekistan played a central role in such an institution before, it can do it again. The metaphor was less about historical accuracy than it was about goals for the future: "[The Silk Road] was an economic route, a trade route, and it was political. But most importantly, it brought people together, acquainted them with each other's cultures, and this is the idea we want to get across," said one spectacle producer. Another said, "It was a place where people didn't cheat each other, all these different nationalities working together in an atmosphere of trust, not signing agreements and counting pennies, but bartering." These ideas about the historical Silk Road reflect modern concepts such as Soviet friendship-of-the-peoples ideology and UNESCO's ideals of cultural exchange bringing about trust and understanding.

It was also a metaphor for how Uzbekistan can participate in cultural globalization without being recolonized by its bigger, stronger neighbors. Even though the country and its culture did not exist as such one thousand years ago, the Silk Road idea asserted Uzbekistan's identity as a major actor in history rather than a mere passive recipient of outside influences. One director argued against the idea that Uzbek culture was solely shaped by external forces when he said, "Why shouldn't we suppose that by way of the Silk Road, which brought cultures together, maybe something interesting from Central Asia was adopted by China, for example? . . . The cultures of the world aren't coming together only now in the era of the airplane and the telephone—they were exchanging ideas ages ago."

The Silk Road Block in Independence Day 1996 reflected these ideas about Uzbekistan's place in the world as well as foreign policy objectives. It was not surprising that a nation's independence day would reflect the country's foreign policy, though I argue that Uzbekistan devoted more time than older, more secure countries might to directing its ideology outward. The 1996 Independence Day spectacle clearly illustrated this, not only in the themes it expressed, but also in the planning process. In July when the planning was still in its early stages, there was a minor diplomatic crisis between Uzbekistan and Russia: the government felt that Russian television had been too critical of Uzbekistan and of President Karimov. This resulted in a backlash against the Russian government in the Uzbek media, which was picked up on by the artists working on the extravaganza. In an early brainstorming session for the Silk Road Block, the historical advisor mapped out the various regions through which the trade route passed. One of the regions was the Crimea, an area that was disputed at the time by Russia and Ukraine. Someone suggested that the familiar churches of Russia's Novgorod, an ancient trade center, be the Slavs' contribution to the Silk Road Block's set design. The director enthusiastically retorted, "Why should we always be giving Russia the credit? Let's give Ukraine the credit for a change, let's do something from Kievan Rus. People know it and besides, the Ukrainian president came on a diplomatic visit not long ago."

Of course, Kievan Rus was not an integral part of the Silk Road, but the facts took second place to the idea the directors wanted to communicate to the audience, in this case through representations of easily recognizable buildings. During the Independence Day planning meeting for this block, Alisher aka said flat out that historical accuracy wasn't important; relating to the viewer is. He left the room briefly, and when he came back and heard the discussion of historical authenticity going on between the historian and the choreographers, he said, "Please, let's not get hung up on details. We need things people recognize. China gets a pagoda. Uzbekistan, what was it called back then? Davron? Nobody knows from Davron, we'll say it is Turon." He went on to say that they would have an inflatable model of the [sixteenth-century] building from the Samarkand Registan with the tigers on it. The original sketch was a less anachronistic Bukharan building from the ninth century, but "this one from the sixteenth is nicer, and people recognize it." And that settled it.

The historian then pointed out that the Slavs were "pagans" during the heyday of the Silk Road and did not build any recognizable architectural monuments. The director instructed the creative team to come up with two variants: Russian and Ukrainian and the final call would be made by Jurabekov, the first deputy prime minister, based on the political situation in late August. Some of the artists seemed to relish the idea of snubbing Russia, but in the end, the elevation of Ukraine over Russia in a block representing a parade of world powers was not accepted by the Orgkom. Russia was represented in the Silk Road Block while Ukraine found itself in the Friendship of the Peoples Block—not as a nation state, but as an ethnic group, one among many with its members in the territory of Uzbekistan.

Another example that shows how low a priority historical accuracy was for the extravaganza directors occurred after an Orgkom review a few days before the holiday. The Orgkom requested that Germany and France be represented in the extravaganza, "to emphasize unity between the East and West." The Silk Road pretty much ended in Southern Europe, and the dances of Asian nations were originally the vast majority of the Silk Road Block. However, Germany was chosen to represent "the West" because of economic ties that had strengthened considerably that year and France because of deepening cultural ties in association with UNESCO's preservation of historical sites in Uzbekistan and Paris's cooperation in holding academic conferences in association with the Amir Timur 660 jubilee.

A similar political decision was made in regard to the national dance to represent Byzantium on the Silk Road. The choreographers originally planned a Greek dance and were surprised when the other members of the creative group listed Turkey as one of the numbers in the block. Hamid aka exclaimed in dismay, "What Turkey? We decided to take Greece from the many states under the Byzantine empire—it is more interesting choreographically and musically. We've already shown Turkey several times, and the choreography isn't so interesting." Alisher aka replied, "No, friends, look, we've already worked this out. Sure, we could choose Spain or Brazil or Mesopotamia, but the thing is we've already ordered the sets from the factory, and we're going to have Turkish architecture. Constantinople. This is what we have chosen so that it will be clear to the viewers what was the main artery of the Great Silk Road." Odil aka interrupted Alisher aka to remind Hamid aka, "The capital of Byzantium was, after all, today's Istanbul. So why go all the way to Greece? Our relationship with Turkey is very good, so let it be Turkey, not Greece." Interestingly, the next day at the recording studio, after Alisher aka left, the choreographers went ahead and asked the composers to track down a Greek song, and a week later they were requesting both Greek and Turkish costumes, but in the end, the Turkish number was the one that got included in the program.

Overall, the Silk Road Block effectively communicated the ideas of internationalism and Uzbekistan's historical legacy, although it was stylistically incoherent due to the haste with which costumes were assembled, the small archive of music the spectacle producers had to draw on (the Indian song was a movie-musical pop song while the Chinese piece was classical, but not very festive), and because of the addition of numbers at the last-minute request of the Orgkom.

THE FRIENDSHIP BLOCK—The slogan "friendship of the peoples" is very familiar to anyone who has studied the Soviet Union. In Uzbekistan, it continued to be a symbol for the desire that all the groups in the multi-ethnic state respect each other and keep interethnic tensions at a minimum. During the Soviet period, friendship in holiday parades was demonstrated by having representatives of each of the Soviet republics march under the flag and seal of that republic, though it is not clear whether these were delegates from the republics or representatives of the republic's titular ethnic group who resided in Uzbekistan.[63] In any case, after independence, these individuals of Azeri or Estonian ethnicity no longer represented the republics of Azerbaijan or Estonia: they were all presented as citizens of Uzbekistan, at least in theory. One of the lead organizers of Independence Day 1996 embarrassed himself as well as the representatives from the Tajik cultural center when he said, "Your holiday [Tajikistan's Independence Day] is coming up soon, too!" There was an awkward silence before one of the Tajiks (who, after all, were citizens of Uzbekistan) icily replied, "It's not *our* holiday." "Well, of course," the first man replied, "you're one of us. I wasn't, ah, you know, our government . . . not to say that . . ." Both parties understood that a nation's independence day holiday was supposed to be a civic, not an ethnic, holiday, but the faux pas belies the underlying ethnic basis of both nation-states.

The purpose of the Friendship Block was to demonstrate the cultures of the peoples who live in the territory of Uzbekistan. The Friendship Block appeared every year in the Independence Day spectacle, and, until 1996, it was part of Navro'z as well. In 1996, it was supposed to be included in the program but, as I mentioned in chapter 1, the organizer of that block fell ill and couldn't put a program together. It seemed that the organizers then decided they could do without it. After 1996, the Navro'z performances of Tashkent's ethnic cultural centers were moved to a different square as part of the postspectacle public entertainment program. In 1994, a reporter stated that the "holiday would have lost much, not just in its brilliance, but in its main idea, were it not for the participation of the national cultural centers' own program."[64] But over the next few years, non-Uzbeks were gradually marginalized by the holiday that was every year more fully devoted to exploring themes of traditional Uzbek culture. The Russian title of the holiday in official documents was *"vsenarodnyi prazdnik Navruz,"* which literally translates to "all-people's holiday Navro'z," but in a conversation with the clerical staff of the holiday's production team, my accidental linguistic deconstruction of the figurative term "national holiday" as *"dlya vsekh narodov Uzbekistana"* or "for all the peoples of Uzbekistan" was a cause for joking. "For *all* the peoples?" one woman laughed, implying that it was clear that Navro'z was a holiday oriented toward Uzbeks. On the other hand, it was equally clear that Independence Day was for the citizens of Uzbekistan.

Holiday organizers described both an outward and an inward face to this block: the outward face was presenting a unified, multiethnic Uzbekistan to international guests, and the inward face was encouraging members of various ethnic groups to participate in their national holiday (Independence Day). In his instructions to representatives from Tashkent's ethnic cultural centers, one holiday organizer explained that he wanted them to put together numbers for the 1996 Independence Day spectacle by putting "their own" people on stage because "it's their homeland. Let the people themselves participate. Besides, you all know your own, right? They'll be recognized on TV." He emphasized that it was important to include all of them in the celebration because "Uzbekistan is a multinational republic. Your participation is obligatory," he said.

There were several large ethnic groups in Tashkent with cultural centers and enough active and talented community members to put together a extravaganza number, but most of them resisted inclusion in the 1996 holiday due to time and budget constraints (the government funds for these centers were largely symbolic). The Korean cultural center had a very active amateur ensemble and was called on several times a year to perform at public cultural events. Likewise, the Tatar and Uighur cultural centers had fairly good talent available, but other centers (Latvian, Lithuanian, and German, to name a few) did not have the same talent pool to draw on. Russians and Ukrainians, however, were well represented in the professional arts communities and could always be counted on to mount an ethnic dance number for a holiday extravaganza. The nationalities that were represented in the final show were chosen partly on the basis of availability and talent and partly on aesthetic grounds, so that no two dances in the same spectacle were too similar. For example, Tatars and Bashkirs are culturally similar, and the holiday producers ruled out asking both groups to work up a dance number.

As I hinted at earlier, sometimes there were unfriendly dimensions to the Friendship Block. During the preparations for the 1996 Independence Day spectacle, the most popular Friendship Block number among the holiday organizers was the Jewish cultural center's dance. However, the dance was cut by members of the Orgkom. I heard various reasons for this decision. In general, the block ran too long and some numbers had to be cut (the Armenian dance was cut, also). More specifically, one Orgkom member allegedly raised the strange objection that it would be impolitic to have a Jewish dance and an Arab dance on the same program (the Arab dance was part of a different block), and another Orgkom member was quoted as saying, "We hardly have any Jews left in Uzbekistan, anyway. Why should we do their dance?" It is true that the majority of Uzbekistan's

Jewish population emigrated soon after independence,[65] and this defensiveness on the part of the Orgkom member reflects what I perceived as a mild but widespread feeling of abandonment on the part of ethnic Uzbeks. Jews in Uzbekistan were not particularly discriminated against, but Uzbeks knew that in order to immigrate to the United States, for example, the Jews from Uzbekistan would have to portray their neighbors as persecuting them, and this caused some bad feelings among the Uzbeks. Their hurt feelings extended to Russians and other ethnic groups who left the land of their birth to "return" to an ethnic homeland. More than once I heard an Uzbek tell a triumphant story of how a Russian or Jewish friend or neighbor immigrated back to Uzbekistan after an alienating experience in Russia or the West.

Particularism and Themes of Ethnic Nationhood

Perhaps because spectacles offer a perfect opportunity to dramatize legends, history, and folk life, the theme of Uzbek national heritage was the most frequently encountered content in both Independence Day and Navro'z, especially in the narrative and Regions Blocks. In Uzbekistan public figures were careless in laying claim to whole epochs of history in the name of the Uzbek nation. When pressed, however, many intellectuals emphasized that while the Uzbeks are the legatees of this ancient history, the peoples in question were not Uzbeks. This is another example of the Soviet legacy for contemporary interpretations of heritage. For example, while Qoraboev claimed all the historical inhabitants of the territory of Uzbekistan (from Paleolithic settlers to the Bactrian and Soghdian civilizations) as "our ancient ancestors," he correctly refers to the Uzbeks, "from the time they arrived [from the north] in the middle ages," as relative newcomers to the heritage of Central Asia.[66] Uzbekistan's national heritage was not limited by Uzbekistan's relatively short political life, nor by the lack of information about the history of the Uzbeks prior to the Middle Ages.

The result of this understanding of heritage was a pastiche of elements from a variety of cultures. The Zoroastrian holy book Avesta, medieval Persian writings, and classical Chinese scholarship had all been claimed by Uzbek academics as parts of a repressed cultural legacy that belonged to the people of Uzbekistan. This came out quite clearly during the seminar for the directors of the regional ensembles that were going to perform in the Navro'z holiday spectacle. One scholar suggested that they work with the theme of the Chinese calendar, making roosters part of their props (an idea that, as I mentioned earlier, was realized in the part of the concert where residents of Tashkent's neighborhoods marched through the staging area).

According to the producers of the holiday extravaganzas, they were carrying out a dual mission: to teach as well as to entertain. Of all the thematic elements, the ones that the spectacle producers had the most fun with were the ones that dealt with the history, legends, and classical traditions of the Uzbek people and their predecessors in the territory of Uzbekistan. Navro'z blocks frequently portrayed myths and legends that cultural elites felt the people should know about but had forgotten, and both holidays usually had at least one narrative block that dealt with a historical topic, such as the Ancestors Block in the Independence Day spectacle of 1993, which portrayed the great medieval rulers of Transoxiana (Timur, Ulughbek, Bobur), who themselves were not ethnic Uzbeks. Various other blocks had virtuoso singers and musicians who presented what had come to be defined as classical Uzbek culture. These classical traditions were not as popular as modified "traditional" or hybrid pop music and were included as pedagogy to round out the complete picture of Uzbekistan's national identity.

FOLKTALES (NAVRO'Z 1996) — The Folktales Block of the Navro'z 1996 spectacle was the focus of the most intense creative energy I saw from the holiday producers in either spectacle. The first reason for this was a reaction to the way Navro'z was produced in 1995 (see the section discussing this below). Hamid aka said, "Navro'z last year especially was very contemporary, very orchestral, and I didn't really like it. I'm not conservative, but Navro'z is a folk festival, so it should have more national music and instruments. We don't need orchestras, even orchestras of national instruments. It should be pure folk."[67] To this end, the scenario for the Folktales Block was based on a recent publication by Yo'ldosh Muqimov, *Navro'z Legend*.[68] Though Muqimov himself spent most of his life as a Tashkent correspondent for Pravda, he had a gift for collecting and preserving folktales, especially those that he remembers his grandmother telling during his childhood near Bukhara. Another source for the scenario was Muqimov's interpretations of the writings of Ibn Sino (Avicenna). Muqimov and the others working on the scenario had the goal of reviving Navro'z rituals while at the same time staking a claim to regional heritage by "making Tashkent the Navro'z capital of Turkistan, and beyond." They aimed to do this by making Navro'z 1996 "deeper, more historical," with "images from ethnography," using the "most ancient things" found in textual sources. One director called the scenario, "almost documentary. The texts are the most authentic, the most original, and this will preserve the continuity of Navro'z."[69] They also took pride in the state's sponsorship for celebrating Navro'z on a massive scale, as Alisher aka expressed: "But I'd like to tell you that, from the information I have, in all the other countries that celebrate Navro'z, there is nothing produced by the government on this scale. They produce a very folksy festival, and in some countries it's not even a day off, as far as I know."[70]

The producers wanted to delve deeper into folklore, not just to educate and revive forgotten traditions, but also to entertain. Nodir aka explained, "It's boring to repeat the same thing year after year. By making it deeper, it will be more interesting for us and for the people. . . . We showed the *sumalak* and all that before, but this time we showed the history, where these things are from."

One of the legends portrayed could be called, "Why We Don't Salt the Sumalak." Sumalak is a traditional Navro'z food (a paste the consistency of peanut butter made from flour and wheat juice), and the legend had it that thirty angels (*se malak*, in Farsi) descended and helped out the sumalak makers, who had fallen asleep and forgotten to put salt in. Another legend was "Bobodehqon," or grandfather farmer, who helps out the young farmers in their spring sowing. A third legend was "Aiamajuz," which illustrated the battle of good against evil and the rescue of a princess and her prince from the forces of darkness by the forces of light. While the extravaganza producers were justifiably proud of their work on this block, I saw little evidence that anyone in Uzbekistan, let alone in the rest of the Zoroastrian cultural zone that celebrates Navro'z, paid much attention to the project of cultural renewal and heritage claim staking.

AMIR TIMUR (NAVRO'Z 1996)—Amir Timur made an appearance in both spectacles in 1996 because it was his jubilee year. The 650th anniversary of the great leader's birth had fallen during Soviet times when

Tamerlane was reviled as a despot and a ruthless conqueror. The 700th anniversary was still very far in the future, and the government of Uzbekistan felt the task of nation building pressing down on them urgently, so they decided to celebrate the 660th anniversary of Amir Timur's birth in 1996.

As I mentioned before, Amir Timur was an all-purpose symbol in Uzbekistan, and he served the Karimov regime by providing a cult of personality by proxy.[71] The rehabilitation of his name set the stage for the rehabilitation of all Central Asian heroes who were repressed by the Soviets, but the government of Uzbekistan took it a step further. The government based its legitimacy in the 1990s in part on its claim to the lineage of Timur's strong state and vast empire. A booklet on good government, attributed to Timur, was widely available in 1996, and President Karimov often made reference to it. The president, in fact, related almost everything about himself or his actions to Timur, leading to a common discourse about Timur as a patron of the arts and sciences, as a strong leader and caretaker of his people, and as a pious but worldly Muslim. Nearly everyone I talked to in the mid-1990s denied that there was truth in Soviet and Western historiography, which tends to emphasize Timur's bloodier side. Nearly every positive characteristic a leader could have was attributed to Timur by members of Uzbekistan's cultural elite, much to the amazement of more serious scholars. Jamshid aka called it the "cult of Timur," expressing disgust at so-called scholars who write about whatever the state wants them to. "Someone is writing a dissertation on the choreography of Timur. What, didn't you know he was a ballet master?" he joked.[72]

Most of the spectacle producers were happy to find ways to include the figure of Timur in the 1996 shows, but they all had their own ideas about how to make it just a little bit more interesting. Since the politicians were not interested in accuracy, the character of Timur wound up in all sorts of strange situations where he merely stood for something else, such as in the Independence Day 1996 spectacle, where the great leader found himself setting the scene for the pageant of the Great Silk Road. In the case of Navro'z 1996, however, the extravaganza producers went to great lengths to find a legend that historically linked Timur to Navro'z. They found one, though I am not certain to what degree they embellished it. The scene showed Timur sampling sumalak and finding it so good he pronounced that if the Prophet (Muhammad) himself had tried sumalak, he would have declared, "Let every day be Navro'z!" This well-chosen scene served a dual purpose: it linked the current government to Timur through their common support for the holiday Navro'z, and it demonstrated that the contemporary secular nature of the Zoroastrian holiday Navro'z was not in contradiction to Muslim identity.

ANCESTORS (INDEPENDENCE DAY '93) AND ALPOMISH (NAVRO'Z '98)— These blocks were coded as having patriotic, ideological, and heritage content. The Ancestors Block presented monologues by actors playing Amir Timur and his descendants, Ulug'bek and Bobur, the latter of whom founded the Mughal Empire in India after he was driven from Samarkand by Uzbek invaders. The litany of Timur, Ulughbek, Bobur (and others) was commonly heard in political speeches and historical articles and symbolically linked contemporary Uzbekistan with great states of the past, as well as linking the president with great leaders of the past. Alpomish was a block dramatizing a scene from the tenth-century literary epic of the same name. One of the Soviet ethnographic beliefs was that every great people should have an ancient literary epic, and *Alpomish* is the national treasure of the Uzbeks, though it doesn't receive nearly as much attention as does the Kyrgyz national epic, *Manas*.[73] Both these blocks were designed to teach the viewers something about history and to instill a sense of pride in Uzbekistan's cultural legacy.

THE REGIONS BLOCK—The Regions Block occupied by far the most time of any type of block in each of the holiday spectacles (see figure 9), indicating both the importance of the territorial composition of Uzbekistan's national identity and the very modern conception that borders should ideally coincide with cultures. As I mentioned earlier, Uzbekistan's divisions into provinces (*viloyatlar/oblasti*) do not always coincide with actual cultural differences, but the extravaganza producers tried to encourage the display of cultural distinctions as much as possible. The regional ensembles received basic instructions on what themes to include in their program. In the case of Independence Day 1996, directors were instructed: "Show the essence of your region and the successes of the past five years," "All songs should have patriotic themes," and "Prepare something different from Navro'z." The ensemble directors were actually brought to Tashkent before the Navro'z 1996 performance for the seminar on organizing a number for an open-air stage. At the seminar, Tashkent academics and spectacle producers stressed that the directors should keep things new yet "true" (to tradition); keep Navro'z and Independence Day distinct; keep up quality and do not let the numbers fall flat like they are a recital of some sort; add local color such as folk games; and use the *Navro'z Legend* book as a source of inspiration and textual basis.

For the spectacle producers, one of the main reasons to focus so much on the Regions Block was the preservation of rich regional cultures. The ensemble from Sirdaryo Region (a purely administrative division within the Tashkent/Fergana cultural sphere) arrived at the Independence Day 1996 rehearsals with the most folkloric piece of all the numbers. Their performance included theatrical business such as singers who enacted traditional bread-baking practices (which were still widespread throughout Uzbekistan) and dancers who had a bit of their performance dedicated to enjoying a slice of melon. "Our region is known for its especially sweet melons," the director explained when I asked why he chose melons as one of his region's "achievements." The body language of the melon-eating dancers was quite well done for humorous effect, but the members of the organizational committee who watched Sirdaryo's performance laughed at it for another reason: apparently it was folksy to the point of being ridiculous to them. In the end it did not matter what the people from Sirdaryo thought was significant about their region, but what the Tashkent organizers thought would be emblematic and glitzy. The people from Sirdaryo put away their bread oven and their melons and in the end were merged into a larger collective consisting of groups from nearby Tashkent and Jizzakh Provinces, both of which have similar customs and achievements. Yet after imposing conformity with the top-down definition, the organizers complained that the regions' performances were too similar and that they failed to express their own regional flavor.

THE CHILDREN'S BLOCK—The theme of family in one sense is a universal theme, but the way it showed up (mainly in the Independence Day spectacles' Children's Blocks) and the way that the producers discussed it indicated that it was somewhat more of an expression of ethnic identity than civic identity, though the two were quite thoroughly mixed in this case. The Children's Blocks tended to feature children who were age cohorts of the nation, so in 1993, the block featured mothers (dressed in both European and Uzbek "national" clothing) walking across the stage holding their two-year-old children, while a narrator read a poem likening mothers to the motherland and children to the future of the nation. In 1997, the children were about to enter school, so there were songs about the joys of education. The children danced in contemporary European clothing to bouncy pop music. Puppets, cartoon characters, and a "main character" such as a schoolteacher, were also common visual and thematic elements. The Children's Block was one block that the extravaganza producers specifically stated should not deal with political topics. The lyrics of the Children's Block songs dealt with patriotism (but not politics), family, respect for elders, and education. "Don't politicize the Children's Block . . . make it more like a game," said one director, criticizing the choice of music in one of the block's numbers. The director wanted the block to be "playful, with songs that fit kids' psychology, that make them want to be playful and to dance. The deeper idea is that there is one Uzbek family, and they are all its children, and that children are the future."

The family and education theme ties the past to the future, linking the value Uzbeks place on large, interdependent, extended families to the idea of building the future through children and their education. Another analogy that came up more than once was the cradle as a symbol of family and country. Interestingly, one year the cradle was a traditional Uzbek *beshik* (in which babies are swaddled to a padded board on top of rounded pieces of wood, colorfully decorated) and another year it was a European pram. The spectacle producers originally had envisioned children representing all the different ethnic groups in Uzbekistan jumping up and down on a large inflatable beshik, until someone pointed out that beshiks are flat boards on which nobody ever jumps, unlike a soft, springy pram. So the director agreed to change it, saying, "Everyone here wheels their children around in German prams anyway."

One block demonstrated the family-related theme of a wedding ritual, a favorite element of Soviet folklore performance that shows up very often in holiday extravaganzas as well as in festivals and contests throughout the former Soviet Union. This block had brides in European white gowns, eyes downcast, accompanied under a canopy by female relatives, and grooms, dressed in European suits with festive Uzbek skullcaps, surrounded by their male friends. The group of brides met up with the group of grooms on stage and exited in pairs, without demonstrating what comes next: a visit to the registrar at the wedding palace, a visit to get blessed by the mullah, or both (most Uzbek couples did both in the post-Soviet era). As in other performances, the colorful, folkloric part of a common ritual was demonstrated while the bureaucratic and religious elements were left out.

Using the content of national holiday concerts and the behind-the-scenes discussions of what went into that content, we can construct a perspective on the ethnic and civic components of national identity that fairly represents the ideals of Uzbekistan's cultural elites as well as some of the realities of their actual views about the ethnic nature of their nation. I have characterized Uzbekistan as having an official ideology of postcolonial civic nationalism in which the valorization of Uzbek culture and history must be understood as a reaction to Russian and Soviet cultural domination. The exclusion of Russian speakers from many of the conversations during the preparation for Navro'z can be seen in this light as a deliberate snub in order to assert that the Russians were no longer in charge and that it was their turn to adapt in order to succeed. At the same time, legacies of Soviet institutions and practices also fostered a strong attachment to elements of civic nationalism that drew on international norms. This can be seen in the unquestioned assumption that the concert should include the Military and Sport Blocks and the national anthem, and that certain blocks should demonstrate Uzbekistan's equivalence with other nation-states. However, underlying this official presentation of national identity were underlying attitudes of ethnic exclusivity, as we saw in the conflicts over the representation of Tajik culture in the concerts. Furthermore, based on anecdotal evidence of discrimination against non-Uzbeks in education and employment, of harassment of Russian speakers in their own neighborhoods, and of the persecution of Muslims who adopt "alien" religious practices, it is clear that the civic ideal is in tension with the realities of Uzbekistan's nationalizing tendencies.

If we assume that these elites were more cosmopolitan, more influenced by Soviet legacies of internationalism, and more Russophilic than the majority of the population, then we can also make some inferences about the extent to which these ideals were shared by the broader population. To be sure, most people in Uzbekistan were much more concerned with the hardships of daily life than with the state's ideology of national traditions and universal human values, but it would not be surprising if the majority of the population were supportive of policies that were more nationalistic than what the Karimov regime initially pursued. Indeed, after 2003 the population seemed to support Karimov's turn away from the West even though it included a turn back toward Russia. However, it also seemed that during the 1990s, there was actually a fairly widespread co-existence of both ethnic chauvinism and ideals of interethnic harmony, and many people throughout the country shared the elite's desire to think of Uzbekistan as a "normal" country and supported the outward expressions of these elements of civic nationhood.

Chapter Four

| | |

CULTURE PRODUCTION AND PARTICIPATION IN THE SPECTACULAR STATE

| | |

It is a common mistake to accuse totalitarianism of a barbaric contempt for culture. . . . The truth is the opposite: in no democratic country has the State valued culture so highly and devoted such constant attention to it.

| Igor Golomstock, *Totalitarian Art* |

During my first few weeks of fieldwork in 1996, I paid several visits to the Tashkent State Institute of Culture to meet with my local academic advisor, Dr. Usmon Qoraboev, an expert on holidays and folk rituals in Uzbekistan who was a member of the Institute's faculty. The Institute of Culture offered courses in both Uzbek and Russian, mostly to students from the provinces, in disciplines ranging from the visual and performing arts to sociology and folklore. The Institute's graduates would usually return to their home regions and become performers or work as administrators in "houses of culture." In line with other aspects of the centrally controlled economy, the Soviet state that created the Institute of Culture in 1974 took upon itself the responsibility of ensuring that its goals for society would be fulfilled by training the right number of workers ("cadres") for a particular cultural task, such as organizing festivals. If villages were to have proper Soviet festivals, it was the responsibility of the state to ensure that there was a cadre in place who knew what to do, and this system of the state planning for the cultural needs of its citizens continued on into the 1990s. Thus one Thursday in February, I met some of the instructors in the Department of Mass Festivals, who presumably prepared cadres like Svetlana, a woman I spent a lot of time with at holiday staff meetings. Svetlana worked in the Mayor's Office in the Directorate for the Preparation of Festivals, which was a post-Soviet phenomenon, created in 1993 to deal more efficiently with the expanding scale of national holiday celebrations in Tashkent after independence.

Later, Usmon aka asked me, "Who prepares cadres in the United States?" I thought about it for a moment and wondered if any universities offered classes in event planning, or whether people who organized festivals all came from backgrounds in theater, television, and film. "I don't think any of our universities have specializations in these sorts of things," I replied, feeling self-conscious that my answers to these comparative questions might have an effect on how my interlocutor judged his own institutions. As I mentioned in previous chapters, the cultural elites I knew were very interested in assessing Uzbekistan's new place in the world, and questions about how we did things in the United States often seemed to contain an implication for how Uzbekistan measured up to "the West." This is not to say that American norms were automatically perceived as better than local norms, just that, in these situations, I was conscious that I was providing what was perhaps a new perspective on how one might do things differently elsewhere. In doing ethnographic fieldwork, especially when "studying up" and working with those who have a high social status, these sorts of exchanges of information are an inevitable part of the research process and have an undeniable effect on the information produced, throwing the assumptions and schemas of both parties into greater relief.[1] However, in my own experience at least, I am certain that my assumptions and schemas were transformed by these exchanges to a far greater extent than were those of my interlocutors.

Because of my informants' interest in "how we do things in the United States," on several occasions, I tried to convey to my interlocutors the very different assumptions people in the United States have about the role of government in culture. When I explained, for example, that the United States does not have a ministry of culture, the response on more than one occasion was, "Well who is in charge of culture, then?!" From the perspective of an Uzbek culture producer who came of age in the Soviet era, it was difficult to imagine that culture could exist without state control. The idea that cultural institutions would direct and support themselves sounded improbable if not alarming to many Uzbek cultural elites, who found the idea of working with the free market more distasteful than working with the state. "In Russia, the houses of culture are now all operating on a commercial basis," one Ministry of Culture employee exclaimed in disgust. "We can't sell our own culture—it's sacred!"[2] While artists resented the state meddling in their creative affairs, the idea of the Ministry of Cultural Affairs playing an active role in the arts was rarely questioned. Because of their desires to renew their national culture, many artists (if they did not give up their careers to earn a living in business) found themselves more invested in the new nationalist state's control of culture than they were during the Soviet period. As employees of the state, the cultural elites I spoke with generally did not seem averse to the idea of creating art that furthered the ideological goals of the state. Following ideological trends was simply part of the process by which producers decided what material to present, but these same producers resented any active interference with their work on the part of government bureaucrats.

Much of my research focused on the production of a kind of culture that was especially resistant to marketization because of its importance to the state. In previous chapters, I analyzed why the Olympics-style spectacle was adopted as the centerpiece of Uzbekistan's holiday celebrations and how that particular cultural form relates both to the desire of cultural elites to be seen as normal members of a global community of nations and to the ability of the state to have a monopoly on the production of meaning. Part of the success of the state's monopoly on meaning, I argued, is related to those properties of spectacle that give participants a feeling of inclusion, without being obligated (or allowed) to respond; the communication is one-way. In this chapter, I will explain in detail how holiday spectacles were organized in Uzbekistan in the 1990s, and I will illustrate the ways that spectacle participants experienced and enacted state power through their performances. I also examine the idea of the complicity of cultural elites in Uzbekistan's nation-building project and explore their motivations for lending their work to support a repressive state.

The Command System of Cultural Production

The cultural elite's somewhat unexpected support for state control of culture had its roots in a universal humanism. According to Miklos Haraszti, in socialist countries, "the supportive state [was] . . . perceived as the protector of aesthetic innovations, the opponent of a degraded (although profitable) mass culture; censorship was embraced as the guarantor of stable values and a constructive humanism."[3] If, as one scholar explained to me, culture is seen in Uzbekistan not as a realm of life but as a level, then artists were aware of a danger that Uzbekistan could become "less cultured" than it was before independence, that their country could fall from its status as "civilized." The state was seen as the guarantor of a high culture based on international standards. Many cultural elites I spoke to believed that if the supply of culture were governed by the demand of popular taste rather than by some sort of absolute aesthetic standards determined by experts and officials, then their civilization would inevitably decline.

However, the idea of civilization and what exactly was threatened by popular taste was a tricky one because of postcolonial legacies. On the one hand, the term "civilization" carried with it a strong connotation of European high culture and popular taste. Yet claims to being civilized were made by those who shared the Uzbek population's disdain for, or lack of interest in, high cultural forms such as opera and ballet. On the other hand, globalized popular culture, with its emphasis on electronic music, high-tech production values, and caricatured female sexuality was wildly popular but seen by the Uzbek cultural elite as a threat to both indigenous art forms and traditional cultural norms. The state in post-Soviet Uzbekistan put the support of traditional and contemporary ethnic Uzbek culture as its main priority, though it did not ignore European high culture and globalized pop culture.

Because of Soviet legacies and because of the concern for the revitalization of ethnic Uzbek culture, it is only somewhat surprising (from an economic point of view) that Uzbekistan's government actually increased central control over culture in the early independence period, especially in the realm of high culture production (pop culture, especially music, was more oriented toward market forces, though its producers were still accountable for the content, if not quality, of their products to the state). For most of the 1990s, the government financed nearly all public cultural activities ranging from the restoration of architectural monuments, to the organization of film festivals, to the physical maintenance of concert halls. The government was still the main source of material support for all cultural institutions including theaters, libraries, museums, concert organizations, educational institutions, and so forth. The state was also responsible for "the activization of the spiritual life and the creative resources of the republic" through the creation of new arts organizations and holidays such as Navro'z and Independence Day.[4]

The importance of state support went far beyond direct material support, however. In the early 1990s when the support for Western high culture began to dry up as part of a postcolonial reaction against Russian cultural dominance, fans of chamber music and ballet sought outside support from European embassies and from nongovernmental organizations such as the Soros Foundation. Mere financial support was not the solution to the problems faced by lovers of European culture since the legacy of government control over culture did not just extend to providing financial support and censorship; a key component to state control over culture was indirect. The state subtly penetrated society through the ownership and management of buildings, through the norms of authority and management, and in various other ways. Grisha, a music critic, explained to me what happened when his organization tried to organize an event showcasing contemporary "classical" (European orchestral) music:

GRISHA: We couldn't get a hall for the concert because we didn't "go through channels," so the director of the hall had no "command" telling him he had to do it, so he refused. He may have even had an order to deny our request. Everyone here is two-faced, saying yes and then doing nothing. It's because they don't have any real reason to say no, they just want to do things the old way. They want someone to come to them and politely request their help with great respect, etc., and above all go through channels.

LAURA: But why don't the people with money and talent want to go through channels?

GRISHA: Because then someone at the ministry or the union or wherever will want to have a say in who gets put on the panel of judges and on the organizational committee, and they want someone else removed, and you get people with personal conflicts, etc., etc.[5]

Even after independence, the bureaucratic control of the state over all aspects of life continued to be seen (especially by the bureaucrats!) as the proper way to do things. Many artists I spoke to seemed resigned to not even trying to work outside the culture bureaucracy because they knew all the trouble it would entail. Still, some organizations made a go of it. Of Uzbekistan's roughly four-dozen theaters, only two were independent: Tashkent's Ilkhom Theater and the Eski Masjid theater from Karshi. The Ilkhom was wildly popular among Tashkent's cosmopolitan elites, but its eclectic and edgy repertoire did not broadly reflect popular taste. But when I assumed that it was the content of the Ilkhom's productions that was the source of conflict (the police regularly harassed the company in the early 1990s), Pavel, a theater critic, corrected me:

PAVEL: The Ilkhom was always [from the 1970s onward] an object of criticism by the government because they bucked the system not ideologically but bureaucratically. They didn't go through the same channels as everyone else, and for that they were labeled oppositional. I don't feel that there was anything especially oppositional about the content of the plays or the politics of the artists. They were harassed even during Soviet times because [director Mark] Vayl isn't an Uzbek, and critics would talk about *korenizatsiia* [the Soviet "affirmative action" policy]. They always looked for alternative sponsors, and now they're fully supported by sponsors.[6]

This was not a case of pure ethnic persecution; other theaters that were oriented toward Uzbekistan's European population, such as the Russian State Academic Drama Theater (formerly the Gor'kiy), continued to receive state support and operated normally in the postindependence period, and tensions between the state and nonstate producers of culture extended to ethnic Uzbek high culture as well. Unlike the Ilkhom, the Eski Masjid Theater based in Karshi was much more closely linked to indigenous theatrical traditions, while at the same time it attempted to transcend the borders that divided the Turkic and Persian peoples of Central Asia. However, the Eski Masjid suffered from lack of state support for its work and occasionally from state interference in its work. This sacrifice of support was one that the theater's leadership was willing to make in exchange for autonomy. A theater critic related the following story to me about what happened back home when the Eski Masjid Theater played a festival in Avignon, France:

KODYR: A French director came and saw them and invited them to this festival. It had all the makings of a good story, something everyone should know about and be proud of, but it hardly got any publicity. Why? Because it was the Eski Masjid theater, which isn't part of the UzTeatr system. Without being part of the state theater system you are not automatically connected to the state publicity organs, the press. You aren't going through official channels! . . . The same bureaucrats are around crushing all sorts of innovation. Who is going to fight with these people? There might be talented people here and there in the organization, but the way things work smoothly is when the ideas come from above and the only ideas coming from above seem to be banal.[7]

The Eski Masjid and Ilkhom theaters were both part of a fading legacy: beginning in the 1970s, the Soviet state supported limited institutional autonomy for youth activities organized by Komsomol clubs, and both Eski Masjid and the Ilkhom were originally Komsomol studio theaters. This legacy is fading because the diversity of state institutions in Uzbekistan actually decreased after independence, giving fewer "home bases" for conflicting interests to take root.

The state in any society is built on multiple institutional locations and furnishes its agents with differing and sometimes conflicting interests.[8] One institutional basis for diversity within the Soviet system was the split between Party organizations, ministries, and other branches of government, and trade unions. The role of Party organizations, especially Communist youth organizations, in the production of progressive and critical art was described in Jeffrey Goldfarb's work on youth theater in Poland.[9] The Uzbek SSR experienced a similar phenomenon, where Komsomol-sponsored youth clubs provided something close to an independent realm of expression:

PAVEL: Originally the [Ilkhom] theater was called the "Experimental Studio Theater of Youth." It was sponsored by Komsomol, but most of its financial support came from the Union of Theatrical Workers, which was headed up by a shrewd man named Rahim Kariev who studied in Petersburg after the revolution and for a while served as the head of cultural affairs in Uzbekistan. He also supervised the construction of the Navoi [Opera and Ballet Theater] and became its director. He was a straight talker who the authorities didn't like but people respected, and he was able to get the Union a great deal of independence, via its own workshop and store. It was he who selected [director Mark] Vayl and who gave the new club so much material help. No one in the club, except the director of the club, who was paid by Komsomol and who managed the budget of the club, was paid, and poverty buys you freedom. Since they weren't dependent on state money, and they were sponsored by the right organizations, they had a lot more leeway.[10]

This version of the Ilkhom's history illustrates both the power of patronage and the importance of institutional autonomy in the Soviet system. After "the Party" ceased to exist, there were no such balances built into the system in Uzbekistan, and the government controlled cultural production more directly than authorities of the Communist Party did.

Administrative bodies that operated as professional organizations nominally independent from the state, the equivalent of trade unions for dancers, composers, and theater artists, lost a great deal of independence between 1995 and 1998. In 1998 these organizations, O'znavo (music), O'zraqs (dance), and O'zteatr (theater), which were responsible for both professional ensembles and specialized artistic education, were brought under the direct administrative control of the ministry. Four of the main professional national dance ensembles, Lazgi (specializing in Khorezmi dance), Zarafshan (Bukharan dance), and Bahor and Tanovar (pan-Uzbek and syncretic dance), lost their former autonomy when they were all incorporated under the directorship of O'zraqs.[11]

Although the state had embraced the rhetoric of the market, culture production in Uzbekistan continued along Soviet lines, unlike in most of the other post-Soviet republics where the state stepped back to a more limited role of protector of the patrimony.[12]

In his thesis on attracting investment in the arts, Bahodir Abdurakhimov, a deputy minister of cultural affairs, focused on four main sources for funding culture in Uzbekistan: the government, sponsors such as local firms or international organizations, foreign organizations interested in cultural treasures, and the donations of individual citizens.[13] Financing culture through marketing cultural goods and services was not an option he mentioned. Furthermore, he underlined the role of the state when he argued that it is the moral task of society to help the state implement new state policies of investment in culture, all of which keep the ministry and

Figure 11. In 2002, the government of Tashkent spent about five million dollars renovating this theater, the Uzbek National Academic Drama Theater (formerly the Hamza Theater). PHOTO BY AUTHOR.

other government organs squarely in the center of the transaction.[14] Government officials, and many culture producers as well, would have agreed that "government investment has always been the main source of culture subsidy. . . . Government sources have had a permanent character since they have been effective in every sort of situation, [whereas] societal, collective and private investments have a temporary character, freely chosen or out of necessity. Self-financing has entered the picture only when not opposed by the government."[15]

Abdurakhimov worked at the Uzbekistan Ministry of Cultural Affairs, which tried to do it all: set policy, enforce regulations, and oversee operations. Even if other sectors of Uzbekistan's economy liberalize (which in the former Soviet republics usually involves setting up an independent regulatory agency and gradually selling off operations divisions to private investors), it is not likely that this will happen to the Ministry of Cultural Affairs (which, as of 2004, had been renamed the Ministry of Culture and Sport). One reason is that the culture business was not lucrative enough to attract the foreign investment that compelled privatization in other sectors. Another reason is the way that Soviet culture production linked the value of culture to the power of the state. Culture was simply too important to the nation to be subject to demand-driven market relations.

The Organization of Holiday Production

The organizational structure that produced Uzbekistan's holiday activities was hierarchical yet collective, as many organizations were under the Soviet system. The structure was hierarchical, but the actual creative work was collective, illustrating one of the contradictions the Soviet creative intelligentsia had to deal with. The synergy of a collection of creative individuals was initiated, structured, and impeded by the demands of the state. The artists themselves had ambivalent feelings about this, expressing their gratitude toward the state for its solicitousness and their resentment of its interference. The main difference in the postindependence period was that the state was perceived to be less solicitous because of economic difficulties, and at the same time less intrusive because of the depoliticization of art since the demise of the Soviet state.

The process of organizing a holiday began with the decree of the president (a one-time occurrence). Then the production of the holiday was at the highest level the responsibility of the state organizational committee for the production of holidays (the Orgkom, for short). This committee met sporadically during the months before a major holiday, but unfortunately, its meetings were closed to me because of the presence of extremely high-ranking officials. The head of the committee was the prime minister, and the committee was composed of the cabinet ministers of Uzbekistan, with auxiliary members from the cultural elite such as poets laureate. The meetings were attended by the lead organizers of the holiday: the deputy mayor of Tashkent, the head director of the holidays, and the head technical director.

A few months in advance of the holiday, the lead organizers put together a team of senior choreographers, directors, and composers, the "creative group." Rustam Hamidov was the main producer of almost every holiday spectacle since independence, and he usually chose the same people for the creative group every year. The conceptual aspect of the extravaganza was sketched out by the lead director and a scenarist, who broke the time up into blocks. The details of these blocks were then left largely to the lead choreographers, who decided what kinds of costumes to order, who would write the music, and what kind of overall visual effect the block should produce. The lead organizers were also in charge of overseeing the "working group," which was composed of technicians and noncreative personnel such as the police and representatives from organizations that supply extras for the show. During the two months prior to the holiday, rehearsals began and the scenario for the spectacle was worked out. The final version of the script was submitted to the Orgkom, which solicited the opinions of experts (for example, historians and poets) and gave their suggestions for changes. The Orgkom also attended a dress rehearsal of the performance to provide similar criticism for the musical and dance portions of the extravaganza.

The way the holidays were produced was certainly no more democratic than the way Soviet holidays were, and some of the organizers I interviewed felt that in some ways it was even worse than Soviet politics of culture. One director said that a lot of work got ruined by people at the holiday reviews who did not have any business being there, such as literary figures who wanted the prestige and financial benefits that came from "participating" in writing the script. One of the most striking incidents (to which I have previously alluded) of the state interfering with the artistic vision of the holiday producers occurred a few days before Navro'z, when the Orgkom decided to cut from the show a dance touching on the sensitive issues of Uzbekistan's Zoroastrian past and the relations between the Turkic and Iranic worlds as exemplified by the story of Siyavush, from Firdawsi's epic poem, *Shahnoma*. The dance had two parts, both of which got nixed: the first part demonstrated a ritual revolving around fire, the second part enacted a game between two sides dressed up as "Turonic" bulls and "Iranic" tigers. The first part was objectionable to the Orgkom because of its ritual content, and the second part was problematic on multiple levels related mainly to relations between Uzbeks and Tajiks and between Uzbekistan and Iran. When I asked Mansur aka how he felt about the way that the Navro'z performance went, at first he used highly charged language about the importance of Navro'z for Uzbek national culture, saying, "To our horror it was recently forbidden, during the dictatorship of the USSR, and now that we have finally been freed from our slavery, now we can have our own ancient holiday, Navro'z." But then he quickly became critical of the way the Orgkom dealt with the Siyavush block, casting his comments about dictatorship and slavery in a different light:

MANSUR AKA: We had all that, but they [the Orgkom] took it away. "That's all just mysticism, we shouldn't emphasize that Siyavush was Iranian," even though his mother was from our territory . . . um, well, there weren't Uzbeks then, so he wasn't an Uzbek, but our, our fellow country-man. His father was Iranian, but his blood was our local, our Asian, Turanian, Turkish, Turkic. Nonetheless, since it was mixed with Iranian blood, they decided it was better not to underline that, to point it out, even though it would have been an interesting scene because of its own history and character. Still, that Siyavush was the leader of Bukhara for thirty years, and when he came, he didn't raise arms against them because his relatives lived there, as if it was was his own homeland. He stayed and ruled Bukhara. But still they decided not to mess with politics.

LAURA: When was that decided?

MANSUR AKA: After the review of the Orgkomitet. They came and watched rehearsals for a few days before the dress rehearsals. At the preliminary rehearsals, about the seventeenth [four days before the holiday]. Then there was the fire worshipping, and the lion and bull—they said, "That's all mysticism, it doesn't have anything to do with us so let's get rid of it." That was what they wanted, and also it ran over an hour and a half, but all the same it's not right that they limited the time. For the sake of art, good god, if it runs five minutes over . . . what's going to happen, a riot or something? But there you go, you can see that if they say it's got to be an hour and a half, it's got to be an hour and a half.[16]

I assumed that this interference in culture production was just the way it had always been, but, based on what I heard, in the mid-1990s it may have been somewhat worse in degree, if not in kind. In my interviews, I heard numerous stories about how the production of performed culture in the Soviet Union was a highly collective process, with artists, critics, and government bureaucrats interacting at numerous points in the pro-duction process.

MANSUR AKA: They always did it like this. The reception commission or the Orgkomitet or their colleagues, or the commission from the

Ministry of Culture which gets theater critics, specialists, dramaturgs together—it always happened like this. Before anything was shown to the public, [what] was called a "public review" [was] assigned to every new spectacle or mass holiday or jubilee, whatever. The Orgkomitet or the artistic union of the theater would come to the show, and after the union discusses the performance and gives its suggestions for necessary changes, then comes the public review. What does that mean? Representatives of the artistic union of the Ministry of Culture, representatives of the Union of Theatrical Workers, and if it's a musical theater, then also someone from the Union of Composers and Conductors —all would come. The drama section of the Union of Writers would be invited, someone from the media would also come. The representatives of these organizations would view the performance and then have a discussion afterward, that is, everyone would express their opinion about the show. Sometimes they would say stupid things, and sometimes they were helpful, sometimes they talked about something entirely different! But in the end, the general consensus would determine whether the show would go on, or to put it on hold and work on it some more, or to shut it down completely.[17]

Several interviewees suggested that between 1991 and 1998 this kind of intensive collaboration and state control began to decrease, but, based on his experience working on Navro'z 1996, one choreographer indicated that perhaps political control over holiday content was increasing rather than decreasing:

LAURA: About the dances that were cut—does that happen often?

HAMID AKA: No. Surprisingly, this was the first time. In my opinion, you can't erase history; good, bad, or average, it's all ours. At one time, in the ancient past, there weren't Uzbeks or Turks, there were some kinds of tribes here, and they were fire worshippers. But in general, Navro'z is considered a Muslim holiday even though that's all relative, since it wasn't originally Muslim but was adopted by the Muslims. But our . . . boys in politics decided that wasn't allowed. . . . They explained that "this isn't ours." [We both chuckle.] And the politicians decided that there shouldn't be an emphasis on the opposition between Iran and Turon, even though they were eventually united. So that our friends in

Iran wouldn't misunderstand. . . . Usually they just give suggestions about little details. They haven't made such big changes before.[18]

The idea that content was rejected because "it isn't ours" is especially interesting in light of the discussion in chapter 3 about the discourse of cultural renewal and the prevalence of Soviet interpretations of Uzbek history and identity. The rejection of popular cultural legacies by the Orgkom in this case reflects how out of touch they are with the vibrant and syncretic culture that is actually embraced by the people (and by many of the less Sovietized cultural elites).

As bothersome as the results of these "outside consultations" were for the Navro'z show, it was many times worse for Independence Day 1996, when a number of poets invited themselves to the dress rehearsal reviews and members of the President's Council demanded extensive changes to the program, sometimes in the name of cutting the length of the show but other times for political reasons (for example, only keeping the dances of countries that the president had visited that year, see chapter 3). Another person who worked on the holiday spectacles agreed that it didn't used to be like this—formerly, only experts were called in to review things. A lot of the innovative and thematically interesting things conceived by the artistic directors got cut, leaving mainly the trite and familiar, and I ended up teaching many of my acquaintances the English saying "too many cooks spoil the soup."

In addition to stifling creativity and allowing the supervision of holidays by political officials, the hierarchical structure of holiday production imposed more general constraints on the creative collective, since it operated as a command system of cultural production. During the process of preparing for Uzbekistan's holidays, artists were pulled from their regular jobs as composers or theater directors by orders from the festival producers, whether they wanted to contribute to the holiday or not. Similarly, bodies were requisitioned for performances like any other supplies such as lighting equipment and props.

This process was not unlike the way mass theatrical presentations were organized during the Soviet period. In his handbook on producing outdoor theater, Silin describes the organizational process of spectacles he was involved in:

> The director and the artists returned with the directorial plan and the preliminary sketches in hand. A series of meetings were held at the

Gorkom [city committee] of the Party. . . . A plan for the holiday was adopted and an Orgkomitet was created to conduct the holiday under the direction of the secretary of the Gorkom, who appointed the director and all those responsible for each part of the work. . . .

In the month before the festival the entire directorial-organizational group arrived in the city, bringing the completed scenario, finished sketches, and the preliminary soundtrack for the rehearsals. The director had secured the necessary materials, the permission for construction and transport, and had concluded all the necessary contracts [with the various ministries]. The scenario and sketches were discussed fully at a session of the Orgkomitet and had been revised where necessary.

Then the Gorkom invited the leaders of all the enterprises and organizations [of the city and surrounding region] . . . and informed them that participation in the preparation would be considered "socialist competition."[19] Every organization was charged with preparing one or two theatrical groups . . . [who] received sketches depicting how their group should look along with a full explanation, text from the scenario, music from the soundtrack, and a schedule of rehearsals. Additionally, an official notice with the signature of the secretary of the Party Gorkom was passed out to all the organizations. . . .

Every day from early morning, the director's assistants, the choir directors, the choreographers, and the movement directors attended rehearsals . . . and every evening at the staff headquarters they discussed the day's events, gave out tasks for the next day, solved organizational . . . and creative problems, and came up with endless explanations, clarifications, and changes.[20]

Other than the references to the Communist Party and socialism, this description suggests how little had changed in the holiday production process since the 1980s.

When I embarked on my fieldwork project, I expected to find Uzbekistan's world of cultural production broken down into three basic groups: culture bureaucrats, political elites, and cultural elites (artists and academics), each with their own agenda for national holidays. I assumed that the bureaucrats would be wrapped up in their institutional constraints and would advocate little change from the Soviet period. I guessed that the political elite would be interested in projecting a new image to the outside world, but at the same time they would want to use the Soviet arsenal of symbols and techniques of control to their best advantage. Thus I expected the politicians to promote a new content within the old forms. Finally, I anticipated that the cultural elite would be engaged in a search for authenticity, a renewal of the pre-Soviet, "true" Uzbek culture, stimulating an explosion of new themes and forms in the cultural realm.

To a large extent, I found that my hypotheses were borne out by what I saw. But I was struck by the great continuity between what I learned about Uzbek culture before 1991 and what I saw in 1996. As I mentioned in chapter 3, it seemed that what was advocated by the cultural elite was not a full-fledged cultural renewal, but rather an expansion of the kind of Uzbek culture that had existed during the Soviet period. Most cultural elites involved in the holiday production process talked about portraying "the most ancient, the most true aspects" of Uzbek culture, but what actually determined their choices in practice were material and temporal limitations, and a Soviet/modern aesthetic that favored novelty and simplicity over authenticity. On more than one occasion, I saw someone pitch a historically or culturally "authentic" idea to the lead director of the holiday spectacles only to receive a polite brush-off. But this reliance on stereotype was common in theatrical productions as well. Directors who wanted to put on plays that, for example, portrayed Amir Timur as a complex man, were discouraged or outright forbidden from deviating from the caricature that had been officially approved by the state.[21] The next few sections of this chapter will examine the role of the participants in this command system of cultural production and analyze the political meaning of preparing the holiday concert for a wide range of the people involved in the process.

The Politics of Participation in Holiday Productions

There were five groups of actors in the holiday production process, each with somewhat distinct institutional locations and interests: artists, bureaucrats, politicians, performers, and audience members. Artists, bureaucrats, and politicians had the most say in how the holiday got produced (what the form and content would be), while performers' and audiences' roles in the holiday spectacle tells us some interesting things about the functions of holiday spectacles. Although some analysts have portrayed the cultural nation-building project in Uzbekistan as a cynical attempt on the part of the leader to warp Uzbek history in a way that will shore up the regime's legitimacy,[22] the sheer necessity of involving multiple actors with different interests demonstrates that this view of Karimov as some sort of puppet master is too simple.

The people involved in carrying out the holiday activities were motivated by a carrot and a stick: the carrot was a bonus, sometimes quite substantial (the equivalent of several months' pay), in addition to their regular government salary paid through their place of employment (which in 1996 was the equivalent of only forty to fifty dollars per month). The stick was the threat of creating professional difficulties for oneself should one refuse to participate. For most of the thousands of extras involved in the main holiday spectacles, the carrot was very small and so was the stick, but for the lead directors and choreographers in charge of the performance, the bonus could amount to the equivalent of several months' salary. The stick rarely was employed because most of the artists involved were workaholics who, for the most part, enjoyed the holiday-planning process. It allowed them to work collaboratively with a group of colleagues who had become quite close-knit over the years.

However, enthusiastic participation was the exception, not the rule. The incentives, both material and otherwise, did not usually outweigh the other demands on participants' time, and I witnessed many examples of foot dragging, avoidance, and outright resistance to working with the creative group. In these cases, often a good scolding from an authority figure or a threat of further repercussions would suffice to move someone from avoidance at least to foot dragging. For example, on a couple of occasions, the director of one of the local theaters was more inclined to work on a project his organization was already committed to than to help with the holiday-production process. In these cases, as I was told, "the authorities [would] explain to them that this was more important." One time, a director was first chewed out by the assistant to the director of the holiday, and when that still did not induce him to make an appearance at the next day's staff meeting, the deputy mayor phoned him and made clear what his priorities should be. The ultimate threat issued by the deputy mayor was, "Do you want me to have to call Jurabekov [the first deputy prime minister]?!" The holiday-discipline stick was wielded by the government at the highest levels, and it was at that point that most people reluctantly agreed to fulfill the task they were charged with.

In spite of all the reluctance, a large proportion of Tashkent's artistic elite participated in some way in these holiday spectacles. There were only two cases I knew of when the creative group did not even bother to ask leading artists to help out. One case was an influential director who had an ongoing professional conflict with certain members of the group, and the other was an artist who had managed to go into business for himself, away from the reach of the long arm of state financial control. One of the holiday organizers suggested that the Ministry of Cultural Affairs "invite" this artist to participate (that is, put pressure on him), but the others realized that such invitations had little influence on independent artists. In other words, the stick no longer frightened them if they were no longer dependent on cooperation from the Ministry of Culture for their careers.

Many of the individuals involved at high levels of the holiday orchestration had taken on multiple jobs to make ends meet, and the holiday preparation strained them to the breaking point. Several of the leading members of the creative staff were nearly ill with exhaustion a whole month before the Independence Day holiday, and one told me that he and another key artist had agreed that if they were asked to do this again next year they would say no and go to the provinces to help organize smaller-scale concerts. "Can you refuse?" I asked, and he made a scoffing sound. Often these high-level people would be absent from important planning meetings, and by late July, the lead director got tired of hearing "He's in Moscow" or "He's at his other job" and yelled, "We will take steps! Girls—take the names of everyone who isn't here by 9:15!" The theaters involved in a holiday show were expected to drop pretty much everything for the month prior to the holiday and devote their personnel to the concert (though this expectation was rarely met). During this time, the theater employees received their regular salaries, and after the holiday, performers and directors received a small bonus. Even though they did not know how much the bonus would be or when it would come, one director explained that they could not really refuse. "But, of course," he said, "we're glad to help, and if we didn't do it, who would?"[23]

During the entire month of July, the spectacle producers agonized about how to get all the bodies they needed because the professional theaters and dance companies were putting them off. Many professional dancers and actors were abroad for the summer, touring with their company or otherwise working outside the country. It was no problem finding students and soldiers to be extras, but the recruitment of actual performers required quite a bit of negotiation and sometimes arm-twisting from the Ministry of Culture. At one of the first rehearsals for the dance numbers, 190 of the 350 performers failed to show up, and the staff blamed this on the chronic absence of the deputy minister of culture who was supposed to be in charge of ensuring the various dance institutes and professional collectives sent their performers to the rehearsal. It was not clear whether the deputy minister simply considered the holiday low on his list of priorities or, as some members of the staff charged, whether he was deliberately trying to make the lead director look bad.

In cases of absenteeism, in addition to threats, both loyalty to the lead director and contractual obligations to the government might be invoked to gain cooperation. On July 16 at the staff meeting for Independence Day, a composer tried to slip out early. First the lead director tried flattering him, saying he was "the best of the best," but they need him to do it better and on deadline this time. Then the composer tried to slip out for the second time, saying,

KARIM AKA: I'll help as much as I can, but I have these other commitments . . .

ALISHER AKA: So you're with them and not us, is that it? I don't need a helper, I need a musical director. You need to stay here and work on these issues with us. In all the government papers it says that you are the head musical director . . . we have 120 minutes to fill up, people!

KARIM AKA: I promise you three songs.

ALISHER AKA: When will they be on tape? How about August first? [In a more jocular tone]: Somebody write this down, Karim Jalalov has promised three songs by the first!

In addition to feeling pressured by other demands on their time, some of the artists involved in holiday planning resented being treated as "workers" who could be told what to do and when to do it. Thus on the twenty-third, the conflict continued. The deputy mayor chewed out Karim aka for missing a meeting and ordered him to produce two songs on tape by the first. "Like a factory!" Karim aka exclaimed and stormed out of the room. This incident of grumbling resistance was evidently quite memorable for the other members of the creative group, several of whom brought it up later. In another incident over lunch one day at the staff headquarters, one of the administrators went on a tirade about how in Kazakhstan and Kyrgyzstan, artists are paid a living wage "but here, great artists are treated like public servants." Then she talked about emigrating from Uzbekistan if things didn't get better.

The first came and went. On August 2, Alisher aka actually turned to me, knowing that, unlike any of them, I wrote everything down, and asked, "Didn't he promise three songs by the first?" "Two," I said, referring to the order of the deputy mayor. By the sixth of August, Karim aka still hadn't produced the songs. Alisher aka was yelling at the heads of the theaters for not having their people available to rehearse the dances for which Karim aka was writing songs. The theater directors retorted, "Well, you weren't ready on the first," which led to another yelling match between Karim aka and Alisher aka. But in the end, what was the "stick" that the holiday producers could use against Karim aka? Unpleasantness seemed to be the extent of it in this case, at least. The next month, Karim aka was promoted to the head of a professional musicians association, apparently suffering no serious consequences for his lack of cooperation.

Outright defiance was not a tactic in the repertoire of resistance of Uzbek cultural elites. One day in August, one of the choreographers told me (jokingly, it turned out) that the directors of the folk groups from the regions were "going on strike" because they were upset that their numbers were being cut. Later when I asked one of the directors about the "strike," she clucked at me and explained, "Uzbeks don't go on strike. It isn't our way." Another director claimed, "It's against the Koran." However, the first director demonstrated what the Uzbek way of protest was: she mounted a heated verbal attack on the Orgkom in front of me and a few of her colleagues, laying out a sequence of events that started with Orgkom decisions to cut musical numbers and ended with crushing the spirits of rural girls whose only escape from the drudgery of milking cows was to dance in the Independence Day show. In the world of culture production, as in many realms of life in Uzbekistan, citizens carried around a bundle of resentments that they were not afraid to express, but rarely acted on. Resistance to authority in Uzbekistan did not often go beyond a culture of complaint, and most Uzbeks were fatalistic about the power that was wielded by those above them in the hierarchy. As Collette Harris has observed about Uzbekistan and Tajikistan, power in family life is structured around a form of patriarchy where not just gender but generation has a strong influence on how people "perform" their identities.[24] In professional life, as well, there is a lot of pressure to perform submission to authority, where authority is defined by bureaucratic position as well as age and gender. These performances of submission, however, should not be mistaken for signs of the legitimacy of authority.

Neither the audience nor the milk maids, soldiers, and professional dancers had input into how a holiday was produced. The performers were simply vehicles for the message, and the audience (with the exception of the Orgkom and the president) was a passive recipient of that message. The main rewards for the relatively powerless extras in the extravaganza (soldiers and students) were a sense of national pride and a small stipend. During the rehearsals for Navro'z in 1996, I talked to some of the young women from the Chemistry Institute about why they were participating in the Navro'z performance. In a cluster of mostly Uzbek women, they responded along the lines of "It's a national holiday, the biggest," and "We are proud to show off our national traditions." A mixed-ethnicity group (Koreans, Russians, and Uzbeks) responded this way, as well, but on further questioning, said things like "They force us to do it," "We get a bonus in addition to our [student] stipend," "It's a break from studying," and they admitted that it was pretty boring and took up a lot of time that could be spent on other things. But they again emphasized that they were proud to be selected.

For others, the reward was an important recognition for their participation in cultural activities. While one official claimed that arts in the countryside were financially supported as much as they had been during the Soviet period, other arts workers from the provinces expressed their concern that, due to the economic situation, the free time of rural people was being devoted to small business pursuits rather than culturally enlightening activities. The director of the ensemble from a remote region who told me that "Uzbeks don't go on strike" predicted dire cultural consequences should ordinary kids from the countryside be shut out of participation in holiday performances because of the poor quality of their performance as judged by the Tashkent experts. "They're going to become disillusioned with dance and quit, which will be their loss and the loss of culture in Uzbekistan."

As for the audiences, most people I talked to enjoyed the festivities surrounding the holiday (the public concerts and street fairs, for example), but thought the holiday spectacles were boring and a waste of money. Understandably, this view was not acknowledged by the artists producing the holiday, who wanted to believe that their work had both educational and entertainment value. Thus, the way that audiences were incorporated in *the minds* of holiday producers had some impact on the way the extravaganzas come out. The artists involved in spectacle production often voiced a very clear idea of what the people liked and wanted from a holiday spectacle, though in reality they had no mechanism for receiving that kind of feedback. When questioned about how they knew what the audience liked and disliked, the common response was, "People tell us, they come up to us on the street and congratulate us." One of the lead directors of the holiday said he knew what people liked and didn't like from the review of the dress rehearsal by experts and critics, and from what the press says. "The press interviews people about their impressions—people like you!— and that's how you know," he said cheerfully.

This willing belief in what James C. Scott calls a "public transcript" is not uncommon among dominant elites.[25] If holiday producers were aware of the "hidden transcript" of the public's dislike of their concerts, they did not acknowledge it. But it is also possible that they were not aware of how the public really felt. Elites receive "a continuous stream of performances of deference, respect, reverence, admiration, esteem, and even adoration that . . . *seem* to transform that domination into the gold of willing, even enthusiastic, consent."[26] Given that members of the public were willing to reproduce this particular transcript, that elites further up in the hierarchy put forth the demands of a spectacular state, and that culture producers were habituated to the way the command system of cultural production worked, there was really very little need for fine-tuning cultural products to audience tastes. The only *audience* that shaped the final performance was the elite audience of critics and bureaucrats who witnessed the preperformance reviews.

Recruiting Participants and the Expression of Group Identities

While the audience mainly existed in the imaginations of culture producers, the performers were living bodies that had to be disciplined according to the artists' vision. There was a clear break in the hierarchy between people who performed on stage and people who had input into the spectacle-production process. Only in rare cases did someone who had creative control over spectacle production appear on stage as a performer. The role of performers in holiday extravaganzas was more similar to that of audience members than members of the creative group, in that they were acted upon as representatives of corporate identities, the most important of which was their identity as citizens of Uzbekistan. For performers and producers alike, participation in the holiday spectacle was a patriotic duty, but for performers and audience members, the holiday extravaganza was a way the state attempted to channel the expression of their identity and to cultivate appropriate cultural understandings.

Fewer people participated in Uzbekistan's national holidays than did during the Soviet period (though numbers ranging from six to ten thousand are still staggering), and the representation of corporate identities shifted. The means of recruiting these thousands was still the same as in decades past, though. During the Soviet period people were recruited through the factories, schools, and neighborhood councils, and they marched under these corporate identities, reinforcing the Soviet idea of solidarity based on shared class interests, as well as rather arbitrary administrative-territorial divisions. After independence, participants were still recruited in this manner, though in a more limited way. The number of participants went down as did the proportion of participants not involved with the arts community in some way. While many "extras" in the holiday performances were from technical universities or the army, people working in Tashkent's factories were no longer compelled (or invited) to take part. People representing the twelve districts of Tashkent marched during the Navro'z spectacle, but not as identifiable groups. They were recruited by district councils, but they paraded through the staging area dressed in whimsical homemade costumes ranging from fairy princesses to traditional Uzbek costume in a sincere attempt to create an indigenous version of the "carnival" genre of performance. The masses of bodies, clad in pastel sweat suits, that paraded around with flags were provided by the army, and those sitting in bleachers, holding colored cards that formed enormous pictorial "backgrounds," were provided by educational institutions, while the featured players on the main and side stages were either professional artists, students of art schools, or members of amateur performance groups (see table 2). Musicians from the army and athletes from various sports teams and clubs were featured performers, as well.

Table 2. "Preliminary Plan of Assignments" issued by the Ministry of Cultural Affairs, delegating responsibilities to various organizations involved in the 1996 Independence Day celebration.

MINISTRY NAME	WHAT THE MINISTRY PROVIDED	PURPOSE
Public Education	1,200 technical high school girls 150 each boys/girls in grades 3–4 180 young athletes 150 young dancers Exhibits, athletic exhibition, contests, and performances	Background—placard mosaics Children's Block Sport Block Theatrical performance, misc. Children's festival on plaza in front of Navoiy Theater*
Higher/Middle Education	2,500 young women and 400 young men	Theatrical performance, misc.
Internal Affairs	400 cadets 100 cadet-firemen Orchestra	Flag bearers Construction, stagehands Performance during sayil*
Public Health	2,500 young women and 400 young men Medical and sanitation services	Theatrical performance, misc. Rehearsals
Communication	Megaphones, television transmitters, telephone lines, and cell phones	Rehearsals, communication among organizers, and transmission of broadcast
Defense	300 cadets Musicians, soldiers 20 pyrotechnicians Musicians, etc.	Flag bearers Military Block Fireworks display Concert during sayil*
Commerce, Local Industry	Necessary goods and materials	Costumes, props, etc.
Cultural Affairs	All Tashkent's theater troupes, professional and regional artists' collectives, and students of the choreography school, the technical school and institute of culture Professional directors and choreographers Entertainment of various sorts	Theatrical performance, misc. and supply of costumes, props, etc. Organizing the theatrical performance Performances during sayil*

Soviet holidays required participation through corporate identities such as the workplace, the military, or one's nationality. The changes in how holidays were officially celebrated in Uzbekistan point to the de-emphasizing of class identity as *expression* (though it was still relevant as *participation*) and a much greater emphasis on entertainment and artistic value. Thus the means of recruiting people to fill up the public space were similar to those of the Soviet era, but there was no longer an idea that this was being done to

ORGANIZATION NAME	WHAT THE MINISTRY PROVIDED	PURPOSE
State Tele-Radio Company	Studio musicians and technicians, recording equipment, and sound editing	Theatrical performance's soundtrack
	Musical groups	Theatrical performance, concerts during sayil*
Federation of Trade Unions	Camp and resort facilities	Intensive rehearsals
	Artistic collectives	Theatrical performance, misc.
	Exhibits, athletic exhibition, contests, and performances	Children's festival on plaza in front of Navoiy Theater*
State Committee on Publishing	Printed matter, images, and sketches	Misc.
State Committee on Sport	Athletes, sport program	Sport Block
	Athletic shoes	Performers in spectacle
	Rooms in Paxtakor Stadium	Rehearsals
Various light industry, petrochemical, and construction concerns	Sewing of costumes, supplying fabric, decorations, helium and air pumps, storage sheds for props, launching area for fireworks, light trucks, etc.	Mostly for main spectacle
Tashkent Urban Passenger Transport	Vans and cars with drivers	Transporting organizers between rehearsal sites, running errands
Uzbekfilm	Costumes, props, fireworks advice	Theatrical presentation

*Indicates a holiday activity that was not part of the main spectacle

demonstrate solidarity, workplace or otherwise. It was simply an efficient way to ensure the supply of unpaid extras to suit the artistic designs of the directors.

One area where corporate identity continued to have symbolic significance (as well as organizational impact) was in the Regions Block. Uzbekistan has twelve provinces (viloyatlar) and an "autonomous region" inhabited largely by the Karakalpaks, who are considered a distinct nationality separate from the Uzbeks but were included in the Regions Block because their "native territory" was within the borders of Uzbekistan. The amateur ensembles that performed in this block were selected by the regional department of culture as being the best representative of the region. One example was the Besh Karsak ensemble from the Urgut District of Samarkand Region. They represented a particular local cultural tradition that was not the same as traditional Samarkandi culture, but they were one of the most active and talented ensembles in the Samarkand Region and were selected almost every year to perform in the holiday spectacles.

During the process of producing holiday performance numbers that express these regional flavors, the local definitions of regional distinctiveness and achievements were disregarded by the Tashkent directors and choreographers, who had professionalism, not identity, at the top of their aesthetic agenda.[27] This stereotyping and standardization was accomplished during the month-long rehearsal period in Tashkent, where the conflict between local and Tashkent artists played out the paradox that the "national culture" demonstrated in a holiday performance should be both folk and professional.

One strategy of passive resistance to the takeover by the Tashkent professionals was exemplified by the group from Bukhara, who arrived late with next-to-no material prepared. They received the full brunt of the fury of the director of the block and the resentment of the other ensembles who had arrived in Tashkent days earlier. Still, this seemed to be a more sensible strategy from the point of view of the ensemble since very little of the music, choreography, theatrical business, and costume that the other ensembles brought to Tashkent ended up in the final performance. The Bukharan ensemble was able to work up its number from start to finish under the guidance of the Tashkent organizers, saving a step in the production process. Again, the authenticity of their performance was less important than the more practical concerns of saving time and effort.

There was a persistent conflict between the desire of the spectacle producers to see amateur groups perform traditional folklore and the desire for novelty and professionalism. The end result was frustration on the part of the ensemble directors and dissatisfaction on the part of the spectacle producers.

> MANSUR AKA: Some of the parts were too similar. . . . Sure, they had different costumes and what all, but really they were very similar. There were too many of them, and in the end they all looked the same. As they say, "better fewer but better," right? Well, we thought, "the more the better!" but we didn't consider that more might be worse.
>
> LAURA: Why did they turn out the same?
>
> MANSUR AKA: Well, they had some element of their own regional characteristics, but in comparison with the professional groups, the cos-

tumes were pathetic, not good quality, simple. They tried to get something across, but they just weren't up to it. Their programs were even cut short, but it [the Regions Block] still dragged on.[28]

One solution the Orgkom and the spectacle producers pushed during the rehearsals right before the Independence Day 1996 spectacle was to cut the weakest ensembles, but this was objectionable politically since it would be an insult to regional leaders if their regions were not represented. It was also objectionable to the performers, who had been living in a Tashkent hotel (at the expense of their regional government) for three weeks and had worked hard to put their number together. The director in charge of the Regions Block reworked the block so that each ensemble was part of a number (though some regions were combined into one number) and so that the block overall was much shorter. Usually the regions based on administrative divisions (rather than cultural or historical divisions), who have less of a sense of distinct identity, were combined with neighboring regions in the final spectacle. Whereas pre-Soviet regional distinctions were based on the successors to the Khanate of Kokand (the Fergana Valley, Tashkent, and surrounding viloyats), the Emirate of Bukhara (Samarkand and Bukhara regions), and the Khanate of Khiva (Khorezm region), the way that the Regions Blocks ended up in both shows in 1996 reflected the following contemporary cultural divisions: 1) Fergana Valley (Fergana, Namangan, Andijan); 2) Karakalpakistan; 3) Samarkand; 4) Bukhara; 5) Surkhondarya; 6) Kashkadarya; 7) Tashkent, Jizzakh, and Syrdarya; and 8) Khorezm.

Thus for the performers in holiday extravaganzas, participating in the arts was important not just for the cultural development of themselves and the nation, but also to represent subnational identities, as weak or strong as those may be. While the holidays' function of reinforcing many kinds of collective identities declined compared to the Soviet period, other kinds of identities were emphasized, as I discussed in chapter 3. Additionally, the performers in these spectacles served an important symbolic function, demonstrating the power of the state through the sheer scale of its pageantry.

The Holiday as Pilgrimage

One aspect of the holiday that had changed relatively little since the Soviet period was the idea that the performance (whether a parade or a spectacle) is oriented toward the preferences of the leader. One choreographer explained that the reason they had ordinary people from Tashkent's various neighborhoods just marching through the staging area during the Navro'z spectacle was so that the people could "go all out and show our president that they're doing well." The performance is also physically oriented toward the leader. Just as the focal point of the Soviet parade was the point where the marchers passed the platform upon which the leadership was standing, the focal point of the Tashkent spectacle was the place where President Karimov sat. Most of the action directed toward the audience began with Karimov, who sat with religious leaders (both Muslim and Orthodox), and high-ranking government officials at center stage. For example, during the Navro'z extravaganza of 1996, cups of sumalak were handed out to audience members, beginning with Karimov.

Just as during the Soviet period, the creation of holiday performances was subject to final approval from the top, and in both cases the performers themselves perceived that their first priority was to please the leader, their second priority was to engage the audience, and their third priority was their own spiritual or material benefit. For many of the ensembles from the provinces, participation in the performance and in the month of rehearsals preceding it was seen as a hardship. While they did receive monetary compensation, and many had a sense of pride in participation, most of them would not have gone had they not been sent. "First you force us to come here, and now you yell at us!" complained one regional choreographer during a dispute with the block director. Later she told me she did not want to be there—none of them did, but "they were just plucked up and brought here."

"It's hard, especially for people who have to leave their families for a month," said a director from another region, "but it goes through the channels of authority [po liniia]. We can't refuse. It's our debt we owe to the government, to our country." I got the impression that the participants were there to make their local leadership look good to the national leadership. I asked one of the members of the creative group why the regional ensembles bothered coming if it was so inconvenient for them. "Because the president can't travel to all those places himself," he said without irony. In many ways, the holidays turned into a ritual of obeisance (or as Yael Navaro-Yashin aptly put it in the case of Turkey, "rituals of statist thralldom") where the not entirely unwilling people were expected to show up to thank the leader for the patronage of the state.[29] Similarly, at the beginning of the O'zbekiston Vatanim Manim song contest mentioned in chapter 3, the show was opened by a reading of the presidential decree regarding the establishment of the annual competition, and the emcees, as well as the lyrics of the first song, specifically thanked the president (who was in the audience) for all that he had done for the nation.

This orientation toward the president was explicitly invoked during the preparations for the holidays. Not only were certain things explained in terms of "this is how Karimov wants it," but decisions brought down from the Orgkom were also personified as Karimov's will. A Jewish dance number that was enthusiastically supported by the choreographers and directors was cut "by the president," according to someone who attended the meeting. And discipline was made to appear as if channeled directly from Karimov through his instruments on the Orgkom. When explaining why the regional collectives had to follow a particular instruction, the phrase "our honorable president said" (*prezidentimiz dedilar*) was used by the government officials quite often. The holiday was also used as a photo opportunity for Karimov. A picture of him picking up a little girl who gave him flowers during a 1993 holiday performance was circulated widely on posters and pocket calendars, and one director of the 1996 independence day spectacle advocated using more child performers because "the stuff with the children would be what would make Karimov clap, and the television would show the child, and then Karimov smiling and clapping," and, by implication, that was what the audience and the politicians wanted to see in the performance.

Spectacle and the Seduction of the Cultural Elite

In the previous chapter, I presented the views of cultural elites on the depoliticization of cultural content, and in this chapter, I have discussed the politics of cultural production. Some of my interviewees also saw culture production as being depoliticized and saw holidays as being freer than they were in the Soviet era, as Nodir aka expresses: "Now, after independence, holidays are completely different. . . . [Before] there were just parades everywhere. It was in the realm of service [to the state]. It was all monotonous. . . . Now the viewer comes and sees the show we've put on, and afterward continues that celebration. They're a participant in the holiday. . . . Things are more free now."[30]

The interesting thing about these assertions that "it's all so different now" was that it did not seem all that different to me as an outside observer. The examples that people gave of how things were in the Soviet era were striking exactly because they were what stood out as being characteristic of Uzbekistan's holidays. Nodir aka asserted that during the Soviet period, holidays were all done by command. However, the contemporary holiday production process was also driven by a command system based on unquestioned authority, not on voluntarism or contracts. Nodir aka claimed that now people do not stand and watch, they participate, too. Yet these holiday spectacles, which were clearly set up to isolate the audience from the performance and, even more strikingly, to restrict audience membership to a small group of the elite, were clearly not examples of democratic participation. While it is true that the rest of the day, apart from the main extravaganza, was open to the public and was designed as a pleasant day out for ordinary citizens, this is not a striking difference from the Soviet period, when holidays were also celebrated with street fairs and public concerts.

The contrast between my perceptions and those of the holiday producers can be explained in two ways. First, since I do not have firsthand experience of the Soviet-era holidays, perhaps the degree to which they were orchestrated by command, restricted in participation, and so forth was even greater than it was in the 1990s. Second, as several of my interviewees pointed out, they had not yet been able to achieve their ideal holiday celebration. In many conversations during the holiday production process, people expressed the idea that now Uzbekistan's holidays were like a carnival, as opposed to the military parade atmosphere of many Soviet holidays. This may have been the perception of the holiday producers because that was their ideal, whether or not they were actually able to realize it. Other agents in the holiday-production process dictated the various aspects of the holidays, so they did not always turn out the way the creative group pictured them at the start of the production process.

For example, the idea that the celebration of Navro'z should be more like carnival, especially Brazilian carnival, came up over and over again in my conversations with holiday producers. This was the ideal toward which they strove because they perceived this kind of festivity to be more authentic, as Mansur aka said, "the way it used to be with us." It seemed that the "authenticity" they admired in carnival was related to popular participation, whimsical individualized costume, and spontaneity, so it is striking that these are exactly the elements that come into tension with the way the holiday is actually produced. In this desire to emulate a globalized cultural practice, as well as in the desire for authenticity and diversity of interpretations, the cultural elites' interests diverged most sharply from those of the political and bureaucratic elites.

But this is my analysis, and in this section I will be presenting a perspective that might well be offensive to my informants because I am arguing that they derive benefits from deceiving themselves.[31] This argument arises from the need I felt to analyze a contradiction between what holiday producers said they were doing and what they actually did, in order to better understand what the nation-building project meant to them and how institutional constraints limited the choices they could make and the ways they interpreted those choices. Here is one of the places in this book where it is important that I highlight my analysis as being the "partial perspective" of an outside observer, equipped with very different theories of agency and power than my interlocutors had. I am invested in my identity as a scholar, whereas they were invested in their identities as artists, and so my goal in writing is to deconstruct power dynamics that they may not be fully aware of, while their goal was to persuade me of the artistic and educational value of their work. It is probably already apparent that I was not entirely persuaded by them, but, on the other hand, they might not be persuaded by my argument either.

The contradiction I examine here comes from my observation that cultural elites involved in holiday spectacles tended to overlook their top-down control over the final product. Many of them asserted that today, holidays were more spontaneous and participatory, and less politicized, than their Soviet counterparts. I was struck, however, by the antipopulist and contrived nature of the holiday spectacles. Earlier, I mentioned that the holiday concerts are entirely lip-synched, in contrast to the expectations of most concert audiences around the world that live music is indeed performed in real time by the person they are seeing on stage. There was, for example, a surprisingly big scandal during the 2008 Olympic ceremonies in Beijing when it was discovered that the little girl in the performance was chosen because she was cute, while the less photogenic girl who was actually singing the song was kept offstage. In the case of the holiday concerts of Uzbekistan, however, there were several reasons for this artificiality. One is that Central Asian audiences had different expectations than other audiences; often outdoor concerts (and sometimes indoor ones, as well) in Uzbekistan were performed to a prerecorded soundtrack. This was for logistical reasons (the acoustics of an outdoor venue, unreliable sound equipment, the precise timing required to coordinate thousands of performers), as well as to keep total control over the content of the songs, and, like in Beijing, to ensure that there wasn't the embarrassment of a less-than-perfect performance.

In addition to the ubiquitous use of lip-synching, spontaneity and participation were actively discouraged by the form and organization of these holiday events. This time in contrast to popular expectations, the public was not allowed to attend, or even get close to, major national holiday concerts. On national holidays and jubilee events (such as the 66oth anniversary of the birth of Amir Timur in 1996), streets were closed off for one square kilometer around the square where the extravaganza was going to take place. Invitation holders had to pass through at least three checkpoints in order to gain admission to the seating area, passing throngs of disappointed, uninvited citizens along the way. Of course, space and security concerns dictated that the performances could not admit hundreds of thousands of Tashkenters, but people I spoke with in 1996 were under the mistaken impression that at least they would be able to get close enough to the central square to view the fireworks on Independence Day.

It was important, however, for the concert organizers to maintain the discourse of participation, authenticity, and spontaneity in order for them to feel that they were accomplishing their nation-building tasks, and the people involved in the higher levels of spectacle production were very good at presenting this illusion to themselves, even when it was clear that their work was very much aimed at a domestic and international elite. For example, when I asked Alisher aka why the Navro'z show was so busy, with so many different elements going on at once all over the staging area, he replied:

ALISHER AKA: During a festival you wander around the streets or across a square, and you look around, and there's someone singing, there's someone dancing. Since we, as viewers, enjoy that, that was our goal, so that the festival wouldn't turn out academic, but popular. Therefore the viewer would be able to see many activities all at the same time. . . . We wanted it to be that in different places, different things were going on in parallel that all related to the same theme. I saw on TV how the diplomatic corps were taped looking here and there, so it was like "I'm actually participating in the event, I'm looking where I want, at what interests me," you see? But it all underlines one main idea: the idea that the viewer should feel like a participant in the festival on the square.[32]

This description of the holiday was patently false. Although holiday concerts evidenced a strict segregation between performers and the invitation-only audience, relied largely on academic interpretations of folk culture rather than actual daily life practices, and were prerecorded so as to guarantee the absence of spontaneity, the spectacle's producers maintained a belief in the new holidays' freedom and inclusiveness. Soviet-era holidays were seen as having been politicized, boring, and coercive. In today's holidays, their producers assert, "The viewer is a participant," because they were more like carnival, as opposed to the military parade atmosphere of many Soviet holidays. But this self-presentation of the holiday was more an ideal than a reality. As Farhod aka said, "I'd like [for] the people themselves, not just artists, professionals, but we the people [to play a bigger role in holiday performances]. Why? Because festivals are for the people, by the people. So in our festivals, the people themselves should participate, organize themselves well. We always would like to see in Navro'z our own traditions in the way of the history of Navro'z. I think we're still just making stabs at this."[33]

Others were more aware of the project they were engaged in, and many saw it as an inherent good:

> IVAN: I don't even think that politics have changed! We've just stopped shouting "Long live the KPSS," that's all. The people are always the people. What do they need? Bread and festivals. For me there is no history! You see, in the end, there are the people. And we have to do something for the people. Listen, earlier there was the orchestra, the folk dances happened, this existed, that existed. The only thing that has changed is the political leadership. But the people are still the people. Give them bread and circuses. Earlier I planned that one thousand people should be on the stage, now it's six thousand. Now it's just more popular.[34]

Though they had very different views of contemporary holidays, both these spectacle producers expressed a concrete disenchantment with Soviet-era ideology and practices. The second director, however, was equally disenchanted with contemporary holidays, and it was no coincidence that he was not an Uzbek and therefore less likely to mislabel mass spectacle as a revival of national tradition. However, like the first speaker, he had been seduced by the prospect of being able to continue doing the work he loved, albeit for a different master.

How do we understand the choice to reject the message of the state and yet participate in its reproduction? The heroic version of totalitarian subjectivity often portrays intellectuals and other cultural elites as having a naturally subversive role in society. Jerome Karabel in his sociological analysis of the relationship between intellectuals and politics calls this the "moralist tradition . . . [which] treats intellectuals not as they actually are, but as they should be."[35] Following Bourdieu's characterization of intellectuals as occupying a position tied more closely to the dominant groups in a society than to the masses, Karabel argues that intellectuals have an interest in the status quo. Intellectuals have a relatively privileged position in the social order, but they are dependent for resources on their links to political and economic elites.

Furthermore, there is an assumption coming from the Western cultural tradition that the natural inclination of culture producers is to be independent and original, but this assumption is grounded in a context of modern individualism and reflexivity. Uzbekistan's cultural elites share some of these assumptions, but they were also grounded in another cultural tradition that emphasized the perfected reproduction of forms, as in the memorization of the Koran or schools of art that strove to imitate the work of the master. These points, when considered in conjunction with the likelihood that some of these artists were hacks (to use the term invoked by an artist I interviewed who avoided at all cost working on holiday spectacles with these "hacks") whose career trajectory was not necessarily related to their talent, lead us to a new understanding of the role of culture producers in spectacular states. The production of kitsch allows the cultural elite to free themselves of the need to engage in a critical creative process; it provides them an easy and automatic route to a cultural product that will satisfy the only truly important audience: the political elite.

My observations of work on these kitschy spectacles reminded me that there can be pleasure in complicity, enjoyment in passivity. As Ritzer argues, spectacle is an antidote to disenchantment and both offer the possibility of playful, pleasurable deception. No one is forced into this self-deception; they go willingly, following only their impulses to seek pleasure in their own cultivation. To the extent that the state continues to be able to make the work of culture producers pleasurable, it will succeed in its seduction of the elite. To the extent that the state is in part constituted by the cultural elite, the elite seduces itself.

What does seduction mean in this context? In Baudrillard's terms, seduction is the willful neglect of truth in favor of the play of power and creation.[36] The act of seduction in Uzbekistan's holiday extravaganzas was mutual. The cultural and political elite gather together and experience collective effervescence, a state of physiological arousal that, as Durkheim argued, makes us more susceptible to the messages we're receiving. In times of collective effervescence, we want to believe, we want the spectacle to be true. This psychological and physiological effect doesn't apply to most of the viewers of the spectacle who watch it on television in their homes, but it certainly applies to the live audience (made up mainly of elites) and most of all to the producers and performers, whose arousal was acute. The presence of the president and the opportunity to interact with him after the performance had a visceral effect on the cultural elites involved in holiday production. After the 1996 Navro'z extravaganza, one director, Mansur, marveled, "The president didn't send one of his lackeys to thank the staff, but rather he himself waited two or three whole minutes for Rustam [Hamidov, the lead director] to make his way down from his post so that he could personally thank and praise everyone. It was such an honor. Can you imagine, the president waiting for a mere director [*rezhisiorchik*]? It was great."[37] The people watched the spectacle inattentively at home while the elite, performers, and the political elites who attended got their "batteries" recharged by the event. They were thus more able to carry out their tasks of nation building with this particular representation of the nation in mind.

One of Foucault's insights into relations of power is that power is not solely a negative, constraining, and external force; it is not always, or even often, the exercise of one's will in spite of opposition: "What makes power hold good, what makes it accepted, is simply the fact that it doesn't only weigh on us as a force that says no; it also traverses and produces things, it induces pleasure, forms knowledge, produces discourse. It needs to be considered as a productive network that runs through the whole social body, much more than as a negative instance whose function is repression."[38]

In Foucault's work, power is also a generative force, producing pleasure, order, and knowledge. Our subjecthood emerges from our agency in existing relations of power, and this means that our very interests and desires are also constituted by power. Thus we respond to the dynamics of power, not just out of fear of the consequences, but because we seek the pleasures of self-fulfillment and external reward that this agency gives us. This insight is very important for understanding the relationship of cultural elites to the state in Uzbekistan. If knowledge and power are mutually constituting, then we must understand what sort of knowledge the state was producing. At the same time, we must also understand that the state, as embodied in particular bureaucrats and government officials, did not coerce artists into producing all or even most of the time. The state didn't simply threaten, though it did so when self-discipline failed, and it didn't just offer rewards (which could be seen as coercive in the economic situation of the 1990s). Power was exercised by the state in the desires of the cultural elites to please their leaders and, even more so, to please themselves.

My emphasis on the pleasures of complicity contrasts with most other accounts of elite cooperation with authoritarian states, which tend to emphasize the ways that complicity produces alienation. Lisa Wedeen analyzes the various ways the Assad regime in Syria relied on externalized and unbelievable expressions of loyalty rather than actually trying to foster loyalty or command belief. She argues that this paradoxical strategy is successful because obeying when we disbelieve requires submission, unlike behaving out of the conviction of our beliefs, which is not anything other than what we normally do.[39]

> Assad's cult is a strategy of domination based on compliance rather than legitimacy. The regime produces compliance through enforced participation in rituals of obeisance that are transparently phony both to those who orchestrate them and to those who consume them. . . . It produces guidelines for acceptable speech and behavior; it defines and generalizes a specific type of national membership; it occasions the enforcement of obedience; it induces complicity by creating practices in which citizens are themselves "accomplices," upholding the norms

constitutive of Assad's domination; it isolates Syrians from one another; and it clutters public space with monotonous slogans and empty gestures, which tire the minds and bodies of producers and consumers alike.[40]

Acting "as if" one is a loyal member of the regime produces complicity, which is much more insidious than legitimacy or hegemony. Wedeen argues that rather than being paradoxical (why would it be a rational strategy for the government to cultivate disbelief among its citizens?), such a strategy proves more flexible and cost effective than more totalitarian techniques of power. What's more, the ritual character of public events, the formulaic structure of official discourse, and the "cluttering" of public space all serve the spectacular state's interest in monopolizing the production of meaning.

Because of the parallels between Assad's Syria and Karimov's Uzbekistan, it is clear that there is more to the spectacular state than Soviet legacies. However, in some ways both Syria and Uzbekistan were inheritors of totalitarian techniques of power refined by the Soviets.[41] Independent Uzbekistan was still marked by many of the characteristics of totalitarian culture noted by Goldfarb: the penetration of the political into the social, economic, and cultural spheres; the use of a specialized official language that attempted to create a truth in accordance with official ideology; and the antipathy to the development of a public space free of the state's monopoly on truth.[42] But Goldfarb's explanation of the role of spectacle in totalitarian culture is too simple. Goldfarb argues that spectacle assuages the cognitive dissonance produced by the conflict between the hegemony of the regime and the widespread disbelief in its official truth. Spectacle simply masks the truth, diverting attention from it and avoiding difficult questions by providing ready-made easy answers of kitsch.[43]

The problem with this analysis of spectacle as distraction is that it focuses too much on either passivity or resistance, without looking at what Wedeen calls complicity, the mundane obedience that demonstrates and reproduces the regime's power through the actions of citizens. Goldfarb's heroes are Polish theater students who dare to ask questions and thereby carve out an autonomous space within the totalitarian culture, even while participating in socialist youth organizations. Wedeen's heroes are the people who glorify the regime in one context and tell jokes about it in another, stubbornly sustaining the gap between performance and belief. A different approach is taken by Alexei Yurchak, who refreshingly has no heroes in his tale of totalitarian culture. Yurchak critiques the dichotomous subject (appearance versus reality, official versus underground) presented in most analyses of socialism as linking agency only with resistance. This stems from a "dissident ideology" that sees socialism as involving "a complex web of immoralities that are calibrated as such against a more moral system, perhaps Western democracy. What may get lost in these accounts is a crucial and paradoxical fact that great numbers of people living in socialism genuinely supported its fundamental values and ideals, although their everyday practices may appear 'duplicitous' because they indeed routinely transgressed many norms and rules represented in that system's official ideology."[44]

Yurchak examines the "hegemony of representation" in late Soviet life, which was so taken for granted that it was not significant enough to merit resistance or even for one to consider whether one believes it or not. In late socialism, mobilizational events such as Party meetings and holiday parades took on a parallel structure: the official event (consisting of shouting slogans, voting, parading) and the parallel event (consisting of gossiping, reading a book, drinking), where a whole other set of practices and meanings were playing out. The parallel structure did not require that the actors support or ridicule the official event, which was, after all, a trivial backdrop to what was going on in "real life."[45]

> For instance, the question, "do you support the resolution" asked during a Soviet Komsomol meeting invariably led to a unanimous raising of hands in an affirmative gesture. However, to participants this was usually an act of recognition of how one must behave in a given ritualistic context in order to reproduce one's status as a social actor rather than as an act of conveying "literal" meaning. In this sense, the raised hand was a response to the question, "are you the kind of social actor who understands and acts according to the rules of the current ritual, with its connection to the larger system of power relations and previous contexts of this type?" To analyze this act only for its truth conditions—as "real" support or "dissimulation" of support . . .—is to miss the point.[46]

Living a "normal" life entailed not getting involved in the official sphere, either as a supporter or as a critic.[47] By recognizing the possibility of normalcy in totalitarian regimes, Yurchak presents a less melodramatic view of how they operate and provides a bridge of understanding of this behavior across regime types. For instance, although many U.S. citizens do not believe in giving their allegiance to an inanimate object, they nonetheless will "pledge allegiance to the flag" when others around them are also doing so (in school, for example). This ritual is neither an actual pledge nor a pretend pledge; it is simply a contextually appropriate action.[48]

Far from being inherently conflictual, as the heroic narrative of the dissident intelligentsia would have us believe, the relationship between artists and totalitarian states can be mutually satisfying, resulting in a "velvet prison" where artists trade freedom of expression for guarantees of material security and social respect.[49] Under the Soviets, after all, cultural elites were well rewarded and occupied a position of high social status. Promising young artists and academics received free, high-quality education, after which they went on to a guaranteed job that offered a decent salary and opportunities for international travel. They had additional opportunities to earn money through participation in special projects and, if they were quite good, from the stipend of "People's Artist" awards. Artists' unions provided housing in convenient locations and provided various social services to artists and their families. Culture was highly valued by the Soviets, and artists enjoyed the respect and admiration of both the political elite and the masses.

Throughout much of the Soviet Union and Eastern Europe, intellectuals and artists were at the forefront of a long struggle to free their nations from the rule of the Communist Party. But when that goal was achieved, did we expect the intelligentsia to suddenly start attacking the new government that they worked to bring to power? When these movements articulated a desire to be free of what they perceived as colonial rule, should we not have expected them to support the new nationalist regime? The heroes in my story are more protagonists than heroes: choreographers, directors, and composers who were offered a regime whose ideals were even more attractive than socialism's. In the early years of independence, Uzbekistan's cultural elite were hoping to unite form and content once again by unleashing their desire to produce culture they believed in. Energized by the nationalist content of the new rhetoric, they became genuinely mobilized in support of the regime, at least for the first few years of independence. By the time I began my research in 1996, many cultural elites were behaving like our stereotypical intellectuals and (privately) voicing criticism of a government that was not living up to their ideals. During my last visit in 2006, it seemed increasingly likely that the seduction was wearing off, that both artists and audiences were growing tired of repetition, and that either the government would have to allow a free exploration of topics or create a more coherent and multilayered official ideology for artists to work from.

SPECTACLE AND THE
IDEOLOGY OF NATIONAL
INDEPENDENCE

If you want a glimpse of heaven, watch Uzbek TV.
If you want a glimpse of hell, come see how we live.

| Contemporary Uzbek saying |

In 2002, I saw a program broadcast on Uzbek TV's Channel 1 that summed up what Tashkent cultural elites might have wanted us to understand about contemporary national identity in Uzbekistan. The story of "Hamroh" ("The Fellow Traveler") started out with a mother fighting with her son about what he is going to do with his life and whether he should be allowed to marry the woman of his choice. The background music was an orchestral pop version of Led Zeppelin's "Stairway to Heaven," reminding us that cultural elites in Uzbekistan have cosmopolitan taste but also hinting at the danger of becoming too much like the West. The mother/son conflict stood for a sort of generational crisis experienced by many Uzbeks who came of age during the Soviet era: while the overt message was "sons don't even listen to their own mothers anymore," the subtext was "nothing is like it used to be. The world is changing too fast." The mother dealt with the crisis by taking a vacation to see an old friend in Urgench, the capital of Khorezm Viloyat. On her train ride, she and her fellow traveler (a young man who exhibited the proper respect that her own son lacked), passed through cities such as Guliston, Jizzakh, and Samarkand, which the mother hardly recognized because they had become so beautiful and modern. The young man informed her of all the wonderful changes independence had brought to their country, and then they were joined on the train by a folklore group who sang for them, just to remind everyone that tradition is just as beautiful and important as modernity. By the time they got to Urgench, the mother and her fellow traveler had become like family, and, in fact, the mother discovers that this young man's sister is the woman her son wanted to marry. The lesson the mother seemed to learn was that although change is frightening, perhaps everything will work out for the best in the end.

This program struck me because it seemed to tie together a lot of the threads of public discourse about Uzbek national identity that I observed in May of 2002. However, change was on its way again, and not for the better. Between 2003 and 2008, Uzbekistan's government responded to a series of domestic and international events with anti-Western rhetoric and policies. The domestic events included terrorist attacks in 2003 and 2004, the increasing visibility of opposition politicians, an increase in public protests related to dissatisfaction with economic policies and anger at the persecution of alleged Islamists, and the dramatic violence that took place in Andijon in May 2005. The international events were the series of "colored revolutions" that took place in Georgia, Ukraine, and Kyrgyzstan between 2003 and 2005. By mid-2005, the government of Uzbekistan had developed a narrative that linked these internal and external events by positing that the United States and other Western governments (and George Soros) were pursuing regime change in the former Soviet Union through nongovernmental organizations (NGOs). Government-controlled television characterized Western participation in the Andijon events as part of a neocolonial strategy: "The reason behind the [Andijon] tragedy is attempts to divide the world by Western states, who are reluctant to give up their spirit of colonialism."[1]

This discourse is rather different from the picture that Uzbekistan was trying to paint of itself in the 1990s. In this book, I have argued that Soviet internationalism was compatible with the preservation of ethnic culture, and this internationalist legacy aided the portrayal of Karimov's "ideology of national independence" as congruent with international norms. This outward orientation in turn linked up with the specific evidence examined here: universal cultural forms such as Olympic-style spectacles were important to Uzbekistan's elites because they served as internationally intelligible forms for communicating the particularism of Uzbekistan's culture. As I have argued throughout this book, European standards were highly esteemed in Uzbekistan, sometimes to the point of being seen as culturally neutral universals. However, this generally pro-Western attitude was not universal among the elite, and Karimov himself expressed various reservations about the imposition of what he saw as specific (not universal) values coming from Europe. ("Not everything that is allowed in European countries can be accepted here.")[2] During the early 2000s, the regime allowed writers to publish criticisms of the West in general terms, especially in connection with the activities of international organizations advocating human rights and civil society. This shift reflected the way that the regime tried to deal with the conflict between international norms and the actual norms in Uzbekistan. On the one hand, the government's earlier strategy was to advocate a wide range of international norms in order to demonstrate that Uzbekistan was a "normal" nation and equal member of the world community. On the other hand, the government didn't like the bad publicity they were getting for violating international norms and desired to avoid the pressure that was being brought to bear on the government by the defenders of those norms. It was one thing for the government to talk about universal human values as part of Uzbek national culture, but it was quite another to be held accountable for upholding international norms.

On the eve of Independence Day 2005, President Karimov gave a speech at the monument to the victims of repression (Shahidlar Hotirasi) that reflected this tension between rejecting international meddling and seeking international acceptance:

In conditions of direct struggle against international terrorism, some powers try to slander our country. A person who considers himself a true son of this land does not have the right to be indifferent or unconcerned. . . . If we live with faith that we have never been worse than others and won't be in the future, if we are convinced that the Uzbek people never has been and never will be dependent, force will never break us. . . . All our compatriots should understand correctly what the goals of the lies and slander about Uzbekistan are and have a firm position with respect to events and independent judgment and views. The aim of the information war following the Andijon events is firstly to lower the prestige of Uzbekistan in the world.[3]

Karimov's rhetoric in 2005 reflected the elite's deep, and perhaps irresolvable, ambivalence between their internationalist, universalistic orientation inherited from the Soviet past and their desire to legitimate the regime on the basis of a unique and valuable national ethos.

By 2008, Karimov's rhetoric had mellowed slightly. In his Independence Day address he returned to the theme of integration with the world community, this time with a surprising touch of humility in recognizing that Uzbekistan has perhaps proved itself a less-than-reliable partner: "Another important factor [in realizing our aspirations is] the integration to the world community, further development of friendly and mutually beneficial relations with near and far neighbors so that [sic] to secure a worthy place and earn yet more trust on [sic] the international arena."[4] However, economic conditions in Uzbekistan continued to stagnate. Political repression and state surveillance continued to escalate to the point where many people had become afraid to talk openly to people outside their inner circle of friends and family. And yet the holiday spectacles continued, with the same form and nearly the same content as they had ten years before. The main difference was that after 2004, both holidays were held in Navoi Park, since Independence Plaza had been filled with barricades to prevent car bombers from reaching government buildings. The dancers and soldiers performing in the concerts were still young and beautiful; only President Karimov had aged.[5] Rustam Hamidov passed the lead directorship of the spectacle to his brother, Baxtiyor, who had an interesting exchange with a reporter on the eve of the Independence Day spectacle in 2008: "A question arises whether this concert will differ from other concerts that had been staged for the past 17 years. The director of this concert, Bakhtiyor Hamidov, said that even if one play is staged 100 times each time it will be a different play. He believes the main aim of the Independence Day concert is to show the high culture of the country."[6]

The reporter's question echoed what I heard from friends and read on Uzbekistan-related blogs more and more often in the second decade of Uzbekistan's independence: people are fed up with official culture and with holiday concerts' unimaginative repetition of stock cultural themes.

The ideology of national independence was seen as inelastic and stagnant, and not just in the realm of the "revival" of national culture. The official ideology promised that Karimov would find Uzbekistan's own unique path to economic development, while what was delivered by daily life was corruption, restriction of economic opportunities for the majority of the population, and impoverishment of the countryside. The ideology stressed the importance of Uzbekistan in the world community of nations, while anyone with access to the internet knew that their government was increasingly marginalized and stigmatized. The problem, though, was not just with policy, it was also with ideology.

Earlier in this book I discussed the idea that spectacle is a technique of power that can be employed in the absence of other totalitarian techniques and that has the benefit of being a positive technique of power (for example, festive) rather than a negative one (for example, repressive). However, for spectacle to have political power, it must be linked to ideology somehow. Spectacular states require a fairly coherent system of ideas to supply content to official culture if the mobilization of mass spectacles is to have the desired political effect. But Uzbekistan's nationalist rhetoric does not fit the definition of the kind of ideology that supports mobilization, that is, "a highly elaborated system of ideas that have the power to actually constrain regimes."[7] Thus, Juan Linz might diagnose the problem of the declining attractiveness of this rhetoric as being an underdevelopment of the ideology: "The lack of ideology . . . limits their capacity to mobilize people to create the psychological and emotional identification of the masses with the regime . . . [and] reduces the attractiveness of such regimes to . . . intellectuals, students, youth, and deeply religious persons."[8]

In this book I have shown that the majority of ethnic Uzbek intellectuals participated enthusiastically in the reproduction of this rhetoric, but that the population seemed to be only mildly interested in what they were offering, in part because the state did not offer incentives for the mobilization of ordinary citizens. Karimov's ideology of national independence was somewhat elaborated, but not constraining, and this kind of elaboration was due only to its piggybacking on the *forms* of the former totalitarian ideology: slogans, programmatic works by the leader, and the requirement of conformity to the official rhetoric in the public sphere. What is lacking is innovation in form, but what people seem to want most is more pluralism, more vibrancy of content. While the experience of participation in the elaboration of the ideology of national independence had a clear impact on the experience and identities of the political and cultural elites, it was not clear that the elite were actually enhancing a system of shared meaning in the broader society. Spectacles probably did not serve the purposes their creators envisioned for them. The assumption that the audience receives the meaning of the spectacle in the way it was intended is unwarranted, as numerous studies on the reception of culture show.[9]

It may very well be the case that, except as part of a larger symbolic universe, Uzbekistan's spectacles had little direct effect on those not directly participating in them. I waited with great anticipation to see if a "rediscovered" folk tale presented in the 1996 Navro'z concert would catch on in popular discourse, but it didn't. Apparently people in some rural areas in the 1990s were interested in learning about the history and celebration of Navro'z from Tashkent TV,[10] but the people in Tashkent who I talked to about these holiday spectacles often watched them only in order to see their favorite pop stars performing in the finale. Still, spectacle was effective at cluttering the public sphere with state-sanctioned discourse as well as at occupying the energies of the creative intelligentsia, many of whom devoted almost a third of their time to producing spectacles at the command of various levels and branches of government. Lisa Wedeen argues that in Syria, the state's monopoly on discourse about history both demonstrates and reinforces the state's power by allowing the regime to broadcast its "freedom to appropriate circumstances for its own uses and to drive competing alternative explanations underground. Second, the regime's ideology, which may not be 'hegemonic' according to the Gramscian understandings of the word, nevertheless organizes public conduct and thereby helps to construct what it means to be Syrian—to be Syrian means, in part, to be fluent in the rhetorical formulas."[11]

Despite the power of this monopoly on symbols, as Wedeen also points out, by saturating the public sphere with the state's domination over society, the state has almost no way to know what people are really thinking. The spectacular state's domination over communication only gives the illusion of control over society. In reality, when the state insulates itself from societal input, it looses touch with social reality and makes decisions based on biased or absent data. The spectacles end up being by and for the elite, rather than an opportunity for society to reflect on itself, or for the state to reflect on society. Contrary to what one might expect, this lack of attention to the public is actually an indication of state weakness. As Verdery pointed out, in every aspect of the socialist economy, the weakness of the state is reflected in its utter dependency on it subordinate units, each of which has an incentive to deceive and thwart the powers above.[12] State control over production is a liability because it means that there are no feedback mechanisms, no market to indicate demand, no independent gatekeepers to evaluate quality or take the pulse of the population. Instead, elites mistake their own opinions about the tastes and needs of the public for the actual tastes and needs of the public, leading to frequently comic and occasionally tragic mismatches between elite and popular perceptions of reality.

In the final analysis, it may be the case that, for many years, Islam Karimov was actually successful in his national ideology and in his campaigns to convince people that he was leading the country to become a great state in the future. In the 1990s, the cult of personality by proxy using Amir Timur had considerable resonance with the people and created loyalty to Karimov. However, after seventeen years of repeating the same slogans about independence and future prosperity, surely even the most enthusiastic of Uzbekistan's spectacle producers must be wondering: isn't it time for a change?

NOTES

Introduction: The Politics of Culture

1. Linguistic notes: in the text I will use the standard English transliteration for place names found in the English language press (Uzbekistan instead of O'zbekiston, Tashkent instead of Toshkent). For all other words and in quotations, I will use the current Uzbek spelling in the Latin alphabet (Navro'z, *viloyat*) and Library of Congress Russian transliteration (*kul'turnyi, sektsiia*). However, I transliterate the Cyrillic of materials printed in Uzbek Cyrillic. I will give the Russian or the Uzbek versions of terms as I encountered them in context.

2. I have posted short video documentaries of these concerts on YouTube. The Navro'z concert video can be found at www.youtube.com/watch?v=DyoMu _DYyiU; and the Independence Day video is at www.youtube.com/watch?v= 9Pbj2txia-s (last accessed 10 March 2009).

3. Kaldor, "Nationalism and Globalization."

4. The approaches to these issues are quite diverse. For example, in Mussolini's Italy, public spectacle was the fascists' preferred means of cultural communication. See Berezin, *Making the Fascist Self*; Falasca-Zamponi, *Fascist Spectacle*. In nineteenth century Bali, royal rituals were "arguments" about what Balinese society was supposed to make of itself. See Geertz, *Negara*. In Renaissance Europe, festivals were a central instrument of government. See Strong, *Art and Power*. According to Lane, in the Soviet Union, ritual was an important means of glossing over conflictive social relationships caused by the lack of political differentiation and the gap between ideology and reality. See Lane, *The Rites of Rulers*.

5. The production of culture perspective emphasizes the context of the creation, distribution, evaluation, education, and preservation of culture, as well as the agency of culture producers. See Becker, *Art Worlds*; Peterson, "Culture Studies through the Production Perspective."

6. For studies that tackle similar issues but with much greater attention to reception than what I have written about here, see Goldstein, *The Spectacular City*; Guss, *The Festive State*.
7. Wedeen, *Ambiguities of Domination*.
8. Allworth, *The Modern Uzbeks from the Fourteenth Century to the Present*; Clark, *The Soviet Novel*; Condee, *Soviet Hieroglyphics*; Dunham, *In Stalin's Time*; Golomstock, *Totalitarian Art in the Soviet Union, the Third Reich, Fascist Italy, and the People's Republic of China*.
9. This point is also made by Goldfarb, *The Persistence of Freedom* and Haraszti, *The Velvet Prison*.
10. Billig, *Banal Nationalism*.
11. For commentaries by other scholars on Uzbekistan's spectacles, see Doi, *Gender, Gesture, Nation*; Hegarty, "The Rehabilitation of Timur"; Liu, "The Perils of Nationalism in Independent Uzbekistan." On how national holidays are celebrated in other post-Soviet Central Asian states, see Eitzen, "Nawriz in Kazakstan"; Schuepp, "Kyrgyzstan Celebrates Spring Holiday." Kazakhstan in the last few years has had celebrations more closely resembling Uzbekistan's than before; that is, they are globalizing their holidays by moving toward the form of the Olympics-style spectacle (see chap. 2).
12. On state-society relations in Central Asia, see Jones Luong, *The Transformation of Central Asia*.
13. March, "The Use and Abuse of History," 371.
14. My definitions of regime types comes from Linz, *Totalitarian and Authoritarian Regimes*. On fascist spectacle, see Berezin, *Making the Fascist Self*; Falasca-Zamponi, *Fascist Spectacle*. On Soviet spectacle, see Chatterjee, *Celebrating Women*; Petrone, *Life Has Become More Joyous, Comrades*; von Geldern, *Bolshevik Festivals*.
15. Uzbekistan had the lowest possible scores on Freedom House political rights and civil liberties indexes. Web site of Freedom House, www.freedomhouse.org, last accessed 24 October 2008. It is arguable that after the brutal repression of the 2005 uprising in Andijon, the Karimov regime now relies on terror to control the population. In 2008 I saw evidence that state security services were recruiting citizens to report on each other for "suspicious" activities related to Islam or contact with foreigners.
16. On Karimov's strategy for consolidating power, see Ilkhamov, "The Limits of Centralization."
17. Hannan and Freeman, "The Population Ecology of Organizations," 929.
18. Powell and DiMaggio, *The New Institutionalism in Organizational Analysis*, 11. On cognitive models, see Meyer and Rowan, "Institutionalized Organizations." On schemas, see Sewell, "A Theory of Structure."
19. Powell and DiMaggio, *The New Institutionalism in Organizational Analysis*.

20. Moaddel, "Conditions for Ideological Production."
21. Spillman, "Culture, Social Structures, and Discursive Fields," 141.
22. Moaddel, "Conditions for Ideological Production," 675.
23. For a thorough analysis of Soviet Uzbek national identity and culture, see Critchlow, *Nationalism in Uzbekistan*. For a more wide-ranging account that is critical of Soviet Uzbek identity, see Allworth, *Central Asia*.
24. As early as 1996, some declared the consolidation of national identity in Uzbekistan as already a success. See Akbarzadeh, "Nation-Building in Uzbekistan," 24. Surveys and public opinion polls were rarely conducted in Uzbekistan, but the ones that were indicated very high levels of support for the government (even taking into account that the figures were inflated by fear) and high levels of patriotism. Polls conducted by the quasi-governmental polling organization, Ijtimoiy Fikr, were published in their eponymous journal (see www.ijtimoiy-fikr.org). However, more recent poll data indicate widespread and deep dissatisfaction with all levels of government. See Dadabaev, "Post-Soviet Realities of Society in Uzbekistan."
25. The state Constitution denotes the "people of Uzbekistan" as all citizens regardless of nationality, and there were no nationality or language restrictions imposed on citizenship, which was granted to everyone who was a permanent resident in 1992. On the distinction between ethnic and civic models of nationhood, see Brubaker, *Nationalism Reframed* and on different models in post-Soviet states, see Laitin, *Identity in Formation*.
26. Akbarzadeh, "Nation-Building in Uzbekistan"; Ilkhamov, "The Limits of Centralization"; Schoeberlein-Engel, "The Prospects for Uzbek National Identity."
27. However, not all the changes were in line with what would be predicted by theories about the power of global models of the nation-state, for example, Meyer et al., "World Society and the Nation-State." Uzbekistan's conformance to global norms is what Risse, Ropp, and Sikkink, *The Power of Human Rights*, would call "instrumental adaptation" rather than internalization.
28. This argument can also be found in Adams, "Modernity, Postcolonialism and Theatrical Form in Uzbekistan."
29. Akbarzadeh, "Nation-Building in Uzbekistan"; March, "The Use and Abuse of History"; Smith et al., *Nation-Building in the Post-Soviet Borderlands*.
30. Laitin, *Identity in Formation*, argues that this Soviet identity was transforming during the 1990s into an identity throughout Russia's "near abroad."
31. Many examples can be found in the official press and in the writings of President Karimov, for example, Karimov, *Uzbekistan*, 6; Karimov, *Uzbekistan on the Threshold of the Twenty-First Century*. For an analysis of elite perceptions of national identity in Kazakhstan, Kyrgyzstan, and Uzbekistan, see Abazov, *Foreign Policy Formation in Kazakhstan, Kyrgyzstan and Uzbekistan*, 18–23.
32. Regev makes a similar argument about rock and roll in " 'Rockization'."

33. Wilk, "The Local and the Global in the Political Economy of Beauty."

34. Kennedy and Suny, "Introduction."

35. Verdery, *What Was Socialism, and What Comes Next?*, 304. For a different, but quite sophisticated take on intellectuals, class, and power in the post-Soviet periphery, see Derluguian, *Bourdieu's Secret Admirer in the Caucasus*.

36. Tishkov, *Ethnicity, Nationalism and Conflict in and after the Soviet Union*, xiv.

37. Montserrat Guibernau, "Anthony D. Smith on Nations and National Identity," 140.

38. Authors who discuss this process in Uzbekistan are Akbarzadeh, "Nation-Building in Uzbekistan"; Ilkhamov, "The Limits of Centralization"; Schoeberlein-Engel, "The Prospects for Uzbek National Identity."

39. von Geldern, *Bolshevik Festivals*; Hunt, *Politics, Culture, and Class in the French Revolution*; Ozouf, *Festivals and the French Revolution*.

40. For other examples of this argument about Soviet cultural legacies, see Rausing, *History, Memory, and Identity in Post-Soviet Estonia*; Humphrey, *Marx Went Away—but Karl Stayed Behind*.

41. On the discourse of normality in postsocialist countries, see Kennedy, *Envisioning Eastern Europe*; Eglitis, *Imagining the Nation*; Rausing, *History, Memory, and Identity in Post-Soviet Estonia*.

42. Cohn, "Representing Authority in Victorian England," 208–9. Partha Chatterjee makes a similar point that there is "an inherent contradictoriness in nationalist thinking, because it reasons within a framework of knowledge whose representational structure corresponds to the very structure of power nationalist thought seeks to repudiate." Chatterjee, *Nationalist Thought and the Colonial World*, 38.

43. Anderson, *Imagined Communities*.

44. On debates about the Soviet Union as an empire, see Adams, "Modernity, Postcolonialism, and Theatrical Form in Uzbekistan"; Beissinger, "The Persisting Ambiguity of Empire"; Hirsch, "Toward an Empire of Nations"; Khalid, *The Politics of Muslim Cultural Reform*; Khalid, "Russian History and the Debate over Orientalism"; Knight, "On Russian Orientalism"; Martin, "An Affirmative Action Empire"; Northrop, *Veiled Empire*; Northrop, "Nationalizing Backwardness"; Slezkine, "Imperialism as the Highest Stage of Socialism"; and Suny and Martin, *A State of Nations*.

45. Brubaker, "Nationhood and the National Question in the Soviet Union and Post-Soviet Eurasia." On the unintended consequences of Soviet nationalities policy, see also Hirsch, "Toward an Empire of Nations"; Martin, *Affirmative Action Empire*; Slezkine, "The USSR as a Communal Apartment, or How a Socialist State Promoted Ethnic Particularism"; Suny, *Revenge of the Past*; Zaslavsky, "The Evolution of Separatism in Soviet Society under Gorbachev."

46. Handler and Linnekin, "Tradition, Genuine or Spurious." In the case of

Uzbekistan, see Abramson, "Traditionalizing Modernities and Modernizing Traditions."

47. Hobsbawm and Ranger, *The Invention of Tradition.*

48. Smith, *The Antiquity of Nations.*

49. Ibid.

50. For Foucault's writings on power, see *Essential Works of Foucault,* and *Power/ Knowledge.* Brubaker, *Nationalism Reframed,* puts forth a similar idea of nationalism as a practice.

51. Monographs based on extensive field research in Central Asia include Collins, *The Logic of Clan Politics in Central Asia;* Dave, *Kazakhstan;* Doi, *Gender, Gesture, Nation;* Jones Luong, *Institutional Change and Political Continuity in Post-Soviet Central Asia;* Levin, *The Hundred Thousand Fools of God;* Schatz, *Modern Clan Politics.*

52. Examples of culturalist explanations for Central Asian political and social institutions can be found in Allworth, *Central Asia;* Gleason, *The Central Asian States.*

53. See Odgaard and Simonsen, "The New Kazak Elite," 31, for an example of the modern, European nature of post-Soviet institutions in Kazakhstan.

54. On postsocialist space as postcolonial space, see Moore, "Is the Post in Postcolonial the Post in Post-Soviet?"; Cole and Kandiyoti, "Nationalism and the Colonial Legacy in the Middle East and Central Asia"; Adams, "Modernity, Postcolonialism, and Theatrical Form in Uzbekistan." On normalcy, see Kennedy, "The Liabilities of Liberalism and Nationalism after Communism"; Eglitis, *Imagining the Nation;* Rausing, *History, Memory, and Identity.* On the hybridity of national identity, see Wanner, *Burden of Dreams;* Humphrey, *Marx Went Away—but Karl Stayed Behind;* Verdery, *National Ideology under Socialism.* On socialist habitus and the reinvention of national cultures, see Verdery, *What Was Socialism,* chap. 4; Wanner, *Burden of Dreams;* Adams, "Invention, Institutionalization, and Renewal in Uzbekistan's National Culture"; Derluguian, *Bourdieu's Secret Admirer.*

55. Bourdieu, *Distinction;* Bourdieu, "The Forms of Capital"; Bourdieu and Johnson, *The Field of Cultural Production.*

56. Verdery, *National Ideology,* 80. For another, equally sophisticated take on these issues, see Derluguian, *Bourdieu's Secret Admirer.*

57. Verdery, *National Ideology,* 86.

58. For a summary of these events and variations on this argument, see Smith et al., *Nation-Building;* Gleason, *Central Asian States;* Khalid, *Islam after Communism.*

59. Williams, *The Sociology of Culture.*

60. Adams, "The Mascot Researcher"; Adams, "Strategies for Measuring Identity in Ethnographic Research."

61. Smith, *The Everyday World as Problematic*, 72.
62. Bhavnani, "Tracing the Contours"; Haraway, *Simians, Cyborgs, and Women*.
63. Wolf, *A Thrice-Told Tale*, 135.

Chapter One: National Identity

1. As Alexei Yurchak points out, derogatory references to the Brezhnev period as an "era of stagnation" come from outsiders or are retrospective; for many former Soviet citizens, the era was something of a golden age. Yurchak, *Everything Was Forever, until It Was No More*, chap. 1.
2. Throughout the book, the names of my friends and acquaintances have been changed to protect their anonymity, and many of my interviewees requested that I not use their real names. Rather than using titles such as Ms. and Mr. when respectfully addressing someone, Uzbeks use first names with the honorific *aka* (for men older than oneself, literally "older brother") or *opa* (for women older than oneself, literally "older sister"). I usually addressed non-Central Asian interlocutors by their first names without patronymics, although using them would have been more polite, but I had too much difficulty mastering the patronymics, and my informality seemed acceptable to most of the people with whom I interacted. Some readers may find it interesting to note that this difference in nomenclature consequently marks the ethnicity of the people I quote in the text.
3. Olick, *States of Memory*, explores similar limitations on the politics of national memory in different cases. See also Gillis, *Commemorations*.
4. Boyarin, *Remapping Memory*; Fentress and Wickham, *Social Memory*; Olick, *States of Memory*; Schudson, "Dynamics of Distortion in Collective Memory"; Schwartz, "The Social Context of Commemoration"; Schwartz, "Deconstructing and Reconstructing the Past"; Schwartz, "Memory as a Cultural System."
5. Halbwachs, *On Collective Memory*, 53.
6. On "local" critiques of "outsider" stories of the invention of tradition, see Briggs, "The Politics of Discursive Authority in Research on 'The Invention of Tradition'," who argues that this particular subject is one where the researcher's analysis is likely to clash with her informants precisely because she is challenging the discursive authority (based on lived experience and local accreditation) of her informants with her own discursive authority (based on her position as a scholar accredited by an outside, usually Western, institution).
7. See, for example, Rausing, *History, Memory, and Identity in Post-Soviet Estonia*.
8. On distortion in social memory, see Schudson, "Dynamics of Distortion," and on "remembering and forgetting," see Anderson, *Imagined Communities*.
9. Schudson, "Dynamics of Distortion in Collective Memory."
10. Brown, "Would the Real Nationalists Please Step Forward."

11. Wagner-Pacifici and Schwartz, "The Vietnam Veterans Memorial."

12. For an interesting study of colonial Tashkent, see Sahadeo, *Russian Colonial Society in Tashkent*.

13. Savage, "Trauma, Healing, and the Therapeutic Monument." Other Central Asian governments preserved memorials to the Second World War, even though they disposed of statues of Soviet leaders from the 1920s. See, for example, Najibullah, "Tajikistan."

14. See Hegarty, "The Rehabilitation of Timur"; March, "The Use and Abuse of History."

15. Roy, *New Central Asia*, 166.

16. For a brief article on the museum, see Adams, "Tashkent Museum Allows for Public Discussion of Recent Past."

17. Lyons, "Where Is the Gold of Amir Said Alimkhan."

18. Roy, *New Central Asia*, chap. 11.

19. For a concise summary of the history of the region, see Soucek, *A History of Inner Asia*. On the making of the Uzbek nation, see Baldauf, "Some Thoughts on the Making of the Uzbek Nation"; Ilkhamov, "The Limits of Centralization"; Schoeberlein-Engel, "Identity in Central Asia" and "The Prospects for Uzbek National Identity."

20. Hirsch, "Toward an Empire of Nations"; Schoeberlein-Engel, "Identity in Central Asia," chaps. 2 and 4. However, Schoeberlein-Engel and other observers have noted that Tajik identity in Samarkand and Bukhara is flexible and that, in practice, the Tajik speakers in these cities also identify with Uzbek as a label. Schoeberlein-Engel, "The Prospects for Uzbek National Identity."

21. Paraphrase of interview with members of Besh Karsak Folk Ensemble, Urgut, October 1996.

22. Smith, *National Identity*, 117.

23. On the battle of Tajik and Uzbek historiography, see Torbakov, "Tajik-Uzbek Relations."

24. For more on Tajikistan's post-Soviet reconstruction of national identity, see Attar, "Nawruz in Tajikistan: Ritual or Politics"; Harris, *Muslim Youth*; Najibullah, "Tajikistan"; Laruelle, "The Return of the Aryan Myth."

25. Hirsch, "The Soviet Union as a Work-in-Progress."

26. Anderson, *Imagined Communities*. On the Soviet case, see Slezkine, *From Savages to Citizens*.

27. Anderson, *Imagined Communities*, 184–85.

28. For a detailed analysis of this process, see Ilkhamov, "Limits of Centralization"; Schoeberlein-Engel, "Identity in Central Asia." For an overview, see Hirsch, "The Soviet Union."

29. Baldauf, "Some Thoughts," 86.

30. Paraphrase of interview with theater director, Tashkent, April 1996.

31. Smith, *The Antiquity of Nations*, chap. 8.

32. Ibid., 221–23.

33. Anderson, *Imagined Communities*, 181–82.

34. See Hegarty, "Rehabilitation of Timur"; Ilkhamov, "Limits of Centralization"; Manz, "Tamerlane's Career and Its Uses."

35. Talk of the Shaibanids was beginning to enter the public sphere in 2002, whereas six years earlier, in a meeting of the President's Council with historians, the policy makers had decided that the Uzbek people just "weren't ready" to learn about the Shaibanids. Amin Tarzi and Vernon Schubel, separately in personal communication.

36. Manz, "Tamerlane's Career and its Uses," 22.

37. Subtelny, "The Timurid Legacy," 15.

38. Ilkhamov, "Limits of Centralization," 320.

39. For more analysis of this phenomenon, see Manz, "Tamerlane's Career and Its Uses" and March, "Use and Abuse of History."

40. Uzbekistan Central State Archive (TSGAUZ), f. 2487 r. 3 y. 1974.

41. Kara, "Reclaiming National Literary Heritage"; Peterson, "History in the Remaking."

42. For a summary of these events and their consequences, see Forced Migration Project, "Meskhetian Turks: Solutions and Human Security."

43. Codagnone, "The New Migration in Russia in the 1990s"; Buckley, "Exodus?"

44. The URL for the website of Birlik is www.birlik.net and of Erk is www.uzbekistanerk.org.

45. Melvin, *Uzbekistan*, 35.

46. Gregory, *The Central Asian States*, 118.

47. For a good summary, see Collins, *Clan Politics and Regime Transition in Central Asia*, 146–50.

48. Ibid., 164.

49. Gleason, *Central Asian States*, 71.

50. Karimov, *Building the Future*, 27.

51. Ibid., 27–30.

52. The best study of Karimov's rise to power and the pacts that kept him there can be found in Collins, *Clan Politics and Regime Transition in Central Asia*. For a similar perspective, see Ilkhamov, "The Limits of Centralization." Ilkhamov argues that these groups are not clans but function more along the lines of regional patronage networks. See also Roy, *The New Central Asia*.

53. Karimov, *Building the Future*.

54. Collins, *Clan Politics and Regime Transition in Central Asia*, 261.

55. Bell, *Ritual Theory, Ritual Practice*; Kertzer, *Ritual, Politics and Power*; Ozouf, *Festivals and the French Revolution*; Spillman, *Nation and Commemoration*.

56. Smith, *Mythmaking in the New Russia.*

57. Ibid., 85.

58. Ibid., 84.

59. Ibid., 97.

60. Interview, theater director, Tashkent, April 1996. Note: unless otherwise noted, quotes are transcribed from tape.

61. During the early 1980s investigators from Moscow uncovered what became known as "the cotton affair," which implicated scores of powerful men, from Brezhnev's son-in-law to regional agriculture ministers throughout Central Asia, in an embezzlement and bribery scheme that involved the falsification of cotton production figures. Most of the blame fell on ethnic Uzbeks, and eventually the head of the CPUZ, Sharof Rashidov, was brought down by the scandal, only to fall ill and die. In contemporary Uzbek social memory, this was a defining moment in the history of Soviet exploitation of Uzbeks, and Rashidov is remembered as a hero and a martyr who fought for the interests of the Uzbek people.

62. Kholmuhamedov, "Sen navro'zni soghinmadingmi."

63. Interview, writer, Tashkent, April 1996. The anecdote was this: once there was a mosque where the imam was short and the muezzin was tall. People would come into the mosque and bow to the tall man first, even though his rank was lower, because he stood out, he was exceptional. This annoyed the short man so much that he had the door to the mosque reconstructed so that it was just his size and "exceptional" people couldn't get in.

64. Interview, scholar, Tashkent March 1996. Unless otherwise noted, all the material in this section about Navbahor comes from Farhod aka in interviews that took place in March 1996 and July 1996.

65. Thanks to Jennifer Hunter for pointing out this analogy.

66. Dominguez, *People as Subject, People as Object,* 151–52. Dominguez doesn't use this term, but the phenomenon she discusses is the same. In Israel, the non-Ashkenazis she studied tended to homogenize their experience through the story that everyone in the group came from a rural setting, they were all in ecstasy upon arriving in Israel, and they all bucked the Ashkenazi system in little mischievous ways (148).

67. Niranjana, Sudhir, and Dhareshwar, *Interrogating Modernity,* 6.

68. Uzbekistan Central State Archive (TSGAUZ), f. 2487 o. 3 d. 37871. 10–40.

69. The Soviet economy was organized around "five year plans" that laid out Moscow's economic goals for all the Union's regions and industries.

70. Uzbekistan Central State Archive (TSGAUZ), f. 2487 o. 3 d. 37871. 31.

71. These accounts were collected in a scrapbook on a circus troupe that I found in the Uzbekistan Ministry of Culture's Department of Popular Creativity. When

I viewed these documents in 1996, they were not formally catalogued and were kept on the shelves of the office.

72. Haraszti, *The Velvet Prison*.

73. *O'zbekiston respublikasi entsiklopediya*, 240–41; Usmon Qoraboev, "Navro'zi olam," 6.

74. Karimov, *Uzbekistan*, 56–57, 64.

75. Allworth, *Central Asia*; Critchlow, *Nationalism in Uzbekistan*; Fierman, *Language Planning and National Development*; Rywkin, *Moscow's Muslim Challenge*.

76. For example, Kirimli, "Uzbekistan in the New World Order."

77. Interview, youth union worker, Tashkent, April 1996.

78. On the political and economic situation in Uzbekistan, see Gleason, *The Central Asian States*; Jones Luong, *Institutional Change and Political Continuity in Post-Soviet Central Asia*. See Ilkhamov, "The Limits of Centralization," on Karimov's attempts to manipulate parliament through the creation of new political parties and the way that regional actors attempted to use these new parties to retain control of parliament.

79. Interview, theater director, Tashkent, April 1996.

80. Interview, Ministry of Culture official, Tashkent, September 1996.

81. For a good overview of the dynamics of national and Muslim identities in Uzbekistan, see Khalid, *Islam after Communism*.

82. These kinds of debates about what kind of covering for women are "nationally" appropriate take place in Turkey, as well. See the discussion in Navaro-Yashin, *Faces of the State*, 67–73.

83. David Lowenthal, "Identity, Heritage, and History," 45.

84. Paraphrase of interview with theater director, Tashkent, September 2002.

Chapter Two: Cultural Form

1. In this paragraph and in other places where I refer to public knowledge about the holiday production staff, all people are referred to by their real names. In references to these individuals in interviews and field notes, their names are changed to protect their anonymity.

2. Handler and Linnekin, "Tradition, Genuine or Spurious," 280.

3. I analyzed eleven holiday concerts in all. I saw the 1996 spectacles in person and videotaped them from television. I also have videotapes of both spectacles from 1995 and 1997, Navro'z from 1991–1993 and 1998, and Independence Day from 1993. Additionally, I used newspaper articles and Ministry of Culture documents as sources of information to triangulate with what I saw on the tapes. When I speak of the characteristics of these holiday spectacles, it should be kept in mind that I am basing my analysis on eleven spectacles and

in my comments drawing on impressions gleaned from a few spectacles I was able to see between 1998 and 2002.

4. This costume typically consists of a solid-color long dress with a wide, flowing skirt; sleeves that are narrow at the shoulder and wide at the cuff; a tailored bodice covered by an embroidered velvet vest in a complementary color; and a flowing head scarf or colorful skullcap. The typical costume for women in folk ensembles is the shapeless dress made of multi-colored *atlas* (*ikat*) silk that is referred to in everyday life as "Uzbek national dress."

5. The term "business" in a theatrical context refers to a kind of nonverbal action that occurs on stage. "Business" often takes place away from the center of attention and consists of little actions that contribute to the verisimilitude of the scene, such as children playing in the background of the party scene of *The Nutcracker*.

6. Giddens, *The Consequences of Modernity*.

7. Robertson, *Globalization*.

8. Elsewhere I analyze this process specifically in the realm of theater. See Adams, "Modernity, Postcolonialism and Theatrical Form in Uzbekistan."

9. Guss, *The Festive State*, 14.

10. Gray, "Uzbekistan."

11. The concept of "cultural field" draws on Bourdieu and Randal, *The Field of Cultural Production*. On global fields of culture, see Adams, "Globalization, Universalism and Cultural Form"; Regev, " 'Rockization'."

12. Paraphrase of interview with a choreographer, Tashkent, October 1996.

13. Interview, theater critic, Tashkent, May 1998.

14. Interview, choreographer, Tashkent, June 1996.

15. Robertson, "Social Theory, Cultural Relativity and the Problem of Globality."

16. Interview, choreographer, Tashkent, June 1996.

17. Interview, choreographer, Tashkent, June 1996.

18. Hobsbawm and Ranger, *The Invention of Tradition*.

19. Doi, *Gender, Gesture, Nation*, 44–48.

20. Interview, choreographer, Tashkent, June 1996.

21. Interview, theater director, Tashkent, April 1996.

22. Appadurai, *Modernity at Large*, 31.

23. Richard R. Wilk, " 'Real Belizean Food,' " 253. See also Wilk, "The Local and the Global in the Political Economy of Beauty."

24. Roche, *Mega-Events and Modernity*, 7.

25. Regev, "To Have a Culture of Our Own."

26. Interview, composer, Tashkent, September 1996.

27. Boli and Lechner, *World Culture*; Meyer et al., "World Society and the Nation-State."

28. Interview, theater director, Tashkent, May 1996.

29. Roche, *Mega-Events and Modernity*, 1.

30. Ibid., 6.

31. *EurasiaNet*, Weekly News Brief on Turkmenistan, "Turkmen Independence Holiday Marked with Military Parade," www.eurasianet.org.

32. A. Baranov and O. Osipov, "Po puti revoliutsionnykh preobrazovannii: voennyi parad i demonstratsiia trudiashchikhsia v Tashkente," *Pravda Vostoka*, 8 November 1986, 1, 3.

33. *Pravda Vostoka*, 2 May 1990, 1.

34. Konovich, *Teatralizovannye prazdniki i obriady v SSSR*, 110–11.

35. See Adams, "Cultural Elites in Uzbekistan" on the invocation of Karimov's will to produce legitimacy.

36. Sharoev, *Rezhissuraa estrady i massovykh predstavleniy*; Silin, *Ploshchadi—nashi palitry*; Silin, *Spetsifika raboty rezhissera pri postanovka massovykh teatral'nykh predstavleniy pod otkrytym nebom i na netraditsionnykh stsenicheskikh ploshchadakh (uchebnoe posobie—chast' ii)*.

37. Silin, *Ploshchadi—nashi palitry*, 20.

38. Ibid., 97.

39. Ibid., 14.

40. Interview, theater director, Tashkent, April 1996.

41. Interview, theater director, Tashkent, May 1996.

42. Clifford Geertz, "Centers, Kings, and Charisma," 152–53.

43. Berezin, *Making the Fascist Self*.

44. Lane, *The Rites of Rulers*.

45. Yurchak, "Soviet Hegemony of Form," 480–510.

46. Rabinow, *The Foucault Reader*, 199.

47. Ritzer, *Enchanting a Disenchanted World*.

48. Debord, *The Society of the Spectacle*, 41–42.

49. Ibid.

50. Durkheim, *The Elementary Forms of the Religious Life*, 236–45.

51. Wedeen makes a similar argument in relation to cults of the leader in *Ambiguities of Domination*, 18.

Chapter Three: Cultural Content

1. For comparative studies that provide an overview of these issues in post-Soviet space, see Kolstø, *Nation-Building and Ethnic Integration in Post-Soviet Societies*; Laitin, *Identity in Formation*; Kolstø, *Political Construction Sites*; Kolstø and Edemsky, *Russians in the Former Soviet Republics*.

2. See Lubin et al., *Calming the Ferghana Valley*. Around this same time, a number of books were published in the West that reflected a sense of alarm over the

potential for violent ethnic and religious conflict in Central Asia. In Rashid, *Jihad*, Central Asia is portrayed as the breeding ground for Taliban-style political Islam, but those familiar with the region found his warnings about religious extremism more than a bit shrill. Central Asia was characterized as rapidly spiraling into crisis in Rumer, *Central Asia*.

3. For examples, see Dawisha and Parrot, *Conflict, Cleavage, and Change in Central Asia and the Caucasus*, and for a critique of these assumptions, see Ferranda and Nolle, "Ethnic Social Distance in Kyrgyzstan"; Megoran, "On Researching 'Ethnic Conflict'"; Schoeberlein-Engel, "The Prospects for Uzbek National Identity."

4. Megoran, "Preventing Conflict by Building Civil Society."

5. Olcott, "National Consolidation."

6. See the argument in Smith et al., *Nation-Building in the Post-Soviet Borderlands*.

7. Brubaker, *Nationalism Reframed*, 5.

8. Ibid., 105.

9. Dave, "A Shrinking Reach of the State?" 134.

10. Ibid. See also Cummings, *Kazakhstan*.

11. Fumagalli, "Framing Ethnic Minority Mobilization in Central Asia."

12. For example, in Ferranda and Nolle, "Ethnic Social Distance," the social distance that Kyrgyz perceive between themselves and national minorities in Uzbekistan (Uzbeks and Russians) is highest among the youngest and oldest generations. The proportion of respondents who answered that they wouldn't accept Uzbeks or Russians as members of their family, as friends, or as neighbors was the lowest among those forty to sixty-four years of age. Ferranda and Nolle, "Ethnic Social Distance," 203.

13. Beissinger, "The Persisting Ambiguity of Empire"; Hirsch, "Toward an Empire of Nations"; Khalid, *The Politics of Muslim Cultural Reform*; Khalid, "Russian History and the Debate over Orientalism"; Knight, "Grigorev in Orenburg"; Knight, "On Russian Orientalism"; Martin, *Affirmative Action Empire*; Martin, "An Affirmative Action Empire"; Michaels, "Medical Propaganda and Cultural Revolution in Soviet Kazakhstan"; Northrop, *Veiled Empire*; Northrop, "Nationalizing Backwardness"; Slezkine, "Imperialism as the Highest Stage of Socialism"; Suny, "The Empire Strikes Out"; Suny and Martin, *A State of Nations*.

14. Hirsch, "Toward an Empire"; Northrop, *Veiled Empire*; Slezkine, "Imperialism."

15. David Chioni Moore has succinctly described the fruitful exchange that could take place between postcolonial and post-Soviet studies and cogently critiqued the neglect of the Soviet case by theorists of colonialism and postcolonialism: Moore, "Is the Post in Postcolonial the Post in Post-Soviet?" See also Adams, "Modernity, Postcolonialism and Theatrical Form in Uzbekistan."

16. This approach to postcolonialism comes from Prakash, "Introduction." Within

the literature on the Soviet Union, Suny, Slezkine, and Northrop also apply this approach. See Northrop, *Veiled Empire*; Slezkine, *From Savages to Citizens*; Slezkine, "Imperialism"; Suny, "Empire Strikes Out."

17. On the hybrid perspective, see Bhabha, "The Postcolonial and the Postmodern," and for a scathing critique of this perspective's divorce from the grassroots, see Ahmad, *In Theory*.

18. Adams, "Invention, Institutionalization, and Renewal in Uzbekistan's National Culture"; Brubaker, "Nationhood and the National Question in the Soviet Union and Post-Soviet Eurasia"; Slezkine, "The USSR as a Communal Apartment, or How a Socialist State Promoted Ethnic Particularism"; Suny, *Revenge of the Past*. On another socialist case, see Verdery, *What Was Socialism and What Comes Next?*, chap. 4.

19. Kennedy, *Envisioning Eastern Europe*. On using the Communist past to critique contemporary capitalist culture, see Szemere, *Up from the Underground*.

20. Hirsch argues that the early Soviet regime was attempting to implement a new nonimperialistic model of colonialism: Hirsch, "Toward an Empire." On Soviet hierarchies of culture in Uzbekistan, see Adams, "What Is Culture?"

21. Slezkine, *From Savages to Citizens*.

22. Schoeberlein-Engel, "Identity in Central Asia," 248–52.

23. Rasulev and Atamuradov, *Internationalizatsiia natsional'nykh kultur*, 13.

24. Ergeshev, *Istoriko-sotsiologicheskoe issledovanie kultury Uzbekistana*, 25.

25. Ibid.; Slezkine, *From Savages to Citizens*, 313–19.

26. This quote is from a document I found in the Uzbekistan Ministry of Culture's Department of Popular Creativity. When I viewed these documents in 1996, they were in loose, uncataloged folders kept on the shelves of the office. Since that time they may have been formally archived. The documents pertained to reviews of the activities of regional theaters during the late 1980s.

27. Djumaev, "Power Structures, Culture Policy, and Traditional Music in Soviet Central Asia." Theodore Levin, *The Hundred Thousand Fools of God*.

28. Konovich, *Teatralizovannye prazdniki i obriady v SSSR*, 111.

29. Interview, composer, Tashkent, May 1996. See also Doi, *Gender, Gesture, Nation*.

30. Interview, choreographer, Tashkent, August 1996.

31. Djumaev, "Power Structures, Culture Policy, and Traditional Music in Soviet Central Asia," 43.

32. I discuss the issues in this section in greater depth in Adams, "Modernity, Postcolonialism, and Theatrical Form in Uzbekistan."

33. Interview, identity confidential, Tashkent, April 1996.

34. Interview, Ministry of Higher Education official, Tashkent, May 1996.

35. Interview, composer, Tashkent, September 1996. For an interesting comparison, see Fernandes's study of the relationship between rap musicians in the

state in Cuba, *Cuba Represent!* Rap as a genre with its roots in social criticism flourished, in part with the support of the Cuban state, which retained its own critical Marxist stance. The government of Uzbekistan's official ideology provided little space for Uzbek rap artists to generate socially meaningful critique, raising the question of whether the genre as it is performed in Uzbekistan can even be called rap. The artists themselves might identify more with hip-hop as a musical genre.

36. Interview, Ministry of Higher Education official, Tashkent, May 1996. On the similar attempts of the Cuban state to work with popular culture, see Fernandes, *Cuba Represent!*

37. Interview, theater director, Tashkent, May 1996.

38. Paraphrase of interview with choreographer, Tashkent, October 1996.

39. Uncatalogued documents I saw at the Ministry of Cultural Affairs Department of Popular Creativity from this time period list "the renewal of Uzbek national culture" as one of the main tasks they set for themselves. This is also the period during which the holiday Navro'z was revived.

40. Paraphrase of interview with choreographer, Tashkent, October 1996.

41. Paraphrase of interview with choreographer, Tashkent, August 1996.

42. For a similar analysis of the way publicity effects change in local versions of local practices in an entirely different context, see Guss, *The Festive State,* chap. 5.

43. Interview, composer, Tashkent, May 1996.

44. On these early Soviet transformations in Central Asian culture production, see Bacon, *Central Asia under Russian Rule.*

45. Paraphrase of interview with Ministry of Culture Official, Tashkent, October 1996.

46. Paraphrase of interview with Ministry of Culture Official, Tashkent, October 1996.

47. Paraphrase of interview with Institute of Culture instructor, Tashkent, May 1996.

48. Paraphrase of interview with music critic, Tashkent, May 1998.

49. Paraphrase of interview with theater director, Tashkent, April 1996.

50. Paraphrase of interview with theater director, Tashkent, May 1998.

51. Paraphrase of interview with theater director, Tashkent, July 1996.

52. Interview, theater director, Tashkent, April 1996.

53. Most of these polls were conducted by governmental and quasi-governmental organizations, but even these polls showed declining satisfaction with economic reforms. See, for example, "Monitoring obshchestvennogo mneniia," *Ijtimoiy fikr-inson huquqlari,* no. 3 (2003), 87; "Uzbekistan: Public Opinion 2000," *Ijtimoiy fikr-inson huquqlari,* no. 2 (2001), 113–16. However, in a survey in 2003, Timur Dadabaev showed a rather dramatic lack of support for the

Karimov regime and for all levels of government. Although 57.7 percent of those surveyed said they "trust" or "partly trust" the central government, 79.3 percent partially or completely distrusted the government in the area of economic policy. Dadabaev, "Post-Soviet Realities of Society in Uzbekistan."

54. Interview, identity confidential, Tashkent, April 1996.

55. Some of these tapes were made by friends, and others were made for me by the state television station. The station was unable to find their copies of the 1994 spectacles, or of Independence Day before 1993. The Navro'z spectacles from 1991–1993 and in 1997 were not taped from start to finish and were severely edited for broadcast, therefore I could not code them systematically. The impression I got from the tapes was that every year the Navro'z spectacle got more extravagant, professional, and elitist.

56. Paraphrase of interview, identity confidential, Tashkent, April 1996.

57. Interview, choreographer, Tashkent, June 1996.

58. Cohn, "Representing Authority in Victorian England"; Chatterjee, *Nationalist Thought and the Colonial World*; Comaroff and Comaroff, *Of Revelation and Revolution*.

59. I discuss this conceptualization in greater detail in Adams, "Modernity, Postcolonialism, and Theatrical Form in Uzbekistan."

60. On a side note, the organizers used this song because it was readily available from the state radio company's archive, despite their misgivings that a) for everyone in the older generation, it was associated with fascist Germany, and b) it was not very "silk road." Similarly, other songs were far from the director's ideal: the Chinese music was folk but not festive, the Indian was festive but pop—the block lacked a certain aesthetic coherence.

61. Uncatalogued documents at the Ministry of Culture showed that in the 1994 Independence Day spectacle the military block did focus on the role of Uzbeks in the Soviet Army's "victory over Fascism."

62. The historic Silk Road ran from China to Eastern Europe and the Mediterranean via three different routes, one of which passed through the territory of today's Uzbekistan. However, the Silk Road was in decline starting in the ninth century, well before the rise of the Uzbek tribes. The inhabitants of Uzbekistan's Silk Road cities, Samarkand and Bukhara, were mostly Turkic, Persian, and Arab.

63. This observation is based on my viewing of various photographs at the Uzbekistan State Photo and Film Archive, but unfortunately, I did not note the particular photographs.

64. *Narodnoe Slovo*, 24 March 1994, 1.

65. Due to changes in emigration laws and successful recruiting efforts by Israeli and American Jews, the Jewish population of Uzbekistan has indeed declined dramatically in the last ten years. About 80 percent of the thousand-year-old

community of Bukharan Jews has left Bukhara, according to a member of that community who stayed. For an overview and analysis, see Cooper, "The Jews of Uzbekistan."

66. Usmon Qoraboev, *O'zbekiston bayramlari*, 6.
67. Interview, choreographer, Tashkent, June 1996.
68. Yo'ldash Muqim o'ghli Otash, *Navro'z naqli*. Otash was Muqimov's pen name.
69. Interview, theater director, Tashkent, April 1996.
70. Paraphrase of interview with theater director, Tashkent, April 1996.
71. On the uses of Amir Timur by the Karimov regime, see Hegarty, "The Rehabilitation of Timur"; Manz, "Tamerlane's Career and Its Uses."
72. Paraphrase of interview with Institute of Culture instructor, Tashkent, May 1996.
73. On the contemporary importance of Manas, see Wasilewska, "The Past and the Present."

Chapter Four: Culture Production

1. The term "studying up" originally comes from Nader, "Up the Anthropologist." On the production of information as a result of the relationship between researchers and their interlocutors, there is a substantial literature which I discuss in Adams, "The Mascot Researcher."
2. Paraphrase of interview with Ministry of Culture employee, Tashkent, September 1996.
3. Haraszti, *The Velvet Prison*, 88.
4. Abdurahimov, "Kul'tura kak ob"ekt investirovaniia," 17.
5. Paraphrase of interview with music critic, Tashkent, May 1998.
6. Paraphrase of interview with theater critic, Tashkent, May 1998.
7. Paraphrase of interview with theater critic, Tashkent, September 2002.
8. Migdal, "The State in Society," 16.
9. Goldfarb, *The Persistence of Freedom*.
10. Paraphrase of interview with theater critic, Tashkent, May 1998.
11. Gray, "Uzbekistan."
12. For an analysis of the implications of elite guardianship of national patrimony, see García Canclini, *Hybrid Cultures*, chap. 4.
13. Abdurahimov, "Kul'tura kak ob"ekt investirovaniia."
14. Ibid., 19–20.
15. Ibid., 21.
16. Interview, theater director, Tashkent, May 1996.
17. Interview, theater director, Tashkent, May 1996.
18. Interview, choreographer, Tashkent, June 1996.

19. Socialist competition, unlike its capitalist counterparts, was seen as a way of contributing to economic and social progress by increasing productivity at the workplace or motivating participation in extracurricular activities. Awards and prizes were given in socialist competitions, but there were political rewards as well.

20. Silin, *Ploshchadi—nashi palitry*, 153–54.

21. See Adams, "Who's Afraid of the Market?"

22. Akbarzadeh, "Nation-Building in Uzbekistan"; Andrew March, "The Use and Abuse of History."

23. Interview, theater director, Tashkent, February 1996.

24. Harris, *Control and Subversion.*

25. Scott, *Domination and the Arts of Resistance.*

26. Ibid., 93.

27. Mary Doi in her book on dancers in Uzbekistan found that this process of experts and professionals defining regional cultures goes back to the very beginning of the development of Soviet Uzbek culture. She also found that this resulted in a standardization and homogenization of dance styles. Doi, *Gender, Gesture, Nation.*

28. Interview, theater director, Tashkent, May 1996.

29. Navaro-Yashin, *Faces of the State*, 153. Navaro-Yashin emphasizes in this chapter the more poplar character of these rituals in Turkey, whereas in Uzbekistan, the direction is very much from the top-down. On rituals of obeisance, see Wedeen, *Ambiguities of Domination*, 6.

30. Interview, theater director, Tashkent, April 1996.

31. To my knowledge, only one of my informants has read my work, and he tends to disagree with my analyses (he thinks I am neglecting the important point, which is the renewal of Uzbek national culture), though he doesn't seem to find my arguments offensive. Other local scholars who have read my work have expressed a positive attitude toward it and have concurred with my analysis.

32. Interview, theater director, Tashkent, April 1996.

33. Paraphrase of interview with scholar, Tashkent, March 1996.

34. Interview, identity confidential, Tashkent, April 1996.

35. Karabel, "Towards a Theory of Intellectuals and Politics."

36. Baudrillard, *Simulations.*

37. Interview, theater director, Tashkent, May 1996.

38. Foucault, *Essential Works of Foucault*, 120.

39. Wedeen, *Ambiguities of Domination*, 69–74.

40. Ibid., 6.

41. Wedeen says that Soviet spectacle producers assisted Syria's government in orchestrating their own spectacles. Ibid., 27.

42. Goldfarb, *Beyond Glasnost.*

43. On socialist kitsch, see also Boym, *Common Places.*

44. Yurchak, "Soviet Hegemony of Form," 484.

45. Yurchak, "The Cynical Reason of Late Socialism," 163.

46. Yurchak, "Soviet Hegemony of Form," 485–86.

47. Yurchak, "The Cynical Reason of Late Socialism," 163–64.

48. This is not to say that in another context, the tension between individual (dis)belief and the imputed meaning of the official ritual does not produce effects analyzable using the "as if" framework. In the context of the debate in the United States about flag burning, for example, the individual disbelief in the flag's status as sacred object can come into direct conflict with the dominant belief that it does indeed have that status. So choosing not to risk arrest or bodily harm for defending flag burners during a protest at which the flag is being burned may indeed be dissimulation. Thanks to Todd Horowitz for spurring this discussion.

49. Haraszti, *The Velvet Prison.*

Conclusion: National Independence

1. Uzbek Television Channel 1, Tashkent, in Uzbek, 11 June 2005.

2. "Uzbek leader calls for careful approach to Islamic Values," UzReport.com, 30 August 2002, www.uzreport.com.

3. Karimov, "Eternal Memory."

4. Press Service of the President of the Republic of Uzbekistan, 2008, www.press-service.uz/en.

5. A video of President Karimov's address at the Independence Day concert of 2008 can be seen on the official press service website, Press Service of the President of the Republic of Uzbekistan, www.press-service.uz/en.

6. "Tashkent readies for Independence Day celebrations," Uznews.net, 26 August 2008, www.uznews.net.

7. Linz, *Totalitarian and Authoritarian Regimes,* 162.

8. Ibid.

9. For example, the classic study on how audiences interpret television shows is Liebes and Katz, *The Export of Meaning.*

10. Zanca, "Remembrance of Navruz Past."

11. Wedeen, *Ambiguities of Domination,* 45–46.

12. Verdery, *National Ideology under Socialism,* 84.

BIBLIOGRAPHY

Abazov, Rafis. *Foreign Policy Formation in Kazakhstan, Kyrgyzstan and Uzbekistan: Perceptions and Expert Assessments.* CERC Working Papers Series 4. Victoria, Australia: Contemporary Europe Research Centre, 2000.

Abdurahimov, Bakhodir A. "Kul'tura kak ob"ekt investirovaniia." Kandidat—Avtoreferat, Akademiia Khudozhestv Respubliki Uzbekistan, Nauchno-Issledovatel'skiy Institut Iskusstvoznaniia, 1998.

Abramson, David M. "Traditionalizing Modernities and Modernizing Traditions: The Forming and Reforming of Ideologies in Post-Soviet Uzbekistan." Paper presented at the American Anthropological Association, Washington, 1997.

Adams, Laura L. "Cultural Elites in Uzbekistan: Ideology Production and the State." *The Transformation of Central Asia: States and Societies from Soviet Rule to Independence*, edited by Pauline Jones Luong, 93–119. Ithaca, N.Y.: Cornell University Press, 2003.

——. "Globalization, Universalism and Cultural Form." *Comparative Studies in Society and History* 50, no. 3 (2008), 614–40.

——. "Invention, Institutionalization, and Renewal in Uzbekistan's National Culture." *European Journal of Cultural Studies* 2, no. 3 (1999), 355–73.

——. "The Mascot Researcher: Identity, Power, and Knowledge in Fieldwork." *Journal of Contemporary Ethnography* 28, no. 4 (1999), 331–63.

——. "Modernity, Postcolonialism and Theatrical Form in Uzbekistan." *Slavic Review* 64, no. 2 (2005), 333–54.

——. "Strategies for Measuring Identity in Ethnographic Research." *Identity as a Variable: A Guide to Conceptualization and Measurement of Identity*, edited by Rawi Abdelal, Yoshiko Hererra, Ian Johnston, and Rose McDermott, 316–41. New York: Cambridge University Press, 2009.

——. "Tashkent Museum Allows for Public Discussion of Recent Past." *EurasiaNet*, 2002. www.eurasianet.org.

——. "What Is Culture? Schemas and Spectacles in Uzbekistan." *Anthropology of East Europe Review* 16, no. 2 (1998), 65–71.

———. "Who's Afraid of the Market? Cultural Policy in Post-Soviet Uzbekistan." *Journal of Arts Management, Law and Society* 30, no. 1 (2000), 29–41.

Ahmad, Ajiz. *In Theory: Classes, Nations, Literatures.* London: Verso, 1992.

Akbarzadeh, Shahram. "Nation-Building in Uzbekistan." *Central Asian Survey* 15, no. 1 (1996), 23–32.

Allworth, Edward A., ed. *Central Asia: 120 Years of Russian Rule.* Durham, N.C.: Duke University Press, 1989.

———. *The Modern Uzbeks from the Fourteenth Century to the Present: A Cultural History.* Stanford, Calif.: Hoover Institution Press, 1990.

Anderson, Benedict. *Imagined Communities: Reflections on the Origin and Spread of Nationalism.* London: Verso, 1991.

Appadurai, Arjun. *Modernity at Large: Cultural Dimensions of Globalization.* Minneapolis: University of Minnesota Press, 1996.

Attar, Ali. "Nawruz in Tajikistan: Ritual or Politics." *Post-Soviet Central Asia*, edited by Touraj Atabaki and John O'Kane, 231–47. London: Tauris Academic Studies, 1998.

Bacon, Elizabeth. *Central Asia under Russian Rule: A Study in Culture Change.* Ithaca, N.Y.: Cornell University Press, 1978.

Baldauf, Ingeborg. "Some Thoughts on the Making of the Uzbek Nation." *Cahiers du Monde Russe et Sovietique* 32, no. 1 (1991), 79–94.

Baudrillard, Jean. *Simulations.* New York: Semiotext[e], 1983.

Becker, Howard. *Art Worlds.* Berkeley: University of California Press, 1982.

Beissinger, Mark R. "The Persisting Ambiguity of Empire." *Post-Soviet Affairs* 11, no. 2 (1995), 149–84.

Bell, Catherine. *Ritual Theory, Ritual Practice.* New York: Oxford University Press, 1992.

Berezin, Mabel. *Making the Fascist Self: The Political Culture of Interwar Italy.* Ithaca, N.Y.: Cornell University Press, 1997.

Bhabha, Homi. "The Postcolonial and the Postmodern: The Question of Agency." *The Location of Culture*, 245–82. London: Routledge, 1994.

Bhavnani, Kum-Kum. "Tracing the Contours: Feminist Research and Feminist Objectivity." *Women's Studies International Forum* 16, no. 2 (1993), 95–104.

Billig, Michael. *Banal Nationalism.* Thousand Oaks, Calif.: Sage, 1995.

Boli, John, and Frank Lechner. *World Culture: Origins and Consequences.* Malden, Mass.: Blackwell, 2005.

Bourdieu, Pierre. *Distinction: A Social Critique of the Judgement of Taste.* Cambridge, Mass.: Harvard University Press, 1984.

———. "The Forms of Capital." *The Handbook of Theory and Research for the Sociology of Education*, edited by J. G. Richardson, 241–58. New York: Greenwood, 1985.

Bourdieu, Pierre, and Randal Johnson. *The Field of Cultural Production: Essays on Art and Literature.* New York: Columbia University Press, 1993.

Boyarin, Jonathan, ed. *Remapping Memory: The Politics of Timespace.* Minneapolis: University of Minnesota Press, 1994.

Boym, Svetlana. *Common Places: Mythologies of Everyday Life in Russia.* Cambridge, Mass.: Harvard University Press, 1994.

Briggs, Charles L. "The Politics of Discursive Authority in Research on 'The Invention of Tradition'." *Cultural Anthropology* 11, no. 4 (1996), 435–69.

Brown, K. S. "Would the Real Nationalists Please Step Forward: Destructive Narration in Macedonia." *Fieldwork Dilemmas: Anthropologists in Postsocialist States,* edited by Hermine G. De Soto and Nora Dudwick, 31–48. Madison: University of Wisconsin Press, 2000.

Brubaker, Rogers. *Nationalism Reframed: Nationhood and the National Question in the New Europe.* New York: Cambridge University Press, 1996.

——. "Nationhood and the National Question in the Soviet Union and Post-Soviet Eurasia: An Institutional Account." *Theory and Society* 23, no. 1 (1994), 47–78.

Buckley, Cynthia. "Exodus? Out-Migration from the Central Asian Successor States to the Russian Federation." *Central Asia Monitor* 3 (1996), 16–22.

Chatterjee, Choi. *Celebrating Women: Gender, Festival Culture, and Bolshevik Ideology, 1910–1939.* Pittsburgh: University of Pittsburgh Press, 2002.

Chatterjee, Partha. *Nationalist Thought and the Colonial World: A Derivative Discourse.* Minneapolis: University of Minnesota Press, 1993.

Clark, Katerina. *The Soviet Novel: History as Ritual.* Chicago: University of Chicago Press, 1981.

Codagnone, Cristiano. "The New Migration in Russia in the 1990s." *The New Migration in Europe: Social Constructions and Social Realities,* edited by Khalid Koser and Helma Lutz, 39–59. London: Macmillan Press, 1998.

Cohn, Bernard S. "Representing Authority in Victorian England." *The Invention of Tradition,* edited by Eric Hobsbawm and Terence Ranger, 165–210. Cambridge: Cambridge University Press, 1983.

Cole, Juan R. I., and Deniz Kandiyoti. "Nationalism and the Colonial Legacy in the Middle East and Central Asia: Introduction." *International Journal of Middle East Studies* 34, no. 2 (2002), 189–203.

Collins, Kathleen. *Clan Politics and Regime Transition in Central Asia.* New York: Cambridge University Press, 2006.

——. *The Logic of Clan Politics in Central Asia: Its Impact on Regime Transformation.* New York: Cambridge University Press, 2005.

Comaroff, John, and Jean Comaroff. *Of Revelation and Revolution,* vol. 2, *The Dialectics of Modernity on a South African Frontier.* Chicago: University of Chicago Press, 1991.

Condee, Nancy, ed. *Soviet Hieroglyphics: Visual Culture in Late Twentieth-Century Russia.* Bloomington: Indiana University Press, 1995.

Cooper, Alanna E. "The Jews of Uzbekistan: A Brief Overview of Their History and Contemporary Situation." *Central Asia Monitor*, no. 6 (1998), 10–13.

Critchlow, James. *Nationalism in Uzbekistan: A Soviet Republic's Road to Sovereignty.* Boulder, Colo.: Westview Press, 1991.

Cummings, Sally N. *Kazakhstan: Power and the Elite*, New York: I.B. Tauris, 2005.

Dadabaev, Timur. "Post-Soviet Realities of Society in Uzbekistan." *Central Asian Survey* 23, no. 2 (2004), 141–66.

Dave, Bhavna. *Kazakhstan: Ethnicity, Language and Power.* Abingdon, N.Y.: Routledge, 2007.

———. "A Shrinking Reach of the State? Language Policy and Implementation in Kazakhstan and Kyrgyzstan." *The Transformation of Central Asia: States and Societies from Soviet Rule to Independence*, edited by Pauline Jones Luong, 120–55. Ithaca, N.Y.: Cornell University Press, 2003.

Dawisha, Karen, and Bruce Parrot, eds. *Conflict, Cleavage, and Change in Central Asia and the Caucasus.* Glasgow: Cambridge University Press, 1997.

Debord, Guy. *The Society of the Spectacle.* Translated by Donald Nicholson-Smith. New York: Zone Books, 1995. First published in 1967.

Derluguian, Georgi M. *Bourdieu's Secret Admirer in the Caucasus: A World-System Biography.* Chicago: University of Chicago Press, 2005.

Djumaev, Alexander. "Power Structures, Culture Policy, and Traditional Music in Soviet Central Asia." *1993 Yearbook for Traditional Music*, edited by Dieter Christensen, 43–49. New York: International Council for Traditional Music, 1993.

Doi, Mary Masayo. *Gender, Gesture, Nation: Dance and Social Change in Uzbekistan.* Westport, Conn.: Bergin and Garvey, 2002.

Dominguez, Virginia R. *People as Subject, People as Object: Selfhood and Peoplehood in Contemporary Israel.* Madison: University of Wisconsin Press, 1989.

Dunham, Vera. *In Stalin's Time: Middleclass Values in Soviet Fiction.* Durham, N.C.: Duke University Press, 1990.

Durkheim, Emile. *The Elementary Forms of the Religious Life.* Translated by Joseph Ward Swain. New York: Free Press, 1915.

Eglitis, Daina Stukuls. *Imagining the Nation: History, Modernity, and Revolution in Latvia.* University Park: Pennsylvania State University Press, 2002.

Eitzen, Hilda C. "Nawriz in Kazakstan: Scenarios for Managing Diversity." *Contemporary Kazaks: Cultural and Social Perspectives*, edited by Ingvar Svanberg, 73–102. New York: St. Martin's Press, 1999.

Ergeshev, I. *Istoriko-sotsiologicheskoe issledovanie kultury Uzbekistana.* Tashkent: Uzbekistan, 1985.

Falasca-Zamponi, Simonetta. *Fascist Spectacle: The Aesthetics of Power in Mussolini's Italy.* Berkeley: University of California Press, 1997.

Fentress, James, and Chris Wickham. *Social Memory.* London: Blackwell, 1992.

Fernandes, Sujatha. *Cuba Represent! Cuban Arts, State Power, and the Making of New Revolutionary Cultures*. Durham, N.C.: Duke University Press, 2006.

Ferranda, Regina, and David Nolle. "Ethnic Social Distance in Kyrgyzstan: Evidence from a Nationwide Opinion Survey." *Nationalities Papers* 31 (2003), 177–210.

Fierman, William. *Language Planning and National Development: The Uzbek Experience*. Berlin: Mouton de Gruyter, 1991.

Forced Migration Project. "Meskhetian Turks: Solutions and Human Security." New York: Soros Foundation, 1998.

Foucault, Michel. *Essential Works of Foucault 1954–1984*, vol. 3, *Power*, edited by James D. Faubion. New York: New Press, 2000.

———. 1980. *Power/Knowledge: Selected Interviews and Other Writings 1972–1977*. New York: Pantheon Books.

Fumagalli, Matteo. "Framing Ethnic Minority Mobilization in Central Asia: The Cases of Uzbeks in Kyrgyzstan and Tajikistan." *Europe-Asia Studies* 59, no. 4 (2007), 567–90.

García Canclini, Néstor. *Hybrid Cultures: Strategies for Entering and Leaving Modernity*. Minneapolis: University of Minnesota Press, 2005.

Geertz, Clifford. "Centers, Kings, and Charisma: Reflections on the Symbolics of Power." *Culture and Its Creators: Essays in Honor of Edward Shils*, edited by Joseph Ben-David and Terry Nicholas Clark, 150–71. Chicago: University of Chicago Press, 1977.

———. *Negara: The Theatre State in Nineteenth-Century Bali*. Princeton, N.J.: Princeton University Press, 1980.

von Geldern, James. *Bolshevik Festivals, 1917–1920*. Berkeley: University of California Press, 1993.

Giddens, Anthony. *The Consequences of Modernity*. Stanford, Calif.: Stanford University Press, 1990.

Gillis, John R., ed. *Commemorations*. Princeton, N.J.: Princeton University Press, 1996.

Gleason, Gregory. *The Central Asian States: Discovering Independence*. Boulder, Colo.: Westview Press, 1997.

Goldfarb, Jeffrey C. *Beyond Glasnost: The Post-Totalitarian Mind*. Chicago: University of Chicago Press, 1991.

———. *The Persistence of Freedom: The Sociological Implications of Polish Student Theater*. Boulder, Colo.: Westview Press, 1980.

Goldstein, Daniel M. *The Spectacular City: Violence and Performance in Urban Bolivia*. Durham, N.C.: Duke University Press, 2004.

Golomstock, Igor. *Totalitarian Art in the Soviet Union, the Third Reich, Fascist Italy, and the People's Republic of China*. Translated by Robert Chandler. London: Collins Harrill, 1990.

Gray, Laurel Victoria. "Uzbekistan." *The World Encyclopedia of Contemporary Theater*, edited by Don Rubin, Ravi Chaturvedi, Ramendu Majumdar, Chua Soo Pong, and Minoru Tanokura, 450–66. New York: Routledge, 1998.

Guibernau, Montserrat. "Anthony D. Smith on Nations and National Identity: A Critical Assessment." *History and National Destiny: Ethnosymbolism and Its Critics*, edited by Montserrat Guiberneau and John Hutchinson, 125–41. Oxford: Blackwell, 2004.

Guss, David M. *The Festive State: Race, Ethnicity, and Nationalism as Cultural Performance*. Berkeley: University of California Press, 2000.

Halbwachs, Maurice. *On Collective Memory*. Chicago: University of Chicago Press, 1992.

Handler, Richard, and Jocelyn Linnekin. "Tradition, Genuine or Spurious." *Journal of American Folklore* 97 (1984), 273–90.

Hannan, Michael T., and John Freeman. "The Population Ecology of Organizations." *American Journal of Sociology* 82, no. 5 (1977), 929–64.

Haraszti, Miklos. *The Velvet Prison: Artists under State Socialism*. New York: Basic Books, 1987.

Haraway, Donna J. *Simians, Cyborgs, and Women: The Reinvention of Nature*. New York: Routledge, 1991.

Harris, Colette. *Control and Subversion: Gender Relations in Tajikistan*. Sterling, Va.: Pluto Press, 2004.

——. *Muslim Youth: Tensions and Transitions in Tajikistan*. Boulder, Colo.: Westview Press, 2006.

Hegarty, Stephen. "The Rehabilitation of Timur: Reconstructing National History in Contemporary Uzbekistan." *Central Asia Monitor*, no. 1 (1995), 28–35.

Hirsch, Francine. "The Soviet Union as a Work-in-Progress: Ethnographers and the Category *Nationality* in the 1926, 1937, and 1939 Censuses." *Slavic Review* 56, no. 2 (1997), 251–78.

——. "Toward an Empire of Nations: Border-Making and the Formation of Soviet National Identities." *Russian Review* 59 (2000), 201–26.

Hobsbawm, Eric, and Terrence Ranger, eds. *The Invention of Tradition*. Cambridge: Cambridge University Press, 1983.

Humphrey, Caroline. *Marx Went Away—but Karl Stayed Behind*. Ann Arbor: University of Michigan Press, 1998.

Hunt, Lynn Avery. *Politics, Culture, and Class in the French Revolution*. Berkeley: University of California Press, 1984.

Ilkhamov, Alisher. "The Limits of Centralization: Regional Challenges in Uzbekistan." *The Transformation of Central Asia: States and Societies from Soviet Rule to Independence*, edited by Pauline Jones Luong, 159–81. Ithaca, N.Y.: Cornell University Press, 2003.

Jones Luong, Pauline. *Institutional Change and Political Continuity in Post-Soviet*

Central Asia: Power, Perceptions and Pacts. Cambridge: Cambridge University Press, 2002.

———. *The Transformation of Central Asia: States and Societies from Soviet Rule to Independence.* Ithaca, N.Y.: Cornell University Press, 2003.

Kaldor, Mary. "Nationalism and Globalization." *Nations and Nationalism* 10, no. 1/2 (2004), 161–77.

Kara, Halim. "Reclaiming National Literary Heritage: The Rehabilitation of Abdurauf Fitrat and Abdulhamid Sulaymon Cholpan in Uzbekistan." *Europe-Asia Studies* 54, no. 1 (2002), 123–42.

Karabel, Jerome. "Towards a Theory of Intellectuals and Politics." *Theory and Society* 25 (1996), 205–33.

Karimov, Islam. *Building the Future: Uzbekistan—Its Own Model for Transition to a Market Economy.* Toshkent: Uzbekiston, 1993.

———. "Eternal Memory." Press Service of the President of the Republic of Uzbekistan, 2005. www.press-service.uz/en.

———. "Ideology of National Independence." *Central Asian Survey* 21, no. 4 (2002), 371–84.

———. *Uzbekistan: The Road of Independence and Progress.* Toshkent: Uzbekiston, 1992.

———. *Uzbekistan on the Threshold of the Twenty-First Century: Challenges to Stability and Progress.* New York: Palgrave McMillan, 1998.

Kennedy, Michael D. *Envisioning Eastern Europe: Postcommunist Cultural Studies.* Ann Arbor: University of Michigan Press, 1994.

———. "The Liabilities of Liberalism and Nationalism after Communism: Polish Businessmen in the Articulation of the Nation." *Intellectuals and the Articulation of the Nation,* edited by Ronald Grigor Suny and Michael D. Kennedy, 345–78. Ann Arbor: University of Michigan Press, 1999.

Kennedy, Michael D. and Ronald Grigor Suny. "Introduction." *Intellectuals and the Articulation of the Nation,* edited by Ronald Grigor Suny and Michael D. Kennedy, 1–51. Ann Arbor: University of Michigan Press, 1999.

Kertzer, David I. *Ritual, Politics and Power.* New Haven, Conn.: Yale University Press, 1988.

Khalid, Adeeb. *Islam after Communism: Religion and Politics in Central Asia.* Berkeley: University of California Press, 2007.

———. *The Politics of Muslim Cultural Reform: Jadidism in Central Asia.* Berkeley: University of California Press, 1998.

———. "Russian History and the Debate over Orientalism." *Kritika: Explorations in Russian and Eurasian History* 4, no. 1 (2000), 691–99.

Kholmuhamedov, Komil. "Sen navro'zni soghinmadingmi." *Fan va turmush* (March 1990), 4–5.

Kirimli, Meryem. "Uzbekistan in the New World Order." *Central Asian Survey* 16, no. 1 (1997), 53–64.

Knight, Nathaniel. "Grigorev in Orenburg, 1851–1862: Russian Orientalism in the Service of Empire?" *Slavic Review* 59, no. 1 (2000), 74–100.

——. "On Russian Orientalism: A Response to Adeeb Khalid." *Kritika: Explorations in Russian and Eurasian History* 1, no. 4 (2000), 701–15.

Kolstø, Pål, ed. *Nation-Building and Ethnic Integration in Post-Soviet Societies: An Investigation of Latvia and Kazakstan.* Boulder, Colo.: Westview, 1999.

——. *Political Construction Sites: Nation-Building in Russia and Post-Soviet States.* Boulder, Colo.: Westview Press, 2000.

Kolstø, Pål, and Andrei Edemsky. *Russians in the Former Soviet Republics.* Bloomington: Indiana University Press, 1995.

Konovich, A. A. *Teatralizovannye prazdniki i obriady v SSSR.* Moscow: Vysshaia Shkola, 1990.

Laitin, David. *Identity in Formation: The Russian-Speaking Populations in the Near Abroad.* Ithaca, N.Y.: Cornell University Press, 1998.

Lane, Christel. *The Rites of Rulers: Ritual in Industrial Society—the Soviet Case.* Cambridge: Cambridge University Press, 1981.

Laruelle, Marlene. "The Return of the Aryan Myth: Tajikistan in Search of a Secularized National Identity." *Nationalities Papers* 35, no. 1 (2007), 51–70.

Levin, Theodore. *The Hundred Thousand Fools of God: Musical Travels in Central Asia (and Queens, New York).* Bloomington: Indiana University Press, 1996.

Liebes, Tamar, and Elihu Katz. *The Export of Meaning: Cross-Cultural Readings of "Dallas."* 2nd edition. Cambridge: Polity Press, 1993.

Linz, Juan. *Totalitarian and Authoritarian Regimes.* Boulder, Colo.: Lynne Rienner Publishers, 2000.

Liu, Morgan. "The Perils of Nationalism in Independent Uzbekistan," *Journal of the International Institute* 4, no. 2, Winter 1997.

Lowenthal, David. "Identity, Heritage, and History." *Commemorations: The Politics of National Identity,* edited by John R. Gillis, 41–57. Princeton, N.J.: Princeton University Press, 1994.

Lubin, Nancy, Barnett R. Rubin, Council on Foreign Relations, Century Foundation, and Sam Nunn. *Calming the Ferghana Valley: Development and Dialogue in the Heart of Central Asia.* Preventive Action Reports 4. New York: Century Foundation Press, 1999.

Lyons, Shawn T. "Where Is the Gold of Amir Said Alimkhan: An Uzbek Metaphor for the Past." *Central Asian Survey* 14, no. 1 (1995), 5–16.

Manz, Beatrice F. "Tamerlane's Career and Its Uses." *Journal of World History* 13, no. 1 (2002), 1–25.

March, Andrew. "The Use and Abuse of History: 'National Ideology' as Transcendental Object in Islam Karimov's 'Ideology of National Independence'." *Central Asian Survey* 21, no. 4 (2002), 371–84.

Martin, Terry. *Affirmative Action Empire: Nations and Nationalism in the Soviet Union 1923–1939*. Ithaca, N.Y.: Cornell University Press, 2001.

——. "An Affirmative Action Empire: The Soviet Union as the Highest Form of Imperialism." *A State of Nations: Empire and Nation-Making in the Age of Lenin and Stalin*, edited by Ronald Grigor Suny and Terry Martin, 67–92. Oxford: Oxford University Press, 2001.

Megoran, Nick. "On Researching 'Ethnic Conflict': Epistemology, Politics, and a Central Asian Boundary Dispute." *Europe-Asia Studies* 59, no. 2 (2007), 252–77.

——. "Preventing Conflict by Building Civil Society: Post-Development Theory and a Central Asian-UK Policy Success Story." *Central Asian Survey* 24, no. 1 (2005), 84–96.

Melvin, Neil. *Uzbekistan: Transition to Authoritarianism on the Silk Road*. Amsterdam: Harwood Academic, 2000.

Meyer, John W., John Boli, George M. Thomas, and Francisco O. Ramirez. "World Society and the Nation-State." *American Journal of Sociology* 103, no. 1 (1997), 144–82.

Meyer, John W., and Brian Rowan. "Institutionalized Organizations: Formal Structure as Myth and Ceremony." *The New Institutionalism in Organizational Analysis*, edited by Walter W. Powell and Paul J. DiMaggio, 41–62. Chicago: University of Chicago Press, 1991.

Michaels, Paula A. "Medical Propaganda and Cultural Revolution in Soviet Kazakhstan, 1928–41." *Russian Review* 59 (2000), 159–78.

Migdal, Joel S. "The State in Society: An Approach to Struggles for Domination." *State Power and Social Forces: Domination and Transformation in the Third World*, edited by Joel S. Migdal, Atul Kohli, and Vivienne Shue, 7–34. Cambridge: Cambridge University Press, 1994.

Moaddel, Mansoor. "Conditions for Ideological Production: The Origins of Islamic Modernism in India, Egypt, and Iran." *Theory and Society* 30 (2001), 669–731.

"Monitoring obshchestvennogo mneniia." *Ijtimoiy fikr-inson huquqlari*, no. 3 (2003), 87–88.

Moore, David Chioni. "Is the Post in Postcolonial the Post in Post-Soviet? Notes toward a Global Postcolonial Critique." *Publications of the Modern Languages Association* 116, no. 1 (2001), 111–28.

Nader, Laura. "Up the Anthropologist—Perspectives Gained from Studying Up." *Reinventing Anthropology*, edited by Dell H. Hymes, 284–311. New York: Pantheon Books, 1972.

Najibullah, Farangis. "Tajikistan: Soviet Era Monuments Quietly Disappearing." RFE/RL, 2007. www.rferl.org.

Navaro-Yashin, Yael. *Faces of the State: Secularism and Public Life in Turkey.* Princeton, N.J.: Princeton University Press, 2002.

Niranjana, Tejaswini, P. Sudhir, and Vivek Dhareshwar, eds. *Interrogating Modernity: Culture and Colonialism in India.* Calcutta: Seagull, 1993.

Northrop, Douglas Taylor. "Nationalizing Backwardness: Gender, Empire and Uzbek Identity." *A State of Nations: Empire and Nation-Making in the Age of Lenin and Stalin,* edited by Ronald Grigor Suny and Terry Martin, 191–220. Oxford: Oxford University Press, 2001.

——. *Veiled Empire: Gender and Power in Stalinist Central Asia.* Ithaca, N.Y.: Cornell University Press, 2004.

Odgaard, Karen, and Jens Simonsen. "The New Kazak Elite." *Contemporary Kazaks: Cultural and Social Perspectives,* edited by Ingvar Svanberg, 17–45. New York: St. Martin's Press, 1999.

Olcott, Martha. "National Consolidation: Ethnic, Regional and Historical Challenges," *Harvard International Review* 22, no.1 (2000), http://hir.harvard.edu/symposia.

Olick, Jeffrey K. *States of Memory: Continuities, Conflicts, and Transformations in National Retrospection.* Durham, N.C.: Duke University Press, 2003.

Otash, Yo'ldash Muqim o'ghli. *Navro'z naqli.* Tashkent: O'zbekiston, 1992.

O'zbekiston respublikasi entsiklopediya. Toshkent: Qomuslar Bosh Tahririiati, 1997.

Ozouf, Mona. *Festivals and the French Revolution.* Cambridge, Mass.: Harvard University Press, 1988.

Peterson, Ken. "History in the Remaking: Jadidist Thought in Post-Soviet Uzbekistan." *Central Asia Monitor,* no. 4 (1996), 23–29.

Peterson, Richard A. "Culture Studies through the Production Perspective: Progress and Prospects." *The Sociology of Culture: Emerging Theoretical Perspectives,* edited by Diana Crane, 163–90. Oxford: Blackwell, 1993.

Petrone, Karen. *Life Has Become More Joyous, Comrades: Celebrations in the Time of Stalin.* Bloomington: Indiana University Press, 2000.

Powell, Walter W., and Paul J. DiMaggio, eds. *The New Institutionalism in Organizational Analysis.* Chicago: University of Chicago Press, 1991.

Prakash, Gyan. "Introduction: After Colonialism." *After Colonialism: Imperial Histories and Postcolonial Displacements,* edited by Gyan Prakash, 3–17. Princeton, N.J.: Princeton University Press, 1995.

Qoraboev, Usmon. "Navro'zi olam." *Guliston,* no. 3 (1988), 6–7.

——. *O'zbekiston bayramlari.* Toshkent: O'qituvchi, 1991.

Rabinow, Paul, ed. *The Foucault Reader.* New York: Pantheon Books, 1984.

Rashid, Ahmad. *Jihad: The Rise of Militant Islam in Central Asia.* New Haven, Conn.: Yale University Press, 2002.

Rasulev, Khasan Gafurovich, and Sadulla Atamuradov. *Internationalizatsiia natsional'nykh kul'tur.* Tashkent: Uzbekistan, 1986.

Rausing, Sigrid. *History, Memory, and Identity in Post-Soviet Estonia: The End of a Collective Farm*. Oxford: Oxford University Press, 2004.

Regev, Motti. " 'Rockization': Diversity within Similarity in World Popular Music." *Global America? The Cultural Consequences of Globalization*, edited by Ulrich Beck, Natan Sznaider, and Rainer Winter, 222–34. Liverpool: Liverpool University Press, 2003.

——. "To Have a Culture of Our Own: On Israeliness and Its Variants." *Ethnic and Racial Studies* 23 (2000), 223–47.

Risse, Thomas, Stephen C. Ropp, and Kathryn Sikkink. *The Power of Human Rights: International Norms and Domestic Change*. New York: Cambridge University Press, 1999.

Ritzer, George. *Enchanting a Disenchanted World: Revolutionizing the Means of Consumption*. Thousand Oaks, Calif.: Pine Forge Press, 1999.

Robertson, Roland. *Globalization: Social Theory and Global Culture*. Thousand Oaks, Calif.: Sage, 1992.

——. "Social Theory, Cultural Relativity and the Problem of Globality." *Culture, Globalization and the World-System: Contemporary Conditions for the Representation of Identity*, edited by Anthony D. King, 69–90. Minneapolis: University of Minnesota Press, 1997.

Roche, Maurice. *Mega-Events and Modernity: Olympics and Expos in the Growth of Global Culture*. London: Routledge, 2000.

Roy, Olivier. *The New Central Asia: The Creation of Nations*. New York: New York University Press, 2000.

Rumer, Boris, ed. *Central Asia: A Gathering Storm*. New York: M.E. Sharpe, 2002.

Rywkin, Michael. *Moscow's Muslim Challenge: Soviet Central Asia*. Armonk, N.Y.: M.E. Sharpe, 1990.

Sahadeo, Jeff. *Russian Colonial Society in Tashkent: 1865–1923*. Bloomington: Indiana University Press, 2007.

Savage, Kirk. "Trauma, Healing, and the Therapeutic Monument." *Terror, Culture, Politics: Rethinking 9/11*, edited by Daniel J. Sherman and Terry Nardin, 103–120. Bloomington: Indiana University Press, 2006.

Schatz, Edward. *Modern Clan Politics: The Power of "Blood" in Kazakhstan and Beyond*. Seattle: University of Washington Press, 2004.

Schoeberlein-Engel, John. "Identity in Central Asia: Construction and Contention in the Conceptions of 'Ozbek', 'Tajik', 'Muslim', 'Samarqandi', and Other Groups." PhD dissertation, Harvard University, 1994.

——. "The Prospects for Uzbek National Identity." *Central Asia Monitor* 2 (1996), 12–20.

Schudson, Michael. "Dynamics of Distortion in Collective Memory." *Memory Distortion: How Minds, Brains and Societies Reconstruct the Past*, edited by Daniel Schacter. Cambridge, Mass.: Harvard University Press, 1995.

Schuepp, Christoph. "Kyrgyzstan Celebrates Spring Holiday." *EurasiaNet*, 2001. www.eurasianet.org.

Schwartz, Barry. "Deconstructing and Reconstructing the Past." *Qualitative Sociology* 18, no. 2 (1995), 263–70.

———. "Memory as a Cultural System: Abraham Lincoln in World War II." *American Sociological Review* 61 (1996), 908–27.

———. "The Social Context of Commemoration: A Study in Collective Memory." *Social Forces* 61, no. 2 (1982), 374–402.

Scott, James C. *Domination and the Arts of Resistance: Hidden Transcripts.* New Haven, Conn.: Yale University Press. 1990.

Sewell, William. "A Theory of Structure: Duality, Agency, and Transformation." *American Journal of Sociology* 98 (1992), 1–29.

Sharoev, I. G. *Rezhissuraa estrady i massovykh predstavleniy.* Moscow: Prosveshchenie, 1986.

Silin, A. D. *Ploshchadi—nashi palitry.* Moscow: Sovetskaia Rossiia, 1982.

———. *Spetsifika raboty rezhissera pri postanovka massovykh teatral'nykh predstavleniy pod otkrytym nebom i na netraditsionnykh stsenicheskikh ploshchadakh (uchebnoe posobie—chast' ii).* Moscow: Ministerstvo Kul'tury sssr, 1987.

Slezkine, Yuri. *From Savages to Citizens: Russia and the Small Peoples of the North.* Princeton, N.J.: Princeton University Press, 1994.

———. "Imperialism as the Highest Stage of Socialism." *Russian Review* 59, no. 2 (2000), 227–34.

———. "The ussr as a Communal Apartment, or How a Socialist State Promoted Ethnic Particularism." *Slavic Review* 53, no. 2 (1994), 414–52.

Smith, Anthony D. *The Antiquity of Nations.* Malden, Mass.: Polity, 2004.

———. *National Identity.* Reno: University of Nevada Press, 1991.

Smith, Dorothy. *The Everyday World as Problematic: A Feminist Sociology.* Boston: Northeastern University Press, 1987.

Smith, Graham, Vivien Law, Andrew Wilson, Annette Bohr, and Edward Allworth. *Nation-Building in the Post-Soviet Borderlands: The Politics of National Identities.* Cambridge: Cambridge University Press, 1998.

Smith, Kathleen E. *Mythmaking in the New Russia: Politics and Memory during the Yeltsin Era.* Ithaca, N.Y.: Cornell University Press, 2002.

Soucek, Svat. *A History of Inner Asia.* Cambridge: Cambridge University Press, 2002.

Spillman, Lyn. "Culture, Social Structures, and Discursive Fields." *Current Perspectives in Social Theory* 15 (1995), 129–54.

———. *Nation and Commemoration: Creating National Identities in the United States and Australia.* Cambridge: Cambridge University Press, 1997.

Strong, Roy. *Art and Power: Renaissance Festivals 1450–1650.* Berkeley: University of California Press, 1984.

Subtelny, Maria Eva. "The Timurid Legacy: A Reaffirmation and a Reassessment." Paper presented at the L'Heritage Timouride Iran—Asie Centrale—Inde XVe-XVIIIe siecles, Tashkent/Aix-en-Provence, 1997.

Suny, Ronald Grigor. "The Empire Strikes Out: Imperial Russia, 'National' Identity, and Theories of Empire." *A State of Nations: Empire and Nation-Making in the Age of Lenin and Stalin*, edited by Ronald Grigor Suny and Terry Martin, 23–66. Oxford: Oxford University Press, 2001.

———. *Revenge of the Past: Nationalism, Revolution and the Collapse of the Soviet Union.* Stanford, Calif.: Stanford University Press, 1993.

Suny, Ronald Grigor, and Terry Martin, eds. *A State of Nations: Empire and Nation-Making in the Age of Lenin and Stalin*: Oxford: Oxford University Press, 2001.

Szemere, Anna. *Up from the Underground: The Culture of Rock Music in Postsocialist Hungary.* University Park: Pennsylvania State University Press, 2001.

Tishkov, Valery. *Ethnicity, Nationalism and Conflict in and after the Soviet Union: The Mind Aflame.* London: Sage Publications, 1997.

Torbakov, Igor. "Tajik-Uzbek Relations: Divergent National Historiographies Threaten to Aggravate Tensions." *EurasiaNet*, Eurasianet Culture, 2001. www.eurasianet.org.

"Uzbekistan: Public Opinion 2000." *Ijtimoiy fikr-inson huquqlari*, no. 2 (2001), 113–16.

Verdery, Katherine. *National Ideology under Socialism: Identity and Cultural Politics in Ceauşcu's Romania.* Berkeley: University of California Press, 1991.

———. *What Was Socialism, and What Comes Next?* Princeton, N.J.: Princeton University Press, 1996.

Wagner-Pacifici, Robin, and Barry Schwartz. "The Vietnam Veterans Memorial: Commemorating a Difficult Past." *American Journal of Sociology* 97, no. 2 (1991), 376–420.

Wanner, Catherine. *Burden of Dreams: History and Identity in Post-Soviet Ukraine.* University Park: Pennsylvania State University Press, 1998.

Wasilewska, Ewa. "The Past and the Present: The Power of Heroic Epics and Oral Tradition—Manas 1000." *Central Asian Survey* 16, no. 1 (1997), 81–96.

Wedeen, Lisa. *Ambiguities of Domination.* Chicago: University of Chicago Press, 1999.

Wilk, Richard R. "The Local and the Global in the Political Economy of Beauty: From Miss Belize to Miss World." *Review of International Political Economy* 2, no. 1 (1995), 117—34.

———. "'Real Belizean Food': Building Local Identity in the Transnational Caribbean." *American Anthropologist* 101, no. 2 (1999), 244–55.

Williams, Raymond. *The Sociology of Culture.* New York: Schocken Books, 1981.

Wolf, Margery. *A Thrice-Told Tale: Feminism, Postmodernism, and Ethnographic Responsibility.* Stanford, Calif.: Stanford University Press, 1992.

Yurchak, Alexei. "The Cynical Reason of Late Socialism: Power, Pretense, and the Anekdot." *Public Culture* 9 (1997), 161–88.

———. *Everything Was Forever, until It Was No More: The Last Soviet Generation.* Princeton, N.J.: Princeton University Press, 2006.

———. "Soviet Hegemony of Form: Everything Was Forever until It Was No More." *Comparative Studies in Society and History* 45, no. 3 (2003), 480–510.

Zanca, Russell. "Remembrance of Navruz Past: Glimpses of a Celebration in an Uzbek Village." CREECA, 2001. www.wisc.edu/creeca.

Zaslavsky, Victor. "The Evolution of Separatism in Soviet Society under Gorbachev." *From Union to Commonwealth: Nationalism and Separatism in the Soviet Republics*, edited by Gail Lapidus, Victor Zaslavsky, and Philip Goldman, 71–97. Cambridge: Cambridge University Press, 1992.

INDEX

ethnic–civic dichotomy, 103, 124, 141–43, 149, 152

ethnic conflict, 44, 103–4

ethnic dominance: Uzbek, 44, 102–3, 125–26, 141–44

ethnicity in regional history, 35–37, 164–65. *See also* Sarts

ethnicity in Soviet era, 11

European culture, 43, 78–85, 108–9, 117–18, 128–36, 150, 156–58, 195. *See also* internationalization; Russification

expression and action, 172

extras, 170–71; recruitment of, 175–77; lack of input by, 173

financial aspects of spectacle production, 1, 70; individual, 169–70, 173

Folktales Block, 145–46

Foucault, Michael: on positive power relations, 188

France, 88, 158–59

friendship of the peoples, 151; Block, 127, 133, 140–44; Square, 30–31

Geertz, Clifford: on ceremony as justification of elites, 96

gender, 150, 172–73; in culture production, 16; in performances, 109, 166; in research methodology, 18

Germany, 43, 83, 129, 136–37, 140–41

Giddens, Anthony: on time and space in modern society, 77

Gleason, Gregory: on Uzbekistan's drive for independence, 46

globalization of culture, 78, 86–88, 135; cradle example, 150; cultural form and, 8, 84–85; theoretical approaches, 77, 85

going through channels, 157–59, 180

Goldfarb, Jeffrey C.: on totalitarian culture, 189

Great Silk Road, 42–43; Block, 138–41

Guibernau, Montserrat: on strategies of national identity, 10

Guss, David: on state use of tradition for legitimization, 79

Hamidov, Rustam (head spectacle producer), 69–70, 86, 92–93, 98–99, 162, 196

Hamza Theater, 69–70, 119, 161

Handler, Richard: on invention of tradition, 71–72

Haraszti, Miklos: on the state as guarantor of culture, 156

Harris, Collette: on social submission, 172–73

hegemony 9, 188–92

heritage, 29–43; controversies over, 65–66; in holiday spectacles, 144–48; state selection of, 59–60, 64–66. *See also* tradition

historiography, modern Uzbekistani, 29, 33

Hizb-ut-Tahrir, 64

Hobsbawm, Eric: on implication of continuity with the past, 11

holidays: comparison with Soviet, 89–92; content analysis of holiday spectacles, 125–33; official, 48; popular vs. political, 95, 125; religious vs. secular, 50; theoretical approaches, 4, 10, 48–49

hospitality, 30–31, 102

humanist ideals. *See* universal values

human rights, 45, 104, 195, 202n15

identities, 176–79; cosmopolitan, 105, 151–52; Muslim, 61–65, 88, 119; regional, 148–49, 177–78; Soviet 33, 49–50, 79, 123; Westernized, 65

professional artists' organizations: loss of autonomy, 160. *See also* Union of Composers and Conductors; Union of Theatrical Workers; Writer's Union

professionalism in cultural activities, 71, 114, 116, 129, 178–79

provinces, 2, 148–49; culture differences from Tashkent, 16, 108, 115–16, 177–79; music competition, 101–2; representation in spectacle, 75, 131, 149, 178–79. *See also* Regions Block

public expectations, 184, 197

public opinion, 49–50, 76, 121, 146, 151–52, 156, 173–74, 192, 196–97, 203n24

Qoraboev, Dr. Usmon, 153–54; on Uzbek ethnicity, 144

Rashidov, Sharof, 30, 52

reflexivity: in research, 18–19, 24, 50, 84, 105–6, 122, 153–54, 182–83

regional variation in cultural products, 115–16

Regions Block, 127, 131, 148–49

religion. *See* Muslim religious practice

representation of foreign cultures, 75;

repression, 57, 60, 64–65, 196, 202n15; religious, 51–54, 61, 64–65, 151; Soviet, 33–34; 54–57, 91; supplemental to spectacle, 98

resistance, 2, 189–92; in holiday spectacle production, 143–44, 169–73, 178–81; Soviet era, 53–58, 80–81

Ritzer, George: on capitalist spectacle, 97; on spectacle as pleasurable deception, 187

Robertson, Roland: on internationalization highlighting local traits, 82; on the nature of globalization, 77

Russia: perception of, 139–40; holidays in, 48–49

Russian: influence on Uzbek culture, 78, 82–84; language and culture, 35, 38, 102–4, 125–26. *See also* Russification

Russians, 31–33, 44, 48, 102, 143

Russification, 47–48, 78–79, 83, 108. *See also* European culture, internationalization

Samarkand: history and heritage, 21, 35–36, 39, 41–43, 107, 148; region's participation in holidays, 177–79

Sarts, 24

sayil (street fair), 56, 58, 110, 176–77

schemas of culture, 3, 37, 101–2, 127–32, 154; Soviet, 55, 132–33

Scott, James C.: on expression and reception of opinion, 174

self-censorship, 57, 132. *See also* censorship

Shosh Maqam (Uzbek music form), 108

Silin, A. D.: on producing outdoor theater, 166–67

Siyavush dance block, 163–66

slogans, 27, 120–22

Smith, Anthony: critique of modernism, 12; on "golden ages," 39

Smith, Kathleen: on post-Soviet holidays in Russia, 48–49

social memory, 24–25, 29, 43, 49

Solih, Mohammed, 45

Soviet holidays, 89–94

spectacle: audience reception of, 173–74; communicative qualities, 3, 96; evolution in Uzbekistan, 98–99; focus on political leaders, 180–81; guidelines for creation, 148–49; illusion of participation, 93–98, 182; in-

Uzbekistan compared to other authoritarian states, 4–5, 96, 188–89, 198
Uzbekistan compared to other post-Soviet Central Asian states, 5, 15, 35–36, 40, 46–47, 49, 89, 95, 103–4
Uzbekistan compared to the USSR: cultural values, 6–10; discursive fields, 6–7, 206n6; diversity of arts, 159; Europeanization, 66, 78–79, 107–9; ideological messages in culture production, 118–23, 155; leader focus, 5; meanings of holidays, 48–50; methods of culture production, 4, 8, 70–71, 122, 153–56, 160–68, 175–80; power and control systems, 5–8; results of cultural efforts, 57, 119, 150–51, 175, 182; role of intellectuals, 9–11

Vayl, Mark (theater director), 158, 160
Verdery, Katherine: on elites' focus on bureaucrats, 13–14; on rivalry of intellectuals under socialism, 10; on socialist strategies of control, 14; on weaknesses inherent to socialism, 199
Vohidov, Erkin (poet), 120–21

Wahhabism, 65
Wedeen, Lisa: on Assad's regime in Syria, 3; on compliance and complicity, 188–90; on monopolization of discourse, 198
wedding rituals, 150–51
Wilk, Richard: on global motivations for local choices, 85
Writers' Union, 53–54, 160, 165

Xalqlar Do'stligi (Friendship of the Peoples Square), 30

Yurchak, Alexei: on participation in monopolized discourse, 96–97; on public support of socialist powers, 191; on ritualized social action, 190–91

zodiac, "Chinese," 74
Zoroastrian legacy, 51, 71, 88, 144, 146, 163–64

Laura Adams teaches in the department of
sociology and the writing program at Harvard University.
She is also the co-director of the Harvard Program
on Central Asia and the Caucasus.

Library of Congress Cataloging-in-Publication Data
Adams, Laura L., 1967–
The spectacular state : culture and national identity in Uzbekistan /
Laura L. Adams.
p. cm. — (Politics, history, and culture)
Includes bibliographical references and index.
ISBN 978-0-8223-4651-7 (cloth : alk. paper)
ISBN 978-0-8223-4643-2 (pbk. : alk. paper)
1. Nationalism—Uzbekistan. 2. Post-communism—Uzbekistan.
3. Uzbekistan—Ethnic relations. 4. Uzbekistan—Politics and
government—1991– I. Title. II. Series: Politics, history, and culture.
DK947.A33 2010
958.7—dc22   2009037284